D1283128

THE RIGHTS OF THE DEFENSELESS

# THE RIGHTS OF THE DEFENSELESS

## Protecting Animals and Children
## in Gilded Age America

SUSAN J. PEARSON

THE UNIVERSITY OF CHICAGO PRESS

CHICAGO AND LONDON

SUSAN J. PEARSON is assistant professor of history at Northwestern University.

The University of Chicago Press, Chicago 60637
The University of Chicago Press, Ltd., London
© 2011 by The University of Chicago
All rights reserved. Published 2011
Printed in the United States of America

20  19  18  17  16  15  14  13  12  11     1  2  3  4  5

ISBN-13: 978-0-226-65201-6 (cloth)
ISBN-10: 0-226-65201-7 (cloth)

Library of Congress Cataloging-in-Publication Data

Pearson, Susan J.
    The rights of the defenseless : protecting animals and children in gilded age
America / Susan J. Pearson.
        p. cm.
    Includes bibliographical references and index.
    ISBN-13: 978-0-226-65201-6
    ISBN-10: 0-226-65201-7
    1. Child welfare—United States—History.   2. Animal rights—United States—
History.   I. Title.
    HV741 .P437 2011
    362.70973'09034—dc22

                                                                    2010042774

♾ The paper used in this publication meets the minimum requirements of the
American National Standard for Information Sciences—Permanence of Paper for
Printed Library Materials, ANSI Z39.48-1992.

# CONTENTS

# ACKNOWLEDGMENTS

Everyone who has ever written a book knows that, for the lucky among us, the hours we spend alone in the library and in front of the computer are augmented by the support of family, friends, and colleagues both near and far. Members of my own family—Mary Alyce and David Pearson, Kenneth Kramer, the late Judith Kramer, Matthew Pearson, and Marjorie Jolles—all helped me immensely. Whether by providing quiet confidence, funny jokes, excellent vintage clothing, crossword puzzle help, free lodging for an itinerant researcher, or simple companionship, each has helped to overcome the isolation and doubt that can come with scholarship.

This project first took shape at the University of North Carolina and I must thank many of my fellow Tar Heels for advice and friendship. Charles Capper, Peter Filene, Jacquelyn Hall, and Timothy Marr all read an earlier version of this manuscript with great care. John Kasson especially deserves praise for many years of faith, careful reading, encouragement and many, many letters of recommendation. The members of my writing group—Matthew Brown, Joshua Guthman, Ethan Kytle, and David Voelker—were amiable comrades and astute readers. Philip Gura, Robert Cantwell, and Joel Williamson all ably responded to early portions of this project. Jan Paris helped me craft one of my first successful grant applications. Becoming friends with Eve Duffy was one of the greatest gifts of my time in North Carolina; I thank Eve not only for responding to my chapter drafts and rambles, but also for her companionship, intellectual and otherwise. And for the runs, the bike rides, and the introduction to the Olive Men and their father.

Along the way I received much-needed financial support for research from Mellon Foundation grants distributed by the Pennsylvania Historical Society and the Library Company of Philadelphia, as well as the Council for Library and Information Resources. The History Department and the graduate school at the University of North Carolina also supported me with teaching assistantships and writing fellowships. I was also fortunate to receive a fellowship from the American Academy of Arts and Sciences. Though a new baby prevented me from accepting the award, I am grateful for the academy's expression of support for my project.

The History Department at Northwestern University has been a supportive and collegial place to be a scholar and teacher. The university provided generous financial support for research and conference travel and, just as important, a fair parental leave policy. At Northwestern I was lucky enough to almost immediately begin a fruitful collaboration with Mary Weismantel. We have since written, taught, and walked dogs together. Mary has always made me feel as though my scholarly interest in crossing the species divide was adventurous rather than idiosyncratic; I am thankful for that.

For assisting me with research and access to materials, it is a pleasure to acknowledge the help of librarians at the New-York Historical Society, the New York Public Library, the Boston Public Library, the Massachusetts Historical Society, the special collections section of the Frances Countway Medical Library at Harvard University, the Pennsylvania Historical Society, the Library Company of Philadelphia, the Bancroft Library at the University of California, Berkeley, the Minnesota Historical Society, the Chicago History Museum, the special collections library at the University of Illinois at Chicago, and the Wyoming Historical Society. At Northwestern, the Interlibrary Loan Office has helped me track down countless primary and secondary sources and the staff of Digital Media Services skillfully helped to prepare the illustrations. I am grateful to the Pennsylvania Historical Society and the Chicago History Museum for permission to reproduce materials in their collections. Ed Vermue of the special collections department at Oberlin College library deserves special thanks for helping this panicked author track down the source for an illustration just in the nick of time.

For reading some version of this manuscript in its entirety and offering insightful comments, I owe a debt to Michael Grossberg, Kate Masur, Sarah Pearsall, Carl Smith, Amy Dru Stanley, and Daniel Wickberg. Francesca Morgan provided sage advice on the introduction. For particularly detailed comments on presentations, I thank Timothy Gilfoyle, Daniel Wickberg, and Sarah Gordon. My editor at the University of Chicago Press, Robert Devens, was relaxed, helpful, and reassuring throughout this process. All of these good people have tried to save me from errors—any that remain are wholly my responsibility.

Michael Kramer deserves something more than mere thanks. He has read the entire manuscript, more than once, and countless drafts of other things—journal articles, book reviews, conference papers, syllabi. He put up with me while I wrote a dissertation, got a job, and shaped this book, all while trying to get his own work done. He calmed my worries, did dishes, cooked emergency dinners, took out trash and recycling, walked the dogs, changed diapers, and otherwise shared with me the inexhaustible, exhausting joys of parenthood. Our son, Tobias, did absolutely nothing to assist with this book. But that is as it should be.

# The Legend of Mary Ellen Wilson

S ometime during the winter of 1873, Mrs. Etta Wheeler, a volunteer for St. Luke's Methodist Mission in New York City, received troubling news. As Wheeler told the story some forty years later, she had been making her usual rounds through the tenements of the Hell's Kitchen neighborhood tending to the souls of the poor and the sick when a "quiet, reserved Scotch woman, truthful and careful of her words," told her that for more than two years she had lived next door to a family that held its only child, a girl, as a prisoner. Locked in the apartment's darkened rooms day and night, the girl was never allowed out, but her cries, which "gave evidence of her unhappy life," trespassed the apartment walls. All the neighbors knew that the child was being terribly beaten, but their appeals to the landlord had fallen on deaf ears. Recently, the family had removed itself to a new apartment down the street.[1] No one knew what to do.

Wheeler went to the family's new apartment house to investigate. She knocked first at a neighbor's door, and entered to find an elderly woman who affirmed that a child did live next door. Like the family's former neighbors, she too had heard it crying frequently. Emboldened by this information, Wheeler knocked on the door of an adjacent apartment and was greeted by a "woman's sharp voice" and an open door. "Being an unbidden guest," Wheeler reported she did not stay long, but she managed to "see the child and gain my own impression of her condition." The child was pale, thin, clothed in a tattered rag of a dress, laboring to wash "a frying pan as heavy as herself." Though Wheeler saw a "brutal whip" lying on a nearby table and glimpsed "many marks of its use" on the child's arms and legs, she claimed that the saddest part of the girl's plight was "written on her face in its look of suppression and misery, the face of a child unloved."[2]

After her brief visual inventory of the girl's sufferings, Wheeler left determined, "with the help of a kind Providence to rescue her from her miserable life." She continued to visit the girl's sick neighbor, learned more of the girl's misery, and consulted with the priest at St. Luke's, with local charities, and with the police about what could be done to help the girl. The charities told Wheeler that they could care for children legally brought to them, but could do nothing to remove a child from her home. The police informed her that they would need evidence, not hearsay, to make an arrest. "No one could tell what to do," she despaired, "there seemed no place of appeal." Finally, at the suggestion of her niece, Wheeler contacted an organization that she felt sure was truly concerned with the plight of the helpless and oppressed: the American Society for the Prevention of Cruelty to Animals (ASPCA). "Why not go to Mr. Bergh," the niece urged, "for she is a little animal, surely." The founder and president of the ASPCA, Mr. Henry Bergh, expressed interest in the case and set his organization's investigative and prosecutorial services to work. According to Jacob Riis, who was then a reporter for the *New York Herald*, Bergh echoed the sentiments of Wheeler's niece, declaring that "the child is an animal. If there is no justice for it as a human being, it shall at least have the rights of the cur in the street."[3]

After Wheeler supplied written testimony of the girl's abuse, the ASPCA's lawyer, Elbridge Gerry, secured a writ to remove her from her home, and on April 9, 1874, one of the organization's agents ceremoniously carried the small girl, Mary Ellen Wilson, out of her home, wrapped her in a blanket, and (after stopping to buy her a lollipop) brought her in his arms to the chambers of the New York Supreme Court's Judge Lawrence.[4] Mary Ellen's abuser was revealed as Mrs. Mary Connolly, who together with her husband had secured the girl from the city's Blackwell Island asylum on a term of indenture when she was just two years old. Mrs. Connolly was convicted of felonious assault and battery, and sent to prison for one year.[5] Several months after the trial, Henry Bergh and Elbridge Gerry called a public meeting to establish a separate organization, the New York Society for the Prevention of Cruelty to Children (NY-SPCC), the first of its kind in the world.[6]

The link that Wheeler saw between animals and children as helpless, oppressed sufferers worthy of legal intervention would prove quite popular in the aftermath of Mary Ellen's rescue. Efforts to protect children and animals from abuse and neglect spread rapidly. The first animal protection society in the United States had begun in 1866; by 1908, there were 354 active anticruelty organizations in the United States. Of these, the plurality, 185 of them, were humane, or dual, societies; 104 were exclusively animal societies; and 45 were dedicated solely to child protection.[7] The decision of Bergh and Gerry to form two separate societies—one for animals and one for children—turned out to be atypical. Most of the "dual" organizations—those that protected both animals and children—called themselves Humane Societies rather than either SPCAs or SPCCs. In 1877, the American Humane Association was formed as the national organization for both animal and child protection. The logic of joining protection for animals and children proved durable into the twentieth century. "The old link that bound the dumb brute with the helpless child in a common bond of humane sympathy," wrote Jacob Riis, "has never been broken."[8] This book investigates the formation of that bond and its institutional, cultural, legal, and political significance.

For the remainder of the nineteenth century, humane organizations divided their time between lobbying for new legislation, public education campaigns, and investigating individual cases of cruelty. Much of their animal protection effort was concentrated on agriculture and industry: the transportation of livestock, the treatment of horses on city rail lines, and methods of slaughter. Later in the century, they began to assume the animal control functions with which they are today associated, taking in strays and running animal shelters. With respect to children, humane organizations concentrated on abuse and neglect but also addressed eliminating child labor in live entertainment and the street trades, and later in the century many child protectionists joined widespread efforts to combat juvenile delinquency, truancy, and children's access to what they believed were immoral or corrupting influences.[9]

In most states, anticruelty organizations were delegated police powers to engage in law enforcement activity. In matters related to animals and children, they were empowered to make arrests and bring cases before magistrates. Though these organizations have been characterized as entirely typical examples of the harsh and punitive scientific charity movement of the Gilded Age, their police powers made them fundamentally different from other contemporary reform and charity groups. They wielded not just philanthropy but state power; they distributed arrest warrants rather than alms.[10] Those they prosecuted could face fines, jail time, and, most severely, the removal of either animal or child from their possession.

In what follows, I examine how anticruelty organizations expanded state power through private means during the Gilded Age. I argue that the linkage of animals with children formed part of an ideology of sentimental liberalism, a rhetoric forged by animal and child protectionists that reconciled dependence with rights and pledged the use of state power to protect the helpless. While SPCAs and SPCCs were in many respects singular, in other ways their story is typical of the last third of the nineteenth century. In the years after the collapse of Reconstruction, during a period of retreat from dreams of equal citizenship, "protection" became a keyword for many reformers and a means of incorporating new functions into the state. Claiming nothing more than sympathy with the suffering of animals and children and a desire to protect their rights, anticruelty reformers made "cruelty" into a social problem, stretched governmental powers, and expanded the state in a typically American way: through private associations.

Mary Ellen's rescue generated more than just a new type of humane organization. It generated powerful rhetoric and compelling narratives of sympathy, progress, and freedom. The effort to make meaning out of Mary Ellen's life began immediately: from the moment she entered the courtroom, her anonymous life of privation ended. As news of her rescue hit the city's newspapers, it was rapidly transformed from a private tragedy into an object lesson. The drama of Mary Ellen's life and rescue were a cause célèbre and the story fast became the founding myth of the child protection movement—a story that is repeatedly told down to this day. In telling and retelling Mary Ellen's story, Americans told themselves other stories about childhood, family, and nation; about the nature of sympathy, Christianity, and cruelty; about the redemptive powers of reform and the possibility for personal and collective transformation.

For nineteenth-century animal welfare reformers, Mary Ellen's story proved the urgency of their mission—to eradicate the sin of cruelty from the human heart. To the leaders of the ASPCA and the New York SPCC, Mary Ellen's case was an historical pivot point, an eruption of progress (of which they were the agents) that began to change children's status from that of mere chattel. "The case of Mary Ellen," claimed one of the New York SPCC's founding members in 1874, "awakened an interest in the heart of every human being to rescue the little waif from the hands of cruelty and oppression."[11] SPCC officials subsequently argued that Mary Ellen's story transformed and redeemed the world by bringing childhood's sufferings into the public sphere and by spawning the first organization dedicated solely to child protection. As the Illinois Humane Society's *Humane Journal* summarized the story less than ten years later, "a helpless, wretched waif in the great city, through her very helplessness and misery, stirred up a social revolution whose waves beat literally upon the farthest shores."[12] At annual meeting after annual meeting, New York

SPCC leaders like Elbridge Gerry, John Wright, and John Lindsay ritually invoked Mary Ellen's case to illustrate both the necessity for the organization and the progress it had accomplished. In one such speech, John Lindsay, SPCC president beginning in 1903, drew a vivid picture of children's lives before Mary Ellen and the SPCC. There was, he claimed, little legislation to protect children, and no one to enforce it. "Public officials were slow to interfere between parent and child," he went on, such that abuse and neglect were given license; children's "exposure to evil conditions and influences, converted them into criminals at an early age, and made them easy victims of depraved adults." By contrast, the SPCC had managed in its short life to nearly eliminate "the worst forms of child-suffering in our community."[13]

Mary Ellen's significance as a pivot point is still repeated in contemporary social work literature. At the end of a litany recounting the historical mistreatment of children (not unlike Lindsay's own), modern authors position Mary Ellen's rescue as "the first step accomplished in establishing the rights of children in the United States."[14] And while nineteenth-century humanitarians saw the link between protecting animals and children as entirely natural, in our own time child welfare professionals find it "a sad commentary that it took a society for the prevention of cruelty to animals to protect the first recorded case of a maltreated child."[15] In addition to being a beacon of light for the future, for many modern child protectionists Mary Ellen's rescue by the ASPCA also sheds a penetrating light on the past, showing how animals received greater legal protection than children. Many social work texts assert (erroneously) that in 1874 there were no laws protecting children, and thus that Mary Ellen was rescued under laws protecting animals.[16] From this illogical ordering of protective priorities, modern child welfare advocates often conclude that "children have been an expendable commodity for thousands of years."[17] Though Mary Ellen's rescue is still invoked as the singular beginning of the movement to end child abuse, for moderns it is tinged with the irony that animal protection preceded child protection, a fact that proves their contemporary efforts all the more necessary and difficult, poised as they are against the accumulated weight of history.

While organizational and social work histories fold Mary Ellen's rescue into a story of progress—inevitable if strangely delayed—SPCAs and SPCCs in general have figured in a quite different story. Written by professional historians, this story's plot revolves around elite and middle-class reformers trying to exercise social control over the working class. Though there are to date no histories of the combined effort to protect animals

and children, scholars who study SPCAs or SPCCs nonetheless emphasize
similar themes. Although humane organizations claimed to care only for
the sufferings of innocent and defenseless animals and children, these historians argue that in reality such groups used "cruelty" as a trope to stand
in for other anxieties—about the unruly and indecorous behavior of the
working class, about immigrants, about industrialization.[18] By this interpretation, it was less the suffering of the abused that upset reformers than
the passions and behaviors it represented on the part of the perpetrators.
Rowdy entertainments like cock fights and insufficiently middle-class
methods of childrearing sparked anxieties about an insouciant working
class of immigrants and the about the challenge of creating a shared culture (with established elites intact). SPCCs are, in the words of social
welfare historian Michael Katz, the exemplars of the "aggressive style of
Gilded Age reform": intrusive, controlling, and intolerant of working-class
family life. Protests against animal and child abuse, according to such historians, mark not the eruptive, revolutionary establishment of rights for
either group, but the effort of reformers to impose bourgeois standards of
decorous behavior on the huddled masses.[19]

In recent years, however, the "social control" interpretation of SPCCs
and SPCAs has become more nuanced. Linda Gordon, Sheri Broder, and
Stephen Robertson have all shown that the populations who came into contact with SPCCs were not simply the victims of meddling society agents.
Case records make it clear that SPCCs launched many of their investigations at the behest of families, neighbors, and even children themselves.
Poor communities often saw the SPCC, or "the Cruelty" as some called
it, as one means of helping them perform traditional functions of behav-
ioral regulation. In some instances, community complaints forced SPCCs
to take on problems—such as sexual abuse—that they had originally not
located under the rubric of "cruelty." In addition to initiating many of the
SPCCs investigations and helping to define the society's agenda, clients
and communities also exercised agency in their negotiations with society
staff. Neighbors might thwart investigations they felt were unjust by refusing to supply information, and women who used the SPCC to shape up
erring or intoxicated husbands might suddenly refuse continued cooperation with agents if they saw improvement in their spouses. While SPCCs
certainly used their power to shape behavior and to define the limits of
acceptable family life, they did not simply impose a middle-class vision of
domesticity on poor and immigrant populations.[20]

Not only is "social control" an incomplete description of how anticruelty organizations functioned on the ground, but also, as other recent

scholarship has shown, it is a reductionist account of the complex and diverse set of motivations that guided the men and women who devoted themselves to SPCAs, SPCCs, and Humane Societies. Many of the women who helped to staff Boston's Massachusetts SPCC, for example, disdained the unfamiliar family ways of the poor and foreign-born, but their interest in changing working-class life also stemmed from a feminist critique of family violence. As with child protectionists, those focused mainly on animal protection were motivated by more than disgust and sought more than simple control. The sentiments behind animal protection were rooted not simply in "bourgeois moral sensibility," but also in abolition, evangelical Christianity, Darwinism, and romanticism. Moreover, as Diane Beers and Bernard Unti have shown, nineteenth-century animal advocates relied as much on moral suasion and public education as they did on coercion and law enforcement, and they undertook a dizzying array of campaigns, many of which had little to do with controlling traditional working-class pastimes and behaviors.[21]

Recent scholarship points to the fact that social control is best conceived as a function rather than a motivation. Campaigns to protect children and animals from cruelty during the Gilded Age undoubtedly exercised social control, but they did so as a function of their avowed aim: to improve the social order by lessening acts of individual violence, relieving suffering, and inculcating a humane sensibility and sense of self-control in others. That anticruelty reformers felt the social order in need of improvement was no doubt a response to the tumultuous times in which they lived. As the closing decades of the nineteenth century were wracked by paramilitary violence and the end of Reconstruction in the South, and the social dislocations of industrialization, immigration, urbanization, panics and depressions, labor unrest, and rising discontent among the nation's farmers, Americans across classes all grappled for ways to explain, and solve, the nation's problems. Anticruelty reformers were among the men and women who were distressed by these rapid changes, and like many of their fellows, they were apt to conflate symptom and cause in their rush to diagnose and cure the nation's social ills. As anticruelty reformers viewed the towns and cities in which they worked, they saw lame, thin, and overworked horses pulling heavy loads, men beating horses and mules, cattle packed tightly into railroads and goaded at stockyards, children begging on the streets, physically abused, or living without enough food, shelter, or supervision. They largely believed that these acts stemmed from their perpetrators' callousness to suffering, willingness to hurt other living beings, greed, intemperance, or a passionate temperament. This temperament, and the acts that it produced, disrupted social order and anticruelty reformers sought to restore that order by appealing both to the heart and to the law.

This book details how such reformers brought together the language of the heart with the power of the law in an ideology of sentimental liberalism. It does not, however, make an argument about what motivated anticruelty reformers. Nor does it provide a history of particular anticruelty organizations. Rather, it is an intellectual and cultural history of the connection between—and consequences of—animal and child protection. It investigates both the rhetorical and the institutional innovations of anticruelty reform, arguing that in many critical respects, anticruelty organizations were a hybrid species. Not only did they link the protection of animals with children, but they brought together the legacy of antebellum moral reform with a postbellum willingness to use the state to regulate social and economic life; they merged an older status-based view of hierarchy and dependence with a newer language of rights; they combined sentimental with liberal language and private with public power. These efforts, pursued on the ground, case by case, reveal how reform was transformed during the Gilded Age—in the link between animals and children, sentimentalism and rights-talk, private life and public power, the "long Progressive Era" comes into view.[22]

"There is not in the whole range of fiction so harrowing a story as the touching and terrible chapter of real life which comes out in the evidence about the treatment of Mr. Bergh's waif," the *New York Times* wrote of Mary Ellen's rescue. Assuming its audience's familiarity with the scores of popular stories of innocent children suffering and often dying at the hands of cruel adults, the *Times* sketched the depths of Mrs. Connolly's depravity by declaring this woman worse than Quilp, the tormentor of Dickens's Little Nell in *The Old Curiosity Shop*.[23] Indeed, Mary Ellen's story as originally reported, and subsequently repeated, bears all the hallmarks of a sentimental tale: it portrays innocence imperiled from without, relies on bodily signs of pain and violation to communicate suffering, and asks of its witnesses that they respond with heartfelt sympathy to the plight of the wounded. The *Times*'s reporter immediately grasped its connection to the stock plots of sentimental fiction, even as he insisted that Mary Ellen's life, in its content and its mere reality, exceeded their bounds. While the literary heyday of sentimentalism had by 1874 largely faded, the reporter's choice to map Mary Ellen to Little Nell reveals its lingering hold; moreover, the narratives spun around Mary Ellen's tortured life show that the sentimental remained a reformist if not always a literary mode long after the Civil War.

Sentimentalism is not easy to define, for its definition tends to change according to its valuation. Detractors charge that sentimentalism is "the ostentatious parading of excessive and spurious emotion . . . the mark of dishonesty."[24] Defenders of sentimentalism, by contrast, argue that it is a coherent ethical modality, "a practice that asks one individual to acknowledge the full, equal humanity of another by appealing to common experiences of relationship, bodily pain, or both"; in this telling, sentimentalism employs emotional appeal to force the "experimental extension of humanity" to new groups on the basis of their capacity for suffering.[25] Whatever their disagreements, both detractors and defenders of sentimentalism are likely to agree that it revolves around feelings. Thanks to a half century of scholarship dedicated to tracing the origins of the sentimental style, both critics and boosters alike are also now likely to agree that sentimentalism is a philosophically rooted genre that positions affect, or feeling, as the grounding of both our common humanity and our morality. Sentimentalists assume that humans naturally have sympathy (or what was once called "fellow feeling") with one another, that this natural sympathy is aroused through the sight of suffering, and that it moves the observer of suffering to try to relieve it.[26] If imagined as an economy, sentimentalism's chief currency is emotion, the conduit is the heart, and the process of exchange produces social bonds, individual ethical development, and moral behavior. The chief goal is virtuous behavior, and the chief strategy to this end is emotional cultivation rather than rational thinking; the heart not the head is the source of moral truth.

By the late eighteenth century such ideas were so widespread that they formed what historians have called a "cult of sensibility" in the Anglo-American world. Spread not just through the texts of their academic and ecclesiastical originators, these ideas frequently took fictional form in novels that revolved around a central character that was also an ideal type—the man (or woman) of feeling. As Philip Fisher has aptly summarized the genre, sentimental plots often revolved around suffering and loss, their themes centered on "imprisonment, the violation of selfhood, power relations in intimate and familiar territory, freedom, the centrality of the family," and their central characters were actual or symbolic prisoners—those whose lives are subject to the whim and will of the powerful.

In antebellum America, sentimentalism informed both domestic-oriented fiction that centered on familial and romantic relationships and reformist tracts agitating on behalf of nonviolence, antislavery, and temperance (to name but a few). As the *New York Times*'s comparison of Mary Ellen to Little Nell suggests, the boundary between fictional and reform texts was porous throughout the nineteenth century. Many reformers—Lydia Maria Child and Harriet Beecher Stowe come to mind—were also fiction writers, and most antebellum reforms relied on moral suasion. Many believed that reading about the evils and suffering caused by war, drink, or slavery could change minds, and most reform movements produced both traditional tracts and fictional accounts of evil and redemption. After the Civil War, animal and child protectionists relied on sentimental tropes in their own propaganda, producing both factual exposes of suffering and commissioning works of fiction such as *Beautiful Joe*, *Our Gold Mine at Hollyhurst*, and *Romance of the Robins*. In such fictional works, and indeed in most of their reform publicity, SPCA, SPCC, and humane society activists took from moral sense philosophers, filtered through antebellum novelists and reformers, the notion that innocent suffering was the problem and sympathy the solution.

Contemporary reportage graphically detailed Mary Ellen's bruised and battered body as the supreme evidence of her suffering. Scarcely an article failed to mention her "black and blue" limbs, while the prosecuting attorney declared that he would present her damaged body as evidence to the jury. The *New York Daily Tribune* reprinted much of Mary Ellen's testimony, including her statement that "mamma has been in the habit of whipping and beating me almost every day; she used to whip me with a twisted whip, a raw hide; the whip always left black and blue marks on my body." The girl went on to describe her current wounds and how they had been made, including a cut on her forehead, inflicted by a pair of scissors. The testimony of the police matron who cared for the girl in custody was also quoted at length, and furthered the sense that Mary Ellen's body was a relentlessly violated one, marred by not just cruelty but also by neglect. The girl was, the matron reported, "very dirty, and it required three distinct washings to get rid of the incrusted dirt."[27]

And though news reports also chronicled the emergence of a new, healthier, and more childlike Mary Ellen, the image of the beaten girl was fixed forever in a photograph taken shortly after she was removed from her home. Two years after her rescue Mary Ellen was living on a farm in upstate New York, but her mangled body was still in circulation. Composer Henry P. Keens affixed her image to the front of the sheet music for his 1876 song "Little Mary Ellen," written to honor her. The same year, Bergh's SPCA featured her picture alongside depictions of abused animals at the organization's booth in Philadelphia's Centennial Exhibition. The *Phila-delphia Times* commented on the grisly display, claiming that to view the SPCA exhibit was "about as pleasant to the senses as an inspection of a thriving morgue in dog days."[28] By publicizing her wounds and repeatedly circulating them, the SPCC ensured that Mary Ellen's story was one that, as the *New York Times* put it, "no one can read without emotion."[29]

Indeed, focusing on the girl's pain and suffering was designed to pro-duce feelings—revulsion, outrage, and, most importantly, sympathy. News-paper accounts of the trial of Mary Connolly, Mary Ellen's abuser, empha-sized the proper reaction, noting that when Mary Ellen took the stand to testify "a crowd gathered and formed a ring of sympathizing listeners."[30] Day after day, respectable New York women crowded the courtroom to watch the proceedings with "the liveliest interest and sympathy" visible on their faces.[31] When Wheeler, Bergh, and the courtroom's spectators (and by extension the newspaper-reading public) turned their solicitous eyes and open hearts toward the beaten girl, they modeled the relationship between familial affections and a more generalizable moral code. The source of mo-rality was, Mary Ellen's case confirmed, an affective orientation nurtured in the domestic sphere, a tendency to sympathy, tenderheartedness, and mercy—precisely the constellation of feelings that her tormentors lacked.

The moral power of sympathy, its transformative qualities, its power to heal wounds and bridge social distances, was also a subtext of press ac-counts of Connolly's trial. Though they lingered over the girl's wounds, news reports and humanitarian propaganda also detailed the emergence of a new, sunnier, more childlike Mary Ellen. Reporters at the trial described the girl's transformation from prisoner to child in glowing terms. If she had been pale, pinched, bruised, dirty, and ragged before her rescue, she emerged during her trial as a smiling, rosy-cheeked, well-clad, and fearless cherub. According to news reports, the change began instantly and was the product of sympathetic solicitude, of emotional investment in the girl. Wrapped in a blanket and surrounded by her benefactors, on the second day of the trial Mary Ellen's face began "lighting up at their expressions of kindness" and seemed already "to have lost some of her feeling of fear." Just three days later the *New York Daily Tribune* reported that "the little child would hardly be recognized now," for she was dressed in a whole new outfit, and the clothing complemented the kindness-induced changes to her "pale little face." By the time of Mrs. Connolly's conviction, the girl "appeared much improved in appearance." Her hair was neat and combed, tied with a ribbon; she wore a pretty dress, a hat, shoes, and stockings. Her face had become "rounded and rosy-cheeked" and this so "completed her

toilet, and so transformed the child that it was somewhat difficult to recognize in her the fear-worn, unwashed, half-clad waif" first brought into
the courtroom.[32]

Emphasis on Mary Ellen's transformation continued after the trial as
"before" and "after" photographs of her circulated. In the SPCC's offices
and on the cover of a pamphlet published by the American Humane Association, the scissors used to beat the girl were framed by a visual narrative of transformation. On the one side, the picture of the girl at the time
of her rescue and, on the other side, the rehabilitated child, freed from her
wounds and transformed by a new "toilet." Mary Ellen's transformation
seemed particularly complete when, years later, child protectionists incorporated further news of her life into their story of her rescue. Not only had
the child gone from wretched to cute during the course of Mrs. Connolly's
trial, but also she had grown up into a respectable, married woman with
two daughters. Unlike many fictional sentimental stories, Mary Ellen's
ended happily. Twenty years after her rescue, the New York SPCC reported
that "the little girl whose abject misery and helplessness" had caused such
a stir "is now the wife of a well-to-do farmer in the State and the mother
of a happy family."[33] Focusing on Mary Ellen's successful rehabilitation
into family life, child protectionists proved the efficacy of reform in general, the transformative power of sympathy, and the benefits of their controversial policy of separating abused children from the parents who had
betrayed their trust as guardians and protectors.

To claim, as I do, that sentimentalism is critical to anticruelty reform
requires rearranging some of what we know about the chronological and
practical scope of the sentimental. As it does for so many other points of
study in nineteenth-century America, the Civil War also typically serves
as a breaking point in studies of sentimentalism. The sectional tensions
of the 1850s and finally the war experience itself, scholars have told us,
profoundly reoriented the moralistic, voluntaristic, and anti-institutional
bent of antebellum reform toward a more pragmatic, more coercive, and
more professionalized, institutional-bureaucratic approach to producing
change.[34] At the same time, the Civil War began a cultural revolution of
sorts, a turn towards "realism" or "naturalism" in literature, a movement
finding its full fruition in early-twentieth-century modernism.[35] In moral
philosophy, the experience of the war years encouraged a new generation
to abandon the moral certainties that they believed had led to war. The
result was, according to recent accounts, both the secularization of American public life and the creation of a nonfoundational philosophy that eventually became know as "pragmatism."[36] Slowly Americans gave up the

misty-eyed conceits of sentimental moral sense philosophy and domestic fiction to embrace the harder edges of the world that they actually inhabited, the one filled with problems of dust, smoke, and poverty that could not be cured by Harriet Beecher Stowe's famous dictum to "feel right." In the domains to which the concept of the sentimental had been applied, then—literature, reform, and moral philosophy—the Civil War is typically thought to mark the beginning of the end.

The rhetoric and assumptions of Gilded Age animal and child protectionists suggests that the death knell for sentimentalism may have been sounded prematurely. In their annual reports and other propaganda, protectionists trafficked in scenes of suffering they assumed would arouse sympathy. In humane education efforts that lasted until well into the twentieth century, anticruelty advocates assumed that "humanity" was identical to sympathy, and that arousing sympathy for suffering animals and children would not only lead to better treatment of both, but to the formation of a moral populace and a better world.

Of course anticruelty reformers did not rely on sympathy alone; for those unreached by moral suasion, they reserved the power to arrest. In their hands, sentimentalism was more than simply a predecessor or an alternative to legal, institutional, or coercive methods of creating social change; rather, power and suasion merged. Speaking a language of sympathy while deploying legal power, anticruelty reformers transformed not only sentimentalism, but also the reach and role of the state. In the postbellum years, sentimentalism remained culturally salient and politically important because claims of suffering and discourses of injury became a way of authorizing action and intervention on the part of both reformers and the state. Sentimental tropes authorized not just feelings but also action that was interventionist and coercive in its nature. Sentimentalism lasted not simply in texts, but in reform practices and in institutions and it helped to shape what Michele Landis Dauber has recently described as the "sympathetic state."[37]

Sentimentally structured as Mary Ellen's tale was, contemporary and subsequent child advocates also hitched its significance to the stability and spread of American liberalism. In its classical form, liberalism is an ideology founded on a belief in human reason, one that cherishes individual rights, limited government, and consensual (or contractual) relations. Associated politically with representative government and economically with capitalism, the vision of history that emerges from liberal quarters enshrines individual freedom from tyranny and dependence as the telos of all history. Plotted on a progressive axis, the liberal version of history moves from monarchical to representative government, from feudalism to market economies, and from personal dependence to individual freedom. Though many of liberalism's central values were articulated by early modern Britons, much of American history has been viewed through this teleological lens, written as if the purpose of the nation was to illustrate and unfold the universal truths of liberalism before the eyes of the world.[38]

The interpreters of Mary Ellen's life placed her squarely within this historical drama, making her individual life into both a harbinger of freedom and progress and an exemplar of the dangers that child neglect and abuse posed to liberalism. The *New York Times* in particular saw in Mary Ellen's fortunes evidence that the failure of the city's charities was mounting a threat to the stability of national values. As the ASPCA's investigators had discovered, Mary Ellen was not the child of the man and woman, Mr. and Mrs. Connolly, who kept her locked inside their home, but they had acquired her legally on an indenture. Though the city's indenture policy required that children be checked on once a year, this had never happened. Her case, intoned the paper, was surely not isolated. The "Commissioners of Charities keeps up a well-stocked child market," it complained, such that just about anyone can get an indentured child from a city asylum. They only had "to go through the formality" of making an application "to obtain the desired quantity of human flesh, on which to work experiments, brutal or otherwise." Linking the city's indenture system to slavery—by then the rhetorical antithesis of a free and liberal society—the paper also suggested that individual rights were violated. But the newspaper went further, warning that farming out children to improper guardians threatened the nature of the American republic itself. Voicing widespread fears that massive European immigration was about to overwhelm the country's character, the *Times* predicted that the city's ill-supervised waifs "will form the nucleus of a class that will in time make cities like New-York as open to the reproach of stimulating beggary as any capital of Europe." While Americans were accustomed to think that "our system has no tendency either to foster or create" permanent classes, the current system of indenturing orphaned and dependent children seemed to threaten the peculiar genius of New World liberalism with the legacies of Old World feudalism.[39]

The wrongs of Mary Ellen's case, the paper suggested, were both personal and political. At the founding meeting of the SPCC, Henry Bergh echoed the *Times*'s concerns when he reminded those gathered that because "those little waifs were destined at a future day to become the fathers and mothers of this Republic," neglecting them was equal to neglect-ing the nation itself.[40] Commentaries like this suggested that the child-centered, affectionate family—the centerpiece of sentimentalism—was also the bulwark of American society's much-vaunted liberty and equal-ity. Far from being opposed, sentimentalism and liberalism merged not only in the family, but also in efforts to remake the family.

Interpreters of Mary Ellen's life also found evidence of the march of his-tory according to the natural laws of liberalism. At the SPCC's inaugural meeting Henry Bergh explained this teleology. "There is a providence in the affairs of men," he declared. "The slaves were first freed from bondage; next came the emancipation of the brute creation, and next the emancipa-tion of the little children was about to take place."[41] The rescue of Mary Ellen by an animal protection agency was not, Bergh implied, an unusual or strange progression, but rather it represented the flow of history, the relationship between sympathy and emancipation, and the link between visibility and freedom. Once their suffering was made public, slaves, ani-mals, and children were freed from the oppressive silence of a pernicious sort of privacy, the privacy of imprisonment. Publicity surrounding Mary Ellen's case focused on the fact that her home had been made a prison. The girl, Bergh told the court, was held in "rigid confinement" and was "unlawfully and illegally restrained of [her] liberty." On the stand, ASPCA lawyers elicited from Mary Ellen the testimony that she had "never been allowed to go out of the rooms" and that she was in fact locked inside them, which meant, among other things, that she had never been allowed to play with another child.[42] Neighbors confirmed that they had seen the girl but once in the two years she had lived near them.[43]

In addition to striking themes of liberty and confinement, Bergh and Elbridge Gerry likewise suggested that they found in Mary Ellen's case a vehicle for proving to the world that "children have rights which parents and guardians should respect."[44] Here Bergh and Gerry connected their much-vaunted sympathy with the girl to her rights, implying that suffer-ing entailed a denial of rights, and sympathy, their recognition. In this formulation, the opposite of cruelty was more than sympathy or love, it was justice. Throughout the second half of the nineteenth century, SPCA, SPCC, and humane society leaders repeatedly claimed that they, un-like other charitable organizations, were in the business of establishing rights, which they identified with the legal protections they provided and enforced. Rejecting moral suasion alone as a reform tactic, the leaders of animal and child protection societies forged a distinctively post–Civil War brand of benevolence, one that combined sentimentalism with liberalism, sympathy with decisive and forceful action, love with justice, and mercy with prosecution.

Speaking the language of rights while amplifying the powers of the state, humane societies stood at the crossroads of what historians typically think of as two versions of liberalism—the one classical and minimalist, the other modern and interventionist. The former focuses on rights as freedom from interference, while the latter seeks to ensure every citizen a modicum of wellbeing and tends to assume that rights are positive as well as negative, that they are not merely formal but substantive.[45] In conventional accounts of American political ideology and state-building, the United States is depicted as tending more toward classical than welfare-state liberalism, as having a "weak" state, and little welfare state at all.

The characterization of the American state as weak has a chronological dimension as well. To the extent that the United States built a more robust welfare and regulatory state, historians usually locate its seeds in the Progressive Era and its full flowering in the New Deal. The Gilded Age, by contrast, is seen as the height of laissez-faire, a time when courts and ideologues embraced the essentially negative "liberty of contract" and combated any and all attempts to use the state to restrain business for the public good. While industrialization fundamentally changed the nature of the American economy and the meaning of liberty, citizenship, and individual rights, Gilded Age moralists and reformers clung to antiquated social theories that attributed success and failure to individual effort and character. Even those who challenged the worst effects of industrialization as unjust—enraged populist farmers or Knights of Labor unionists—failed to fully comprehend the new order, instead hanging onto a producerist republicanism that had no place in the agglomerated world of the corporation.

The Progressive Era, by contrast, is often depicted as the period when at least some Americans came to terms with the true nature of industrialization, realizing that it required new ways of organizing both thought and action. In a variety of ways, Progressives replaced liberal individualism and the shibboleth of "liberty of contract" with corporatism. Social scientists described an interdependent and interconnected world in which individual fortunes were controlled by external forces and responsibility was redistributed. Reformers realized that the state was the only force powerful enough to control business, and they increasingly asked it to regulate the conditions of both production and consumption. During this period important, if rudimentary, social insurance and social welfare programs were also launched—workman's compensation and mother's pensions are the best-known examples. And it was during the Progressive Era that reformers first turned to the federal government to regulate what had become a truly national economy.[46]

All of these factors—the intellectual abandonment of individualism, the reformist commitment to state regulation, and the turn to the federal government—are criteria that historians typically use to distinguish both the laissez-faire Gilded Age from the state-building Progressive Era and classical from modern liberalism. But a steady stream of scholarship has begun to change crucial aspects of how we understand both the nature and the historical creation of the American state. In a recent survey of such scholarship, legal historian William Novak sought to put an end to what he called the "myth of the 'weak' American state." As Novak argues, the characterization of the United States as a weak state is based both on an exceptionalist myth—that the United States is different from the Old World—and on a normative definition of "the state" that is derived from the centralized governments of Western Europe in the nineteenth century. Employing a model of the state that privileges centralization and standardization, historians tend to identify periods of state-building exclusively with the amplification of federal power and regulatory capacity. Thus between the end of the Reconstruction—with the seeming death of activist government and federally guaranteed citizenship—and the flurry of reform in the Progressive Era, there seems to many historians to have been a retreat, a rejection of the activist state.

These conceptual blinders prevent scholars from detecting the tremendous range and depth of governmental activity throughout United States history, much of it occurring at the local and state level. Abandoning a normative definition of the state, Novak argues, we can see how the American state has achieved an "extraordinary penetration of the state through civil society to the periphery." Among the chief characteristics of American statecraft are a reliance on the rule of law, dispersion of authority among local, state, and federal governments, and the interpenetration of public and private authority "to accomplish public objectives." The study of anticruelty organizations—which were active on the local and state levels, used law and law enforcement to achieve reform, and were private organizations used for public purposes—contributes to this revised understanding of how the state has functioned in America.[47]

There is reason to believe, moreover, that just as historians have too quickly characterized the American state as weak, so too the conventional portrait of the Gilded Age as a period of laissez-faire and harsh individualism may be something of a stereotype. Historians have begun to depict the years between 1865 and 1900 as a period of governmental expansion, arguing that fighting the Civil War amplified the power and scope of the national government in ways that outlived Appomattox.[48] But the state-building fluorescence during the Gilded Age becomes even more pronounced if we direct our analytical gaze away from federal politics to local and state governance. Here we find that the postbellum years were a period of tremendous governmental activity and what contemporaries called "state interference" in social and economic affairs. Indeed, late-nineteenth-century students of government remarked on this fact. Perhaps the most famous example is the Englishman James Bryce's *American Commonwealth*, first published in 1888. A survey of American government, Bryce's treatise included a chapter on laissez-faire. Bryce acknowledged that many Americans were sentimentally attached to the *idea* of laissez-faire, but he argued that this ideology was honored in the breach. This was particularly so in the late nineteenth century when "new causes are at work in the world, tending not only to lengthen the arms of government, but to make its touch quicker and firmer." Among the "new causes," Bryce cited not only the complexity of modern civilization but also "a quickened moral sensitiveness" to which "the sight of preventable evil is painful." Modern men wished to use government to manage an industrialized and interconnected society and to palliate social problems. Turning exceptionalist myths on their head, Bryce concluded that "The new democracies of America are just as eager for state interference as the democracy of England and try their experiments with even more light-hearted promptitude." To gauge the depth of Americans' practical commitment to state "interference," one need turn to the state legislatures; but Bryce confessed that state-level regulations were "so numerous and so various" that it was hard for him to select the choicest examples.[49]

Local and state regulations did present an embarrassment of riches. Bryce's American contemporaries were as likely to complain of "statutory enactment without limit" as they were of government inaction. Growing out of common law traditions, state and local governments had long used their "police powers" to enact rules conducive to public health and safety. During the last third of the nineteenth century, many local governments established health and safety standards in building construction, created municipal health organizations, installed sewer systems, and increased public ownership of utilities. And state legislatures were even busier. Not only did they continue their longstanding practice of promoting the development of infrastructure such as roads and railroads, manufacturing, and agriculture, but most also began to regulate the conduct of business. States enacted laws ensuring the purity of certain foods, liquors, and medicines, promoting or requiring vaccination, establishing minimum requirements for certain professions (such as teachers, doctors, pharmacists, dentists, lawyers, and ship pilots), requiring public inspection of the accounts of banks, insurance companies, mutual aid organizations, and railroad companies, and prohibiting monopolies. States also tackled the "labor question," mandating inspection of factories, regulating wages and work contracts, and restricting the working hours and conditions of children, women, and, in some cases, men. In all, state legislatures passed over sixteen hundred laws regulating the terms of labor before 1897.[50] To combat moral decline, states regulated, licensed, and, in some cases, prohibited the liquor trade, banned gambling, prizefighting, obscene literature, and lotteries. And, of course, animal and child protectionists lobbied for legislation that added to this number, generating rules that reshaped personal conduct across a number of relationships. These manifold regulations both grew out of and spawned the institutional growth of municipal and state government, increasing their size, power, and bureaucratic complexity.

Reconceptualizing both the nature of the American state and re-thinking its historical development allows us to see that the Gilded Age, while it had its committed laissez-faire ideologues, was a period both of state expansion and the creation of new justifications for state intervention. Among the agents of this transformation, I argue, we should place SPCAs, SPCCs, and Humane Societies. While Bryce argued that Gilded Age legislatures were busy extending the "arms of government," Humane Societies often referred to themselves as "the arm of the law." They were "arms" in two senses—they acted both as appendages to established law enforcement, and as extensions of it, reaching out into new domains. As I shall detail, their role in transforming the liberal state was both rhetorical and institutional. Rhetorically, they made "cruelty" into a social problem and wedded sentimentalism to liberal rights discourse to expand public responsibility for animals and children. Institutionally, as private organizations delegated police powers, they extended the "arms of government" because they helped create and enforce new laws. As organizations that relied on the rule of law and that blended public and private authority, humane organizations are typical of an American approach to statecraft. The expansion of government power under private auspices enabled Gilded Age Americans—animal and child protectionists among them—to perpetuate what James Bryce had identified as their favorite fiction: that even in the midst of ever-increasing "state interference" they remained a people committed to liberty and voluntarism above all else.

Writing ten years after Mary Ellen's rescue in the *Bay State Monthly*, Ernest Nusse surveyed the formation and current state of societies for the prevention of cruelty to children. Recounting the girl's rescue, Nusse lauded the formation of SPCCs, which he called the guardians of "the rights of childhood." Though he drew heavily on the words of Elbridge Gerry, the New York SPCC president, Nusse, like newspaper reporters ten years earlier, praised Henry Bergh as "a man who has never been deaf to a cry of despair," who cared as much for children as he did for animals. Nusse found no illogic or surprise in the rescue of a child by an animal protection organization but argued that they were united not just by the historical accident of Mary Ellen's rescue, but also by "a philosophy which rightly esteems that cruelty commences with the animal, only to end fatally with the human being." Humane organizations were especially necessary in the United States, Nusse concluded, since the country and its citizens were so "adverse" to permitting even necessary functions "to be concentrated in the hands of public officials." Happily, though, he surmised that organizations like the SPCC and SPCA served to correct the deficiencies of the limited liberal state, providing protection where the chaos of privacy might otherwise reign.[51] In combining the story of Mary Ellen's rescue with themes of sympathy, rights, and the amplification of liberalism, Nusse was typical rather than original. In his typicality he nonetheless reminds us that however we may judge their efforts, we should not forget that anticruelty reformers brought together more than simply animals and children. The memory of *that* strange union has been all but lost, making it possible for modern child welfare advocates to look back in shock on Mary Ellen's rescue by an animal protection society as a "sad commentary" on children's value in nineteenth-century America. As we shall see, however, the nexus of animal and child protection was neither sad nor strange, but was instead tightly bound to the crosshatched threads of sentimentalism and liberalism.

# "The Child Is an Animal": Domesticity, Discipline, and the Logic of Joint Protection

A lmost as soon as little Mary Ellen Wilson's case had been resolved, her rescuers founded a separate entity, the New York Society for the Prevention of Cruelty to Children (NY-SPCC). Immediately following the formation of the New York SPCC, reformers organized SPCCs in Brooklyn, Buffalo, Baltimore, San Francisco, Philadelphia, and Wilmington, Delaware.[1] Though Mary Ellen's case proved to be the impetus for a new form of organized child protection activity, the decision of Henry Bergh and Elbridge Gerry to separate the protection of animals and children ultimately proved to be atypical. As child protection spread outward from New York City, most existing and subsequent anticruelty societies combined child with animal protection under one institutional mantle. Most often, these "dual" organizations were known by the name of "humane society."

Anticruelty reformers rarely felt the need to discuss, or justify, their decision to combine child with animal protection. On the rare occasions when they did reflect on this choice, reformers usually averred that combining the two functions was a practical rather than an ideological matter. But the reality was much more complicated. In fact, combining child with animal protection was in many ways a profoundly impractical choice: protecting animals and protecting children turned out to involve very different sets of problems and priorities. Far from being simply expedient, the institutional fusion of animals with children was dictated as much by a cultural as a practical logic.

Popular and humanitarian literature identified children and animals as similar, capable of forming intense emotional bonds and reciprocal relations, and incorporated animals-as-pets into the emotional order of domesticity. In addition, popular authors and humanitarians applied new ideas about punishment, discipline, and rearing equally to animals and children, incorporating both within a disciplinary regime of kindness. Associated with middle-class domestic ideals, the regime of kindness consigned both beasts and babes to a similar position in the household's affective economy, assigning them a mutual role as objects of sentimental investment. The sentimentalization of both children and animals was, in turn, critical to the increased moral attention given to both over the course of the nineteenth century. For within a philosophy that regarded familial feelings as the exemplar of all morality, membership in the family was equivalent to membership in humanity at large, a necessary precondition for the extension of rights within the framework of sentimental liberalism.[2]

First among the so-called dual societies for animal and child protection to emerge in the wake of Mary Ellen's case was the Illinois Humane Society, founded in Chicago in 1869 as the Illinois SPCA. In 1877, the society's board decided to incorporate child protection under its mantle. To reflect its new functions the organization changed its name to the Illinois Humane Society (IHS).[3] From his perch as the president of the national American Humane Association, former IHS president Edwin Lee Brown promoted the moniker "humane society" as the appropriate label for all organizations that combined animal and child protection.[4] The name was meant to suggest that animal and child protection were joined by principle rather than accident or convenience. Twenty years after this titular change, IHS president John Shortall concluded that the decision to join the two functions had "been amply justified . . . by the fact—as I believe it to be—that no Society for the prevention of cruelty to animals—perhaps none for the prevention of cruelty to children—has been organized since that date." That is, no single-function society had been formed since 1877, but instead "the title 'Humane Society' has been commonly adopted, and both services united thereunder."[5] Likewise, when the Woman's Christian Temperance Union (WCTU) began to oppose cruelty through its National Department of Mercy in 1890, it gathered both animals and children under its protective mantle.[6] In some states animals and children were even linked as government wards. In Colorado, for example, the state's twenty-year-old humane society became an arm of the government in 1901, and was renamed the State Bureau of Child and Animal Protection. From this platform, Colorado's Humane Society and WCTU activists (unsuccessfully) petitioned Congress for "the creation of a Federal Government Board, whose duty it shall be to study the conditions of, and suggest methods for the protection of children and dumb animals."[7]

Anticruelty activists seldom devoted much effort to explaining the decision to combine animal and child protection functions. Sometimes, however, reformers explained that animals and children were joined by their common helplessness. More to the point, reformers pictured animals' and children's helplessness as grounded in a single, common source: their speechlessness. Most humane societies adopted the SPCA's motto, "We speak for those who cannot speak for themselves." This emphasis on animals' inability to speak was clearly borrowed from antebellum abolitionists, who described themselves acting as "mouth and utterance" for the enslaved and asserted that "we open our mouth for the dumb and plead for our brethren who cannot plead for themselves."[8] Though abolitionists claimed that slaves could not speak for themselves, they often specified that slaves were dumb because of social, not natural, conditions. The Lynn, Massachusetts, Women's Anti-Slavery Society, for example, praised Frederick Douglass's ability to "plead for those, who, by American laws, cannot plead for themselves." Slaves were forbidden from making legal testimony against whites, and this rule served abolitionists as a metaphor for their larger condition.[9] The difference between speech and silence was, abolitionists imagined, the difference between freedom and slavery; voicelessness was powerlessness.

For animal and child protectionists too the trope of speechlessness stood in for the inability to act physically, legally, and politically on one's own behalf. Reformers continually emphasized that "small animals, small children, young lives—they are all the same as far as the need of protection and gentleness is concerned." Of children, New York SPCC president Elbridge Gerry wrote that their "very innocence and helplessness present a cogent plea from which few can turn away." Though not literally mute, children were represented in anticruelty literature as without "the power of speech to make known their injuries," and like animals, without a voice because their "appeals for mercy and protection are unheeded" or because they are "afraid to complain and seek protection and help." Creating analogies between the situation of animals and that of children, most humanitarians agreed with Henry Bergh when he declared that "I regard a helpless child in the same light as the dumb animal. Both are God's creatures. Neither can protect themselves."[10]

Though Bergh and other anticruelty reformers sometimes explained the relationship between animal and child protection in terms of common helplessness, more often they rested their case on practical grounds: as in the case of Mary Ellen Wilson, citizens brought established SPCAs complaints of cruelty to children, and since there was no one else willing to investigate, they did it themselves. Indeed, there is much evidence to suggest that Etta Wheeler's impulse to bring a child-cruelty case to an animal protection organization was not singular. From its very earliest days, the Pennsylvania SPCA received complaints of cruelty to children and the Massachusetts SPCA likewise had to publicly remind its supporters that it did not prosecute cruelty to human beings. In spite of such disavowals, in 1876 the MSPCA did intervene in a case involving over-worked child acrobats.[11] Likewise, the Illinois Humane Society did not seek child-protective functions but took them because, as IHS board member Mrs. C. M. Fairchild recalled, "the abuse of children, as beings likewise with animals not able to speak for or defend themselves, was brought to the attention of the Society."[12] Whether reformers wanted to address cruelty to children or not, they were often forced to confront its existence by a public that saw animal and child protection as logical corollaries.

This public demand was not without its merits. Animal protection societies *were* equipped to intervene in cases of child cruelty and neglect in ways that most existing charities were not. As the New York SPCC's first president, John D. Wright, explained, many charities already existed to aid children, but they "assume the care and control of their inmates ONLY AFTER THEY ARE LEGALLY PLACED IN THEIR CUSTODY."[13] An agency modeled after the SPCA would, by contrast, actually ferret out cases of cruelty and, when necessary, remove children from the custody of their parents. Already granted police powers by their state charters, and already engaged in the business of receiving complaints, sending officers into the field to investigate, collect evidence, and bring the results before local magistrates, some SPCAs saw child protection as simply a matter of applying the same methods to different objects. In combining moral suasion with law enforcement, the SPCAs had created a unique organization that promised to pick up the slack left by city police departments. "The laws already exist for the protection of children and animals," explained the superintendent of the Wisconsin Humane Society, "but the police force is necessarily occupied with the gravest and most obvious cases of crime. Before the organization of this Society, no friendly and powerful hand had been especially delegated to rescue these children and animals from lives of misery and abuse, and to bring them, by an order of court, under the merciful care of humane people."[14] To some members of the general public, and to some anticruelty reformers, extending animal protection services to children made sense from a procedural standpoint: anticruelty organizations were specially empowered by the law in ways that could benefit children as well as animals, and the casework method developed in animal protection could be easily transferred to children as well.

There were, then, some practical reasons to join animal and child protection. On the surface, cruelty toward animals and children appeared the same—so too did the methods for alleviating it. But many humane societies experienced the merger as profoundly impractical. For one thing, anticruelty organizations found it difficult to divide attention and time between animals and children. In 1880, just three years after it had begun child as well as animal protection, the Illinois Humane Society assured its supporters that although the child cruelty caseload was increasing apace, "all cases of cruelty, whether toward children and animals, are carefully investigated and dealt with." In spite of this assurance, anxiety about the society's ability to adequately perform both functions proved persistent.[15] As President Shortall himself acknowledged during an 1897 speech, the decision to incorporate child protection within an existing SPCA was arrived at with some difficulty. Some of the organization's members feared "that with a horse and a child at the same time calling for help, the horse would be likely to suffer, at least by delay."[16] With limited staffing, money, finite time, and two different populations to serve and protect, how could humane societies avoid giving priority to either animals or children? How could the two functions complement rather than compete with one another?

The right balance proved hard to achieve. Some evidence suggests that, at least in the case of the IHS, animal and child protection did not easily fit together. During the late 1870s and early 1880s, IHS leaders considered breaking out child-saving functions into a separate organization. Just two years after joining animal and child protection, Shortall expressed anxiety at the 1879 annual meeting that, when faced with a choice between remedying cruelty to an animal or a child, "where one of these must be postponed, it will be that of cruelty to the brute."[17] The next year, Shortall again used his annual presidential address to argue for "the necessity of the organization of a branch of this Society which shall assume exclusively the protection of children from cruelty" since their "overworked city agent" could not handle all the complaints that came his way. That year, Shortall appointed and headed a special committee to investigate the formation of a separate SPCC.[18] However, by the next year's meeting Shortall had relented. His special committee reported that child protection "thus far has not lessened nor impaired the efficiency of our animal protection service." Further, the committee asserted that child protection "seems at present naturally and legitimately to belong to the work of the Humane Society" since no other state or local organization was prepared to absorb it. "Without our seeking it," they went on, "the work has come to us, we are doing it, and the public sentiment demands that we continue to do so." They resolved, therefore, simply to seek additional funds from the public to enhance their ability to "prosecute this work of protecting children (as well as animals) from cruelty, abuse and criminal neglect."[19] By 1884, doubt about the appropriate merger of animal and child protection had officially been abandoned. At that year's annual meeting, one of the society's founding directors and the author of the state's anticruelty legislation, John C. Dore, proclaimed that "prevention of cruelty to children and to dumb beasts, are part and parcel of the same work, and it is very fortunate that we never separated the two as I think was once considered."[20] Like the members of the general public who brought children's cases to animal protection organizations, Dore believed that animal and child protection were naturally aligned.

Though Shortall realized that it was not possible for the IHS to disaggregate into two separate societies, he did not, in the end, agree with Dore. Instead, after raising the issue of competition between animal and child cases, Shortall proposed a way out of the conundrum: the two caseloads could safely be combined precisely because they had so *little* in common. "There has been no collision of interests" between animal and child protection, Shortall somewhat disingenuously reported in 1897, because "the action of the Society in the separate fields is too dissimilar in process"—the children's cases being more complicated and requiring more lengthy involvement than those of animals.[21] Shortall's claim was echoed by William DeLoss Love, the president of the Connecticut Humane Society. Love also found that animal and child protection presented quite different problems. "The dual aim of a humane society, as an organization for the protection of both children and animals, inevitably leads to the study of diverse problems," he wrote. "The two conditions seem to have nothing in common except their helplessness."[22] As with Shortall, Love concluded that children's cases were more complex and protracted. Yet the Connecticut Humane Society, like the IHS, was not prepared to abandon either species among its charges.

Shortall and Love were right—the problems of animals were very different than the problems of children. Internal reports from the IHS's own officers illustrate the "diverse" problems facing those who would protect both animals and children. In an October 8, 1884, report to President Shortall, IHS agent O. L. Dudley described how he had spent his day. In the morning, Dudley had inspected a horse market and investigated a complaint about a whipped horse. Finding no witnesses to the whipping, Dudley returned to the office. While there, "a lady brought in a little girl 8 years of age." The girl, it turned out, was the sister of two other girls that Dudley had, the week prior, placed in Chicago's Home for the Friendless orphan asylum. All three girls, Dudley reported, were "driven away from home by a drunken step mother." After taking the third sister to the home, "[I] went and hunted up the father and brought him to the office and he signed surrenders giving all three of these girls to the Home for the Friendless."[23] Tracking commerce in and cruelty to horses in the morning, Dudley spent his afternoon presiding over the dissolution of a family. The problem facing the dual society was not simply, as some IHS members had feared, that either animals or children might be favored, but rather the disparate caseload facing officers such as Dudley.

When humane societies represented their chief purpose as the prevention of cruelty toward animals and children, they suggested that the problems confronting both populations were the same. Both suffered physical violence and were helpless to stop it. But as Dudley's report suggests, physical suffering of the sort typically imagined as cruelty formed only a portion of the caseload. Physical violence, or actions that caused physical suffering, were, moreover, a much larger portion of the caseload for animals than for children. In 1894, for example, the Fox River Valley branch of the Wisconsin Humane Society narrativized some "specimen cases" alongside statistical information about its yearly work. Among the animal cases described in the annual report, the society prosecuted offenders for dog fighting and for beating, overworking, and overdriving horses. Among the cases involving children, the society prosecuted some instances of physical cruelty: a child whose ear had been bitten by her parents, a case of father-daughter incest, an infant exposed to the cold for too long by its intoxicated parents. But the society also reported removing boys from a "gambling den," taking girls from a "lewd dance," and rescuing a child from a "drunk and dissolute" home. This disparity was not unique to the Fox River Valley. The annual reports of the St. Paul, Minnesota, Humane Society also illustrate the "diverse problems" dividing animal from child protection. In 1899, for example, the St. Paul Society reported tending to 801 animals. Of these 801, the society reported that a small minority, forty-nine, were cases of "general cruelty" and eighteen of "torturing." The vast majority of cases involved offenses against horses such as working them when galled, lame, or overloaded, or leaving them unblanketed in winter weather. Among the other animal cases, the society found homes for cats

and dogs, ordered poultry watered and fed, and "humanely killed" homeless cats, dogs, and injured livestock. During the same year, the society
tended to some 314 children's cases. Sixty-seven (or about 21 percent) of
these were cases of physical abuse, while another eighty-six (or 27 percent)
were cases of abandonment or neglect. Sixty-three were cases of destitution in which the child was placed in a home away from its parents. The
society also reported reprimanding minors for smoking, being in saloons,
working underage, and working in theaters. The majority of the St. Paul
Society's children's cases, in other words, were not episodes of physical
violence or even attempts to relieve bodily suffering.[24] Indeed, much of
the children's caseload—in the Fox River Valley, in St. Paul, and at anticruelty organizations throughout the country—centered on problems of
poverty, such as abandonment, neglect, and destitution, and on the protection of children's morals rather than their bodies.[25] So different were the
animal and child cases that many dual organizations had separate committees, departments, or officers dedicated to each client population. And
as the century wore on, the corporate body dedicated to dual protection,
the American Humane Association, began to formally divide its annual
meeting into separate sessions on animal and child protection.

In spite of the fact that animal and child protection cases proved to be
very different from one another, members of the public brought children's
cases to animal protectionists, and animal protectionists accepted the responsibility for them. As we have seen, when protectionists explained this
to themselves and to their supporters, they argued simply that animals
and children were alike in morally relevant ways—both were helpless—or
that the choice to combine functions was expedient, not ideological. But
neither the argument from expediency nor from common helplessness can
fully account for the union of animal and child protection. For, as we have
seen, the union was actually impractical. Helplessness, moreover, is too
capacious a category to explain this particular pairing. Why not women
and children? Animals and women? Children and the aged? The candi-
dates for helplessness, in other words, were numerous, but only the link
between animals and children proved institutionally persistent.

The origins of the institutional link between animal and child protection
lay not simply in expedience, the moral relevance of helplessness, or even
in the peculiar case of Mary Ellen Wilson. Rather, a cultural link between
animals and children had been solidified in the antebellum years by domestic ideology. Over the course of the nineteenth century, the legal and

cultural status of both children and animals changed as each was transformed from an economic to a sentimental investment, from being adjuncts in the family economy to the center of family affections. Domestic
ideology not only positioned both children and pets at the center of the
family, but also promoted new ideas about discipline that were shuttled
back and forth across the species line.

As historians have detailed, the ideology of domesticity reshaped
American notions about the purpose of the family, its home, and particularly about the economic role of women and children. Although the process occurred unevenly across racial, class, and geographic lines, in general
the development of a market economy removed the production of essential
goods from the home and provided women with readymade food, clothing,
and other labor-saving devices. The consequences of such shifts were as
much cultural as economic. As economic changes created a conceptual
and spatial division between home and work, moralists crafted a new role
for the home as the center of virtue, religion, and tender feelings.[26]

The same shifts in the economy and household production that increasingly separated home and work also contributed to the development of new
ideas about childhood. When households had been sites of production and
the centers of the family economy, children, like their mothers, had been
productive agents and necessary laborers. Common law held that fathers,
but not mothers, had a near absolute right to the control and custody of
their children and a right to their labor power, as children were routinely
employed in household labor and apprenticed out to work in other households. As James Kent put the matter in his antebellum *Commentaries on
American Law*, a father "is entitled to the custody of their [his children's]
persons, and to the value of their labor and services" during minority.[27]
From the colonial period through much of the nineteenth century, common law chiefly framed the relations between parents and children as a
"labor relationship," analogous to that between masters and servants
and, more distantly, that between masters and slaves. Fathers or masters
were obligated to provide educational, religious, and nutritional support,
while children were duty-bound to offer obedience and labor. In a tightly
organized household-based economy, such a high premium was placed on
obedience that while laws prohibited guardians from "unreasonably" punishing children, courts interpreted reasonableness quite liberally, giving
fathers, masters, and teachers wide latitude. Thus, while fathers did not
enjoy an unlimited power over their offspring—fathers' rights depended
on the performance of their duties—children were regarded less as indi-

viduals with distinct interests and rights and more as constituent units in the overlapping and hierarchically ordered domains of the household and the economy.[28]

By the mid-nineteenth century, however, the structural and ideological edifice of middle-class domesticity had transformed children into objects of sentimental, not economic, value. Once seen as miniature adults, by the antebellum period adults all over the Western world were coming to view children as unique beings and childhood as a prolonged and protected period of dependence. Middle-class families had fewer children, removed them from the labor force, and extended their schooling. Prescriptive child-rearing literature proliferated to guide American mothers in cultivating their children's health and character.[29] This new emphasis on childhood as a special time of life in which maternal guidance and cultivation of character were necessary to prepare for adulthood was undergirded by changes in educational theory and Protestant theology. Both emphasized children's essential goodness and malleability, positioning them as innocents in need of protection and guidance rather than as sinful creatures in need of discipline and salvation. Earlier generations who had subscribed to the stern, Calvinist doctrine of original sin believed that the task of child-rearing was to break the child's will in order to bend him toward God. But the rise of liberal protestant doctrines that stressed a loving, even maternal, God, universal salvation, and gentle conversion also affected popular ideas about children and childrearing. Instead of seeing children as wicked, many antebellum advice-givers stressed their innate goodness and viewed religious and moral instruction as a process of shaping rather than breaking the child. At their most extreme, liberal Protestants imagined children as uncorrupted angels, closer to God and true religion than their parents. In her 1844 advice manual, *The Mother's Book*, Lydia Maria Child expressed this position, reminding her readers that "children come to us from heaven, their little souls full of innocence and peace." In addition to being pictured as angels, popular religious literature and fiction was populated by the image of the "child redeemer" whose innocence and simple piety—and often untimely death—converted those around him or her.[30]

The assumption that children were innocent and pure was also fed by the growing influence of romanticism on American thought. If liberal theologians and manual writers such as Child positioned children as closer to God, romantics found the reason for this in children's proximity to nature, which they understood as the source of truth and goodness. Echoing the image of the child-redeemer promulgated in more mainstream religious texts, American transcendalist Ralph Waldo Emerson wrote that "we distrust and deny inwardly our sympathy with nature," but "infancy is the perpetual Messiah, which comes into the arms of fallen men, and pleads with them to return to paradise." Here Emerson located the source of religious truth in nature and positioned children as its especial conduits. In contrast to earlier religious and childrearing ideals that stressed innate depravity and proper socialization, romantics believed that children were innocent at birth and that socialization all too often tended to corrupt rather than realize man's true nature. The closer one could be to the original state—symbolized both by nature and the child, the better.[31]

Romantic reassessments of nature affected not only children, but also animals, and configured the link between the two positively. Like children, animals often served romantic writers as exemplars of purity and innocence. And because romantics saw animals as more than mere brutes, or symbols of human will and passion, they positioned animals in a similar symbolic space with children: close to nature, uncorrupted, a conduit to truth. The association of animals with children (and children with animals) was not new, but romanticism and domesticity transformed its valence from negative to positive. Where seventeenth- and eighteenth-century parents feared children's animality, nineteenth-century parents were less troubled by it. As historian Karin Calvert has shown, colonial American parents feared infant "creeping" or "crawling" because they believed that the habit of walking on all fours was not a developmental phase, but a dangerous approximation of animal locomotion that would, if left unchecked, consign the crawling child to a fallen life among savages and beasts. Belying a sense of both the distance between and the perilous proximity of man and animal, colonial Americans employed all manner of artificial means to make their children erect as soon as possible. Early American children's books accordingly portrayed animals not as friends but as distant underlings, useful helpmeets, or dangerous and savage beasts.[32] By contrast, in the antebellum years, parents came to accept infant crawling as yet another charming instance of children's separation from adult modalities. Children's apparent animality was also reinterpreted. Where seventeenth- and eighteenth-century parents might have thought their children like animals because they expressed unrestrained passions and an unregulated will, nineteenth-century parents increasingly understood the animality of children as natural and untroubling. "The baby is an animal," wrote one mid-nineteenth-century author, "and so the child should be—and its devotion, on the whole should be to its body." It was normal for children to want to run, scream, and play, and, in the words of the parenting manual author George Ackerly, "every effort to restrain them in their youthful gambols is as unnatural as it would be to confine the deer in the midst of the forest." Indeed, by the mid-nineteenth century the sheer physicality of early childhood was so accepted among middle-class parents that they were more likely to fret over the unnatural mental development of their young children—their "precocity"—then than they were to fear their declension into sin and savagery.[33]

It was not only the symbolic, but also the material relationships between children and animals that antebellum Americans came to see as manifold and positive. This was due in large part to the ways in which domesticity inflected the practice of petkeeping and the deep connections that the ideology of petkeeping forged between animals and children. Like children, pets too served as icons of home and family for mid-nineteenth-century Americans. As sources of labor and food, animals had long been a part of the household economy. Despite the economic changes wrought by urbanization and industrialization, animals did not disappear from the nineteenth-century American landscape. Laboring animals were as ubiquitous a part of the town as they were of the country, central to familial as well as to industrial life. Well into the nineteenth century, even town-dwelling middle-class households were likely to keep some useful animals like chickens, livestock, or a horse on their property. Increasingly, however, middle-class families also sought out economically useless animals—birds, cats, dogs, guinea pigs, mice, or squirrels—whose sole function was to provide companionship; pets provided an object of emotional investment for family members, especially children. By mid-century, an accelerating market in pets and pet supplies was established, making animals and their accoutrements widely available.[34]

Pets were more than simply a new market niche and petkeeping more than a mere habit acquired by middle-class families. Rather, keeping pets was a practice closely linked to domestic ideology, as pets were transformed, like children, into beings that had sentimental rather than economic value. The similar status of domestic animals and children—their mutual function as, first, laborers, and second, as cherished objects of emotional investment—is reflected in the etymology of the word "pet." From its sixteenth-century origins, "pet" had referred simultaneously to a "spoiled child" and "a domesticated, fondled, young animal."[35] In the preindustrial family-subsistence economy, when both animals and children were chiefly labor sources, "pet" was a pejorative term—an association reflected in the word's third meaning, to be in a "pet," or "fit," as in the sort of tantrum in which a spoiled child would indulge. Long associated with economic uselessness and the misinvestment of (adult) emotional energies, the esteem of the "pet" rose with industrialization and the separation of home and work. In mediating the transition from laboring to bourgeois family, and the moral separation of home and marketplace, the care of pets, plants, and children provided a model of what literary critic Lori Merish has called "sentimental ownership," in which the proper relation of persons to things was defined by emotional investment rather than rational calculation, and the economic and status inequalities of both the traditional patriarchal family and the market were masked by "norms of emotional interdependency."[36] Sharing a similar role as cherished and dependent, both animals and children were designated as "pets" throughout the nineteenth century, but this had come to signify preciousness rather than petulance.

Animals and children were connected not simply by the term "pet" or the economic changes that eroded their status as economic agents, but also by the way in which the ideology of petkeeping positioned relationships with animals as critical to child development. Under the rubric of domesticity, the presence of pet animals in the home was, as historian Katherine Grier has shown, transformed from an indulgence of the idle rich to a morally mandatory activity for the middle classes. Consistent with the notion that the home was an arena of fellow-feeling and heart-cultivation, antebellum advice books aimed at the middle class instructed parents that children who cared for pets would learn to be gentle, kind, and benevolent toward man and beast alike.[37] "Nothing will possibly be so efficacious in softening the feelings of children towards animals," predicted one author, "as to bring them up in the society of domestic pets, such as a gentle-tempered dog, a cat, or a bird."[38] Because the care of pets taught children to be kind and gentle, the activity provided an opportunity for children to reproduce and internalize familial affection, acting toward pets as their own parents did toward them. "I have always found the presence of lower animals and pets in the family favorable to gentle and humanizing feelings in the highest degree," wrote E. Oakes Smith. For "the care of them calls out the necessity of attention and watchfulness, providence and forecast, in order to supply their natural requirements. Thus the boy and the girl unconsciously acquire neatness and order and that development of the sympathies without which the character is hard, worldly and mechanical. . . . and the sentiments thus engendered exercise a wholesome influence upon their whole after-life."[39] By teaching children that relations with animals were governed by the same rules as those with humans, middle-class parents naturalized an idealized version of family life and prepared their children to assume their future roles as tenderhearted, self-disciplined mothers and fathers.[40]

A story published in an antebellum keepsake book, "Mary and the Kittens," illustrates the extent to which petkeeping was understood to offer young children lessons in domesticity. Mrs. Puss, the cat who lives on Mary's farm, has given birth to a litter of kittens. A young male farmhand swoops the kittens up and delivers them to Mary, declaring that they must be drowned—the most common method of feline population control. Mary refuses to allow this, and announces that she will find homes for the kittens. Upon hearing this, Mrs. Puss begins to purr and rub up against her, indicating that Mary has successfully aligned her feelings and actions with that of the mother cat. Once Mary has found homes for all her feline charges, however, she feels sad instead of rewarded, "as though she had lost all that she loved, all that loved her." Having made caretaking central to her identity, Mary is relieved of her sadness only when she begins a stroll around the farm and finds that the chickens run up to her, the tame starling calls out her name, and Hector the dog and Billy the goat rush to greet her. Surrounded by these animals, "Mary's sadness passed away and her heart grew glad again, for she felt that there was always *something* to love, and something to love us."[41] As practiced in her dealings with animals, Mary had learned more than kindness; she had also learned to constitute herself through creating, and caring for, families. With a heart full of love, the story suggested, Mary would continue to create happy families wherever she went.

The antebellum understanding of petkeeping as both domestic and didactic was readily absorbed by animal protectionists in the postwar years. Humane education advocates involved in the WCTU, the AHA, and countless local organizations too assumed a connection between petkeeping and their campaign for character education. Every classroom in the country, wrote one such proponent, should have a pet so that its pupils' attention can "be called to the silent appeals of those dependent upon us for food and protection."[42] Children should have pets, suggested another, so that "by their early acquaintance with animals" they will "unconsciously acquire considerable knowledge of natural history, and their experience with their pets is not only a pleasure in itself, but a step in education."[43] During the summer months, Boston's Animal Rescue League formed "Kindness Clubs," in which youngsters took charge of formerly homeless animals and thereby helped not just the animals, but all of society since, remarked the league's director, "if children are taught to be kind and considerate of the rights and comforts of the lower animals the chances are that they will make far better citizens."[44] Here the familial relation of pet to child was used as a model for citizenship, as though the qualities of sympathy and tenderheartedness that made for a good caretaker were identical to those that made for a good citizen.

The animal protection movement's proliferating humane education textbooks also emphasized the links between sympathetic feelings, family organization, and the principles undergirding the republic. An organizer in the WCTU's Department of Mercy, Emma Page published her textbook *Heart Culture* in 1897, announcing that she aimed "to arouse and stimulate a sense of humanity, of honor, of justice, and of honesty in every detail of daily living and to continue the development of sympathetic interest and care of all forms of life."[45] Pets were integral to this project, as they provided an opportunity to learn how to care for others and thus served as a means of developing the capacity for intersubjective identification, which Page defined as the basis of moral judgment. Opening the book's section on pets, Page remarked, "it is worth while for us to study carefully the rights and needs of the beings about us, whether they be human or dumb, and be mindful of them." Learning the proper care of domestic animals, she suggested, "may tend to create a greater feeling of responsibility and sympathy for the creatures we have made dependent upon us." And sympathy is, in the end, she told her young readers, "the most important lesson of the many lessons you have to learn."[46] With that in mind, Page's petkeeping instructions explicitly encouraged her young readers to equate animals with human children. In the matter of feeding, for instance, she asked them whether it would be right for a human mother to forget to feed her baby just because it was helpless and could not ask for its food. Assuming that all would condemn this behavior, Page guided her readers to analogize from babies to animals, and posed the moral of the story as a rhetorical question: "Then is it not cruel to neglect dumb animals, and leave them to suffer from cold, and thirst, and hunger, just because they can't tell us what they want?"[47] In a somewhat contradictory series of associations, Page assumed that her young readers could identify both with the baby left unfed and with the mother, as she asked them to transfer their feelings from baby to animal, and then to transform these into guideposts for proper motherly caretaking.

Page's moral lesson exemplifies one longstanding function of petkeeping as a didactic enterprise: to teach children to become adults who can exercise self-control in their dealings with equals and, more importantly, subordinates. As dependent beings, animals afforded children an opportunity to act as miniature adults, mirroring both the relation between parent and child, and between God and man. These lessons in ideal adult behavior were, unsurprisingly, gendered.[48] Girls, naturally assumed to be sympathetic and good, practiced their mothering skills, as did Mary when she rescued Mrs. Puss and her kittens. In a story that enshrined the same ethic of kindness, a young girl rescued a wounded cat, nursing it back to health under her constant care. So reared, the girl's cat learned to live with her pet bird, who had presumably been similarly brought up. "The bird and kittie [sic] live at present on amicable terms," the story concluded, "eating and drinking together with that polite and respectful demeanor which should characterize family relationship."[49] Thanks to her natural mothering instinct, the girl not only repaired physical wounds, but did what all good women should do, subduing household conflict and inculcating self-control through kind treatment.

If mothering seemed to come naturally to the girls who populated such stories, boys were generally depicted as needing a bit more refinement. Humane authors were loath to attribute innate evil to anyone, even boys, so they assumed that greater male violence was a bad habit acquired very early on and continually reinforced by the favorite pastimes of boys (which included stoning frogs, capturing butterflies, poking cows with sticks, and chasing cats).[50] Not only were boys deemed more "thoughtless" of others than girls, but also they were more likely to occupy positions of power as adults, making their unchecked passions a source of more potential danger. Significantly, if girls were most often credited as the creators of happy families, the most common charge against boys was their destruction of home life, symbolized by their penchant for stealing birds' eggs and nests and for shooting them with guns and slingshots.[51] Scarcely a humane publication failed to upbraid boys for these practices. In these admonishments boys were asked alternatively to imagine themselves as baby birds, frightened or lonely upon being kidnapped, or as mother birds, brokenhearted at the destruction of the nest. In *The Birds Nest & Other Stories*, Young Harrie, for instance, brings home a bird's nest to his mother, who tells him that he must put it back where he found it or "when the parents would find out that their young ones were missing, they would be much distressed and would hardly know what to do, for they had as much affection for their young, as a human being."[52] Likewise, humane publications featured first-person stories from bird mothers, pictures of dead bird babies and wrecked homes, and role-reversal scenarios in which boys were snatched from their homes by giant, menacing birds.[53] Meant to develop empathy in boys, reformers seemed to hope these didactic fantasies would transform boys from home-wreckers to home-defenders. "There are very few good children," declared one humane author, "who have had proper instruction who will not protect the houses and cradles of the infant birds as they would that of their own baby sister or brother."[54] To ratify this point, the same publications never tired of holding up as exemplars men like Abraham Lincoln and Theodore Parker, who had either restrained themselves from acting on cruel impulses, or actively restored a rent avian domesticity.[55]

The utility of pets and an ethic of kindness toward animals were not, however, limited to scenarios in which children benevolently ruled over animals. In addition to being surrogates on whom children could practice their grown-up behaviors, pets were also cast as moral exemplars for children, beings from whom they could actually *learn* genteel values. In this respect, no animal was more heralded than the loyal family dog. Jacob Abbott, the popular author of "Rollo" books for children, provided an early example of dog-as-model. His 1854 collection of stories, entitled *Bruno; or, Lessons of Fidelity, Patience, and Self-Denial Taught by a Dog*, left none of its lessons to the imagination. Bruno was loyal to his master, most proud and happy when he had a duty to perform, and willing and eager to learn. During the course of Abbott's book, Bruno exalts in the quintessential heroic deeds of the canine race—saving his master's life and the life of his master's child, running off thieves, ferreting out missing objects in the dense forest, and leading lost travelers to their proper path. "Learn from the example of Bruno," Abbott advised, "to find your happiness in the diligent and faithful performance of duty."[56] Humane leaflets in subsequent years repeated stories of dog heroism, suggesting not only that their deeds made dogs worthy of respect, but also that these humble heroes were character models for children everywhere.[57]

As petkeeping became a defining feature of bourgeois family life, humanitarians assumed not only that pets were morally good for children to have, but also that animals and children naturally gravitated toward one another. In part, this imagined gravitation derived from a shared role in the household. Over the course of the nineteenth century, the portrayal of domestic animals as servants was eclipsed by their representation as children.[58] Consonant with this, both domestic pets and children were positioned as family-constituting beings that attracted emotional investment and care and provided a channel for the performance of the middle-class family's purported raison d'être: nurturance. Depicted elsewhere in humanitarian literature as capable of forming families based on deep and lasting emotional ties, animals also served to complete human domestic fantasies by standing in as surrogate children.[59]

Published in the juvenile journal the *Riverside Magazine*, "Marrying for the Sake of a Dog" tells the story of a man named Cabassol, who had believed that a family could consist of man and dog alone. For many years, he was quite content to live with his faithful dog Medor, given to him by a woman who was moving away. One day, however, after several years of happiness together, Medor began to "howl and whine in the most piteous and unaccountable manner" right in the midst of eating his supper. As it turned out, he had detected the presence of his former mistress, whose presence made the dog roll "in an ecstasy of joy." She had come to reclaim the dog. Cabassol would not relinquish Medor for any fee and, after much argument, proposed instead that they let the dog decide. Man, woman, and dog set off, with Medor "frisking about them in great glee," happy for their togetherness as the trio marched to the top of a nearby hill. At the top, Cabassol set off down the northern slope while the woman descended the southern edge—whomever Medor followed would be his true master. The dog, however, had given each "half his heart" and raced back and forth between the two until he collapsed from exhaustion back at the top of the hill. Medor was not too tired, however, to wag his tail feebly when his master and mistress reunited beside him as he lay panting. Cabassol and the woman realized that it would "break his heart" to separate Medor from either one of them. The only solution, clearly, was for the two to marry. "And so they married," the story ends, "to please the dog."[60] While the story can be interpreted as the melting of a man's heart as he learns that he needs the soul-nourishment of a family, it is through the dog-as-child, through its needs, affections, and attachments, that domesticity is configured. Just as children might learn proper "heart culture" through their pets and practice ideal family relations with them, so too adult families are both completed and formed through emotional investment in the pet-child. Every family ought to have a dog, wrote another author on the same theme, "for it is like having a perpetual baby in the house."[61] To have a perpetual baby was, in the context of nineteenth-century bourgeois family ideals, to continually enact the family's emotional constellation and reason for being.

*Little Pet*, a children's book published in 1872, amply illustrates the sentimental coupling of animal and child both within the family and under the term "pet." The subject of the story is a young girl aptly called "Pet," whose birth is the cause of much exultation: "What joy there was in the house when baby Pet was born! How happy were papa and mamma, and how proud was nurse to see the plump baby and kiss her little soft cheeks!" As the object of so much properly channeled affection, she is a "pet," and her story details her daily activities from infancy through age eight, when she has to begin the transition out of childhood by going to school. During this protected preschool phase of her life, her companions and activities almost wholly consist of or relate to animals. She is never shown playing with other children, but instead with her "Noah's Ark" toys, rollicking with her cat and dog and lamb, learning to spell her first words, such as "cat" and "dog" and "horse" and "doll." As a pet, the girl's time is absorbed in intimacy with like beings who seem to exist as both her equals and her playthings, but with whom she finds ready companionship and through whom she begins to learn the skills that will make her an adult. When she turns eight, Pet receives a new name, Addie, signaling her transformation from pet-child to school-going young lass. She matures and leaves the family's nest, while her animal companions stay behind, fulfilling their roles as perpetual babies.[62] The equation of Pet's loss of childhood with her disassociation from her animal friends is a theme repeated by many nineteenth-century authors who nostalgically represent the pains of assuming adulthood with the loss of childhood pets. Their animals remain, for such authors, a means of accessing and symbolizing the falling away of their own innocence in the passage from dependence to adulthood.[63]

The positive valence of animal and child pets was not lost on humane society activists, who similarly portrayed animals and children as connected within the domestic sphere. "Two Little Pets" (fig. 1), a picture from the *Humane Journal*, deploys this linkage, as does the image of "Children and Young Animals" (fig. 2) from the same publication. The young girl and her dog in figure 1 illustrate the popular practice of posing children with pets for portraits, and affirms the middle-class status of the dyad—the girl, through her clothes, and the dog, through his non-utilitarian size and his residence on his little mistress's lap. The portrait shows both the connection that child and dog have with one another, and their mutual status as objects of a sentimentalizing gaze.[64] The children and their lamb in figure 2 seem, at first glance, to tell a different story. The scene is pastoral, but the children are in a field, possibly having labored there, and their pet is a lamb—an ambiguous pet to be sure. For although one of the original denotations of the word "pet" was "cade lamb," a lamb brought up by hand, the lamb is a useful animal, an item of stock that, unlike the family dog or cat, will be expected to produce milk, wool, and perhaps even meat.[65] Like the

*TWO LITTLE PETS.*

**Figure 1.** Animals and children as pets. *Humane Journal* 10, no. 3 (March 1882), 43.

girl-pet who transforms into Addie, the lamb will leave the protected phase of its life and enter an animal adulthood of labor and eventual death. The text accompanying this picture offers, however, another and more positive interpretation of the scene, one that recasts both the children and their lamb in the familiar terms of middle-class domesticity. "The sympathy between young animals and children has often been marked by observers," the caption begins. Noting that "the young of all domesticated creatures exhibit similar traits of character," the text explains that this is because they are all "naturally buoyant of temperament," and because "the exuberance of their animal life renders it necessary that they should expend their excessive stock of spirits in some positive manner." Hence, sheltered from the "cares of active life" and "relieved of trouble as to their own support, they naturally take to play" together—children, dogs, and lambs all "gamboling and tumbling and running and hiding" in mutual sport. And though the scene at hand does not show animals and children at play together, it nevertheless depicts another phase of the "close friendship that

*CHILDREN AND YOUNG AMIMALS.*

**Figure 2.** Animals and children as pets. *Humane Journal* 8, no. 11 (November 1880): 3.

may exist between young animals and children."[66] Identifying animals and children as similarly dependent, nonlaboring, carefree, and overflowing with "animal," or physical, energy, the text erases the labor of both in order that they may occupy the innocence afforded middle-class pets.

Beyond occupying a similar space in the family cast of characters, children and animals were also represented as having a special emotional connection that drew them toward one another. As the *Humane Journal*'s explanation of the "natural sympathy" between children and animals suggests, the imagined likeness between the two rested on more than just status and family role. Humanitarians and popular authors assumed, sometimes unconsciously, that animals and children shared a space of subjectivity not available to adults. Their mutual sympathy is the subject of *The Pet Fawn*, a story about a girl named Mary and the deer that her uncle has given her as a present. With the deer Mary finds solace and friendship, seeking out the fawn whenever she is feeling badly. "The fawn would seem to understand her sorrow, licking her face, and trying to show its sympathy, and Mary would feel that in her pet she had one real true friend."[67] Mary and the fawn represent a world unto themselves, a dyad outside the adult world (the place that seems to cause Mary's suffering), and their bond is immediate and natural, depending on empathy rather than language.

Humane publications echoed the themes of *The Pet Fawn*, frequently printing stories of children who had found the truest companionship in empathetic relations with animals. "Miss Murphy," by Francis Orr, describes how John, a sickly boy, is sent out West to live on his uncle's ranch in the hopes that the clean country air will bolster his health. John feels at home there only after he befriends the eponymous young calf. Like John, Miss Murphy is separated from her mother, and after hearing her bellow and cry all day long, the boy realizes that the calf is lonely and misses her mother. He goes to her in the yard and speaks gently to her, commiserating with her sadness. As he talks, he cries, missing his own mother, and the calf begins to lick his hand "sympathetically." "That was the beginning of a strange friendship which was not long confined to the cattle yard." John realizes that Miss Murphy is a perfect friend because they are in the same situation, lonely and away from their mothers. The two go everywhere together, and when John is too sick to come outside, Miss Murphy stands by his window as a silent comforter. As the calf grows, so too does John, who "seemed to absorb strength from her." Finally, the power of the bond between these two "pets" reconstitutes John's family—his parents move out West to be with him and open a dairy farm, thus insuring that he can continue to spend his days around cows (that, fortunately, will not be killed for meat).[68] With animals, the children of these stories find comfort and empathy that the adult world seems unable to offer.

This shared subjectivity was also manifest in the use of talking animals in children's literature. Animals talked to children in Western literature in ways they did not to adults. While the phenomenon of talking animals in literature has a long history, it was not until the late eighteenth century that children's authors began to offer animals as individual protagonists with whom children could identify. Prior to that, talking animals were a staple of fable and satire, a means for either imparting moral lessons or critiquing social pretensions. Beginning with Englishwoman Sarah Trimmer's 1786 *Fabulous Histories*, later known by the title *The History of the Robins*, the nonsatirical talking-animal genre flourished, and was aimed almost strictly at children rather than adults.[69] Stories with talking animals and autobiographies of dogs, cats, mice, and horses proliferated on both sides of the Atlantic throughout the nineteenth century, and only some of these were the work of avowed animal protectionists.[70] For their part, humanitarians encouraged children not only to identify with animals on the page, but also to enter imaginatively into their minds and give them voice, effectively replicating the structures of talking-animal fiction in their own words. Humane education curricula suggested essay topics for children that included "How I Found a Home," which could be written in the voice or either a cat or a dog, "What My Dog Would Say to Me If He Could Talk," "The Autobiography of a Work Horse," and "A Letter from the Horse to His Master."[71] In their humanitarian guise, talking animals certainly taught lessons and remained critical observers, but this strategy depended on an identification of children with animals rather than the topsy-turvy fantasy world of earlier animal satire.

The almost total equation of talking animals with children is evinced by the changing fortunes of Englishwoman Anna Sewell's internationally famous *Black Beauty* (1877). Sewell did not write the story for children; rather, she intended its audience to be the late adolescent and adult male grooms and drivers of horses, and the book contains a healthy dose of technical horse-keeping instruction.[72] However, its combination of talking animals and moral didacticism made it too attractive to keep away from children, and Sewell's London publisher soon issued "school editions" of the novel. Likewise, in the United States *Black Beauty* was first published by the American Humane Education Society in 1890 at the behest of Massachusetts SPCA founder and president, George Angell, who immediately identified it as a key text in his humane education mission. Though some in the United States took up the cause of distributing Sewell's novel to horse-tenders and drivers, most reflexively categorized it as a children's book. Simpler versions of the story, with comprehension questions included, were serialized for younger children in the *Humane Journal*, and the book was widely adopted in public school classrooms (it came recommended by the U.S. commissioner of education, William T. Harris), and as a component of missionary education campaigns among the children of Native American and African American populations.[73] Its utility in humane education efforts that were directed primarily at children only partly explains the rapid rise of *Black Beauty* as a children's book; a full explanation reveals a larger culture that assumed that children and animals were naturally sympathetic to one another. Making her protagonist speak in first person, Sewell traded on sympathy, and while humanitarians wanted everyone to have sympathy with animals, they, like others, readily assumed that children were more likely than adults to achieve this bond. As helpless innocents, animals and children were closer to one another than was either to the corrupt and hardened world of adult humans.

In 1871 Jacob Abbott, the author who had, in 1854, taught children moral lessons through his canine character Bruno, published the manual *Gentle Measures in the Training and Management of the Young*. Though Abbott normally aimed his didacticism at children, now he sought to reach their parents. The aim was, as Abbott explained, to teach parents how to establish and exercise their authority through the eponymous "gentle measures." The language Abbott chose to describe his techniques was drawn from horse training, where the art of "gentling" rather than "breaking" horses into submission had been popularized. Indeed, the frontispiece illustration to *Gentle Measures* suggested the connection between training horses and children (fig. 3). The illustration shows a couple riding in a horse-drawn carriage that has drawn up in front of a well-appointed home. The woman passenger points toward the home's porch, where a small child sits waiting on a rocking chair, while a groom attends to the horse. The picture is captioned "Authority," but the referent seems both multiple and ambiguous. The couple has authority over their horse, the groom who attends them, and over the child who is waiting obediently for their return. But it is the horse and their relationship to it and the groom that occupy the visual center of the picture—the child is in the background— suggesting that the "authority" in question begins with the couple's relationship to the horse and extends to the child.[74]

Abbott's metaphoric and literal use of animal training as a source

AUTHORITY.

**Figure 3.** Discipline across the species line. Jacob Abbott, *Gentle Measures in the Management and Training of the Young* (New York: Harper & Brothers, 1871), frontispiece.

for childrearing techniques is a particularly vivid example of the ways in which new ideas about discipline, developed in the bosom of the family, were shuttled back and forth across the species line throughout the mid to late nineteenth century. In addition to economic and cultural trends that sentimentalized animals and children as perpetual babies, as family-constituting beings, and as natural intimates, the cultural equations between the two were both forged and reflected in changing ideas about training and discipline. As we shall see in chapter 3, humanitarians considered cruelty to animals and children similar in nature and logically linked, with animals serving as object lessons in cruelty to human beings. But it was not just the *improper* treatment of children and animals that reformers considered identical—ideals for the proper management of animals and children were also remarkably similar. Positing both as essentially innocent and good, reformers argued that the character of beasts and babes was alike ruined through cruelty and redeemed through kindness. If animals or children behaved badly, owners and handlers, or parents and teachers, need look no further than themselves for the cause.

The notion that animals and children were good until made bad by their superiors reflected not just the changed assessments of animal and child nature discussed above, but also a widespread revaluation of the role of punishment in education and character training. Based on similar suspicions about the effects of physical punishment on both the whipper and the whipped, antebellum reformers had railed against corporal punishment in schools, prisons, and the navy. Educators, moralists, and other would-be advisors advanced the notion that those in authority should "substitute kindness and suasion for corporal punishment."[75] Besides brutalizing the souls of all involved, corporal punishment's detractors framed it as an ineffectual method of training that compelled a cursory, outward obedience while leaving the mind and the soul untouched.[76] Only by being kind and winning the affections of one's charges, whether they be employees, children, or sailors, could true allegiance, and thus lasting obedience, be obtained.

In place of physical corrections, reformers substituted what Richard Brodhead has called "disciplinary intimacy" or "discipline through love."[77] In both antebellum novels and childrearing manuals, discipline was refigured as an affective and intimate process. Parents or schoolmasters were advised be kind to their charges to gain their love and trust. Once a child identified with an authority figure, he or she could be ruled through the granting and withdrawal of affection, and would eventually come to internalize the authority figure's likes and dislikes, accepting the rules both as the condition of love and acceptance and as the right ordering of the world. This would yield, reformers hoped, a far more thoroughgoing effect on a child's character than would external blows, with their power to touch the body alone, or, worse, actually to harden a rebellious heart.[78]

By the time that humane societies took up the cause of child protection, they did not need convincing on this point, though they believed that many others still did. "The lash," protested the Wisconsin Humane Society, "never changed a child's nature." On the contrary, "it embitters, arouses and cultivates the very worst parts of the child's nature." Every child can, however, assured the society, "be managed by kindness and affection," the only paths to true character formation.[79] Anticruelty activists also attributed bad behavior on the part of children to prior mistreatment rather than an originally sinful nature.[80] Writing in the 1882 edition of the *Humane Journal*, B. A. Ulrich advised parents to abandon the strategy of trying to break the child's will. Not only would weak-willed children make poor citizens in a republic since they would not be likely to stand up for themselves, but also punishing a child for a bad temperament was a misassignation of responsibility. "The child," Ulrich wrote, "should not be blamed for [its character], for the cause rests with the parents, and not with the child. *The child is innocent of its own creation.*"[81]

Other anticruelty publications echoed this sentiment. "The Effect of Parental Severity upon Children," by Samuel Smiles, advanced the notion that "the child does not make his own temper; nor has any control, while a child, over its direction." Rather, "if the parents have conferred an irritable temper on the child, it is their duty to exercise self-control, forbearance, and patience" to correct it. Physical punishment would, Smiles predicted, only make matters worse by instilling a love of tyranny and violence in the child that would end in "inflicting pain upon school-fellows under their own age, and upon dumb, sentient creatures." As a further corollary, Smiles claimed that children's cruelty to animals reflected a brutal nature that itself was caused by cruelty. "There is an enormous amount of cruelty practiced upon animals," he observed, "originating, we believe, in the physical punishment which has been received in the family or in the school."[82] Likewise Thomas Hill's encyclopedic humanitarian tract, *Ways of Cruelty*, voiced the classic sentiment that the problem with cruelty to children was that it both "debases" its inflictor and "brutalizes the nature of the child" who receives the blows.[83]

As with children, reformers identified physical punishment of animals as a wholly unjustifiable method of management by arguing both that its recipients were by definition innocent of their alleged transgressions and that their behavior would be *worse* rather than better as a result of its infliction. Humanitarians most often exemplified their claims with the horse, to which their drivers and riders looked for predictable and controllable behavior. Thomas Hill's entry in *Ways of Cruelty* on "A Good Disposition Spoiled by Whipping" claimed that "it is always unfortunate for the helpless to be at the mercy of the cruel, so it is a sad misfortune to the horse to fall into the hands of an ill-tempered master" not only because of the physical suffering endured, but also because "however kind the disposition of this horse may have been in the beginning, it is soon spoiled by this cruel treatment."[84] The ASPCA similarly emphasized the faultlessness of horses in their 1866 pamphlet *A Brief Account of Some of the So-Called Vices Practised by Horses*, claiming that all instances of equine rebellion—balking, kicking, biting, and so on—were plainly the result of bad treatment rather than ill will or bad intentions on the part of the horse. Profoundly shaped by individual experience, horses do not forget their past. Therefore, "before joining in the cry against equine vice," advised the text, "always investigate the act which is adduced to justify the prejudice," and see if the horse might not, based on its prior treatment, be acting in a more or less reasonable manner.[85]

Reformers also included other animals in their ruined-through-cruelty

narratives. In humane recitation contests, for instance, children were assigned to retell a story proving that a cow with an inclination to kick had
been improperly "broken" by its owners. Cats, too, came in under this defense. "Cats are stigmatized as treacherous, ungrateful, thievish, deceit-
ful, and so on through the entire list of adjectives of that class," claimed
Kate Thorn. But this, she went on, only shows that they have been poorly
treated. A properly fed, petted, and loved cat will neither steal from nor
betray its keepers. Dogs, likewise, wrote animal defender T. T. Munger,
absorb "the spirit of the household, almost as quickly and as fully as a
child, and they tell no lies about it," behaving well or ill according to the
company that keeps them.[86]

The rise of an affective ideal of discipline thus changed relations not
just among humans but also between humans and animals. As with children, many believed that animals could be controlled through love rather
than force. Antebellum children's books and later humane publications
alike looked with a kind of sentimental orientalism on Arabian horse-
training methods, which they characterized as kind and familial. Arabs,
informed the children's *Natural History of Beasts*, never beat their horses,
but let them live in their tents with them, as members of the family. As
a result of such kindness, their horses were never disobedient, and never
kicked or bit. Similarly, a sermon preached by Samuel Osgood in 1867 instructed that Americans could learn from Arabs how to bring out a horse's
natural gentleness and kindness and to use this rather than force in training.[87] Later in the century, humanitarians offered "Arab Horse Maxims"
and Arab practices as evidence that this sort of kindness was the best way
to rule a horse.[88]

The extent to which the family had been reconfigured as a site of "disciplinary intimacy" was reflected in how often approving authors noted
that "the Arab's horse is said to be as dear to him as his children" and that
horse and family "live in the same tent." Writers frequently supported this
contention with another legend—that an Arab, in the midst of selling his
horse to a Frenchman, had reconsidered and refused to sell the steed. "'To
whom it is,' he exclaimed, 'that I am going to yield thee up? To Europeans,
who will tie thee close; who will beat thee; who will render thee miserable; return with me, my beauty, my jewel! And rejoice the hearts of
my children.'"[89] The incorporation of the horse into the family circle was
evinced by its residence in the tent, by its "deservedly high place in the affections of the family," and by the Arab's refusal to sell the animal, whose
dearness was measured in the currency of family life—emotions—rather
than in that of the marketplace.[90] Further, the horse's status as a member

of the family seemed to be the source not just of the Arab's kind treatment of his horse, but also of its natural and easy obedience.

As Jacob Abbott's appropriation of the language of horse training in *Gentle Methods* suggested, the cult of Arab horse rearing was supplemented by the proliferation of manuals for training animals avowing that "kindness is the whip" best used to compel animal obedience.[91] Likewise, a new style of homegrown animal trainer—the popular "horse tamers" or horse whisperers—traveled from town to town, dazzling crowds with their instant and nonviolent control over unruly horses, creatures formerly trained, like children, by having their wills "broken."[92] And though he had his rival in Sullivan, the famous Irish horse "whisperer," the American horse trainer Willis J. Powell touted himself as the first to discover how to "gentle" rather than beat a horse into submission. Powell claimed to have come to his gentling methods in 1814, and he spent much of the rest of his life traveling from town to town, performing his feats before audiences and promoting his belief that "a gentle hand may lead an elephant by a hair." Not content to extol gentling's benefits as a system of training alone, Powell presaged humanitarian interest in training methods when he claimed that his own taught mankind "a moral lesson of patience and gentleness—virtues as necessary to get along through life among men, as they are when used in taming horses."[93]

Although Powell's junior in the taming business, Ohio native John Solomon Rarey (fig. 4) was by far the most legendary of American horse trainers and the one most revered by anticruelty activists. Throughout the 1850s and 1860s, he traveled widely in Europe and the United States, displaying a Barnumesque knack for putting on shows, gaining publicity, and insinuating himself into the good graces of European royalty.[94] Published in 1861, his *Taming; or, Breaking the Horse by a New and Improved Method* assumed that every horse was "naturally of willing and gentle disposition," and aimed to demonstrate how "in contrast to the usual mode of training by harsh words, a sharp whip, and cruel worrying," the horse may "easily, quietly, and safely . . . be tamed by kindness." Echoing the contemporary theoreticians of disciplinary intimacy, Rarey reminded readers that the real aim of horse training was "to work on his [the horse's] understanding rather than on the different parts of the body."[95]

Not surprisingly, animal protectionists championed Rarey's methods and extended his fame in the service of their cause. During a stay in London (see fig. 4), Britain's RSPCA awarded Rarey a medal of honor to thank him "for introducing to the public his humane method of taming and managing animals."[96] American animal protectionists too were eager to

CRUISER TAMED.

**Figure 4.** A new method of discipline: Rarey and Cruiser. *Harper's New Monthly Magazine* 22, no. 131 (April 1861): 616.

claim their native son. A story in *Our Dumb Animals* by Reverend T. Jackson contrasted previous horse government with that promoted by Rarey. Jackson's friend had acquired a cheap horse, beautiful but with a "sullen and savage" temper thanks to having been "cruelly trained by careless persons." The horse's new owner resolved to employ Mr. Rarey's methods to try and reverse the damage and to "develop the good qualities so long dormant." So determined, the man visited his new steed each day, feeding him by hand and talking gently to him, "exercising over him a sort of mesmeric influence," until he won the horse over. Through his kindness, the new owner established a deep and lasting bond with the horse and was able to control him, even in the middle of city traffic, with just his voice, "the voice of friendship."[97] In reformers' eyes, Rarey had worked a revolution in training and given the lie to every man who claimed that he could only govern his horse—a purportedly wild and unwilling beast—through physical power. Accounts not just of Rarey but also of a more general capacity to control horses through treats and voice and to redeem the vicious through gentleness flooded the pages of humanitarian publications.[98]

Indeed, for many in the nineteenth century, the power of kindness seemed limitless and few animals beyond its grip. To many of his spectators, Rarey's method of "gentling" horses was vindicated by his legendary taming of a zebra from London's zoo. Naturalists had long pronounced the zebra incorrigible and untamable, but in a show at London's Roundhouse, Rarey "put the learned philosophers in science to shame, vindicating the power of kindness" by bridling the zebra.[99] Other animal training manuals, like Jesse Haney's *Art of Training Animals*, extended Rarey's lessons to "all kinds of animals," including donkeys, zebras, dogs, monkeys, and birds. Like Rarey, Haney claimed that physical punishment "inhibits the animal and lessens their talent," and is "both cruel and unwise." He maintained that animals could easily be taught and controlled through the granting and denial of rewards. "Withholding the accustomed reward when he fails or but imperfectly performs his duty," advised Haney, "is much more effective than any corporeal punishment."[100]

While dime museums, menageries, and circuses continued to pit men against lions, tigers, and other wild beasts in a contest of wills that was anything but loving and familial, some wild animal tamers came to extol kindness and to insist that even the allegedly unregenerate—wild beasts such as lions, tigers, and bears—"may be tamed, and will show their affection, when treated with kindly attention to their wants."[101] The *Humane Journal* reprinted an article from the *New York Commercial Advertiser* whose headline blared that "The Most Savage Animals May Be Ruled by Kindness" and which recounted the experiences of several animal keepers in the Central Park and Philadelphia Zoos, who developed intense bonds with their charges. So pleased was he with the success of a friendly approach to his wards that the Philadelphia Zoo's tiger keeper declared that "I have an idea that lions, tigers, and leopards might be domesticated like the cat."[102] Indeed, relations of kindness so defined the family that susceptibility to kindness became a kind of precondition for animal domestication, the incorporation of animals as adjuncts of the human family. A few months later, the cover of the same magazine displayed a scene of two small children riding atop the back of a bear in a forest setting. Amazed onlookers gaped at the bear's tolerance as the picture's caption explained to the onlookers outside the frame that this bear was "controlled by kindness," a trait here represented by the natural goodness and gentleness of children.[103] The bear's willingness to let small children crawl on its back at once illustrated the transformative power of kindness and the innate bond of trust and affection between animals and children.

The suggestion that kindness could bring out the innate goodness of even wild animals was not confined to humane publications. Throughout the nineteenth century, "Happy Family" exhibits—featuring "hundreds of living beasts and birds of opposite natures, trained to live together in the most perfect harmony"—were a popular feature of menageries, which billed them as examples of "Enemies by Nature Made Friends by Art."[104] The art, of course, was kindness, and this was once again made synonymous with familial intimacy. Anyone who sees such an exhibit, claimed one children's book, will "have his mind awakened to the extraordinary effects of habit and gentle discipline" that make it possible for all to coexist, "the weak without fear, and the strong without desire to injure." "It is impossible," the book concluded, "to imagine any prettier exhibition of kindness."[105] Humane publications cited the "Happy Family" exhibits as evidence not just of what kindness could achieve, but also as evidence that the earth's natural state was peaceful and harmonious. Wild animals living together in peace represented, to many, the prelapsarian moment before Adam had brought sin and enmity to both man and beast. Rarey's teaching, one commentator suggested, showed nothing less than "the spell through which man should have dominion over the beasts of the field, the law that was ordained in the very beginning of time."[106] Contemporary acts of kindness, in other words, not only harkened back to that time, but also hastened its return. Reformers recalled that Christ had been born in a manger, surrounded by animals, who, along with Mary and Joseph, were his first intimates; they thus also looked forward to the moment when the truly innocent nature of animals and children would be manifest as the lion, lamb, and child would assemble themselves into a tableau vivant version of Edward Hicks's peaceable kingdom.[107]

Changes in the government of animals and children, both of which moved from violent will-breaking to "disciplinary intimacy," were neither confined to domestic relations, nor simply parallel, but they instead intersected as anticruelty activists and others—such as Abbott in his *Gentle Methods for the Training and Management of the Young*—explicitly likened the one to the other. The comparison of animal and child training was, in turn, part of a larger culture that interwove the treatment of animals and humans, shuttling lessons in discipline back and forth across the species line and applying them to crime, prisons, lunatic asylums, and families alike. In the years during and following his European and

American tours, Rarey's name, for example, became synonymous with the more general turn from violent correction to "discipline through love." His contemporaries suggested that his lessons in the law of kindness begged the question: "why should it stop short of 'humans'?"[108] One author compared Rarey's reform of equine treatment with the reform of insane asylums—much like horses in their stables, the insane were once shackled and chained and kept in damp and dark cells, but were now assured that "the law of kindness, in all well-regulated institutions, alone prevails."[109] Reviewing the French criminologist M. Prosper Despine's *Psychologie Naturelle*, Oliver Wendell Holmes, Sr., claimed that Despine "borrows a lesson from our famous countryman, Rarey, whose treatment of horses was founded on a patient study of equine psychology." Associated with the movement from a punitive to a reformative approach to legal punishment and imprisonment, Despine and Irish prison reformer Crofton were likened by Holmes to Rarey because of their mutual assumption that no man is "utterly incorrigible" and "that hope and not fear is the chief motive to be addressed to the criminal." Nineteenth-century reformers wanted to believe that, like the misunderstood horse, man was never utterly bad and most were susceptible to the human equivalents of apples, lumps of sugar, and carrots.[110]

"The Rarey Method," a story in an 1863 issue of *Harper's New Monthly Magazine*, shows the interrelation of human and animal discipline and the extent to which both were identified with the family circle. At the outset, we meet Sophia Moody as a member of the audience in a New York performance by Rarey. We quickly learn that Sophia Moody is unhappy in her marriage, constantly bickering with her melancholy and stingy husband. She wants the finer things in life—a larger house, piano lessons for her daughter, more fashionable clothes and furnishings. He is grumpy and hoards his considerable earnings, seeming to take no pleasure in his family. Seeing Rarey perform, Sophia is rapt because "she had a very unmanageable partner to deal with at home" and figured that if a testy horse could be overcome by this combination of "firmness and gentleness," so could Mr. Moody, whose character was "considerably in accordance with his name." She resolves to no longer express anger at her husband, but instead to "manage" him through the granting and withdrawal of affection. She begins her gentling regime by seeing that Mr. Moody has better meals and affecting a solicitous and sweet demeanor in his presence. "The Rarey method thus happily initiated was pursued with signal success," and all was happy for a time in the house. "The servants became punctual, industrious, and attentive," as Sophia is overseeing them more to make the house and food better for her husband, thus extending her new management throughout the household, and Mr. Moody himself is changed, bringing home gifts, taking his wife and family out in the evenings, and granting his wife and daughter's wish for piano lessons with the famed and expensive Mr. Weiss. The gentleness portion of Rarey's method underway, Sophia soon has to apply "firmness" when her husband balks at her suggestion that they move to a larger house, preferably a brownstone on Park Avenue. He is outraged, and she discontinues both her pleasing manner and good food for several weeks, during which she longs to make up, but refuses to capitulate, realizing that "a great principle was at stake. This day must decide whether she were to mount and ride her steed, guiding him henceforth, as she listed with bit and bridle, or whether she were to descend again to the coaxing and experimenting of the last few months." She continues her firmness, but without resorting to violence, tantrums, or threats. Finally, inevitably, Mr. Moody gives in, buys his wife the new house, and is altogether changed by the experience, becoming a warm and sociable man. Now, the story closes, "the brown stone and its intimates flourish," and Mrs. Moody "never forgets to whom she owes this rise to empire, and her photograph book contains an admirable *carte de visite* of Mr. Rarey."[111] Although it satirizes marriage and womanly manipulation, "The Rarey Method" nonetheless points to widespread application of Rarey-ism and its associated principles of animal management through kindness to a variety of social institutions including the home. Further, it underscores the essential goal of all such management—not kindness itself, but kindness in the service of more effective and efficient control, whether of husbands, animals, children, criminals, or lunatics.

Humanitarian and popular authors, however, were more likely to compare animal and child management than they were to liken the control of balky horses to obstinate husbands. Usually, they compared animals to children, suggesting similar methods for their control. Horse manuals began to recommend personally rearing one's horses from their youth, after the Arabian model, since "horses are like children" and it is thus better "to instruct and watch over them all the time to prevent them doing wrong, than to have to break them after they have done wrong." Rarey credited the discovery of his method to both being raised around horses and having the opportunity to raise and observe colts from birth through maturity, thus molding and educating rather than breaking them.[112] Writer Paul Ketchum likewise advised horse owners that if young colts are treated with love and affection from the start, "there will be no more need of breaking them than there is of calling upon Rarey to break your grown children."[113] Several authors stressed that the idea of "breaking" an animal should go the way of "breaking" children's wills. Thomas Hill, for instance, pointed out that "teachers are rapidly becoming wiser in the ways of training children" and that "fifty years have wrought a complete revolution in methods of government." Whipping has been replaced by "appeal to the higher nature of children," and the rod has been replaced by love. "Thus," he continued, "let us hope that the improved sentiment of the age will demand" that more humane methods be used for animal rearing as well, "and may this opposition to physical punishment increase until the feeling that it is as wrong to whip one of these [animals] as it is now known to be a mistake to strike a child."[114]

Sometimes humanitarians moved beyond the broad principles linking the treatment of both animals and children to offer specific tips for their management. An article in *Our Dumb Animals*, for instance, noted that mankind once thought it necessary to break a child's will when it refused to do something. We have since learned, it went on, that it is much easier to distract a child than force it into submission, and the same applies to horses. When confronting a balky horse, the article advised, make like it is a child and distract rather than beat it, and the horse will soon be moving again, having forgotten its resistance entirely.[115]

Most often, humanitarians likened animals to children to argue for better treatment of the former, but occasionally, as in Abbott's case, this formula was reversed and animals provided a model for rearing children. One article, for example, inverted the relationship suggested above, claiming that strategies for overcoming balkiness in horses were an ideal formula for overcoming children's resistance.[116] An article on "How to Bring Up Children" extended beyond the helpful-hints genre to take note of general principles, advising parents to observe the changes in animal training where "kindness and patience [is] being substituted for the harshness and severity of former times" and where, from all accounts, "this change is universally regarded as a great improvement." The wisdom of corporal punishment for children is, the author acknowledged, a subject of much debate, but "we are inclined decidedly to the opinion that the principles and rules which have proved so advantageous in the training of animals" would work just as well for children since we know that "every species of barbarous punishments—of punishment which permanently impairs the self-respect of a child—is injurious."[117] Just as animals may be governed by kindness, so too can children; and just as ill treatment might ruin an animal's temperament, so too the child. Changed methods of discipline had taught, on the whole, that "children as well as dumb animals are easiest governed by kind words and kind treatment."[118]

Humanitarians left their reasons for combining the activities of animal and child protection largely unexplained and unexamined. To the extent that they said anything on the matter, anticruelty organizations tended to explain their joint activities in terms of both sheer necessity and the common defenselessness of animals and children. Subsequent analysts have largely repeated these explanations, ignoring the substantial and widespread cultural associations between animals and children as petted members of the family and vital elements in its affective glue. Declines in the functional utility of children and the rise of petkeeping as critical to the family's moral function both contributed to the widespread cultural assumption that animals and children shared a special bond as natural intimates and family-constituting beings. This presumed bond was further elaborated by the incorporation of both animals and children within the ascendant regime of management-through-kindness, an ideal that positioned the essence of the family—love—as the moral template for a wide range of social institutions.

The desire to manage both children and animals through affection rather than violence also reflected changed attitudes about the inevitability of violence, pain, and suffering. As many reformers sought to create a society free from suffering, they adopted a theory of violence that linked cruelty to animals with cruelty to human beings. Animal and child protection were logically related, then, not only through sentimentalism and domesticity, but also by the idea that cruelty toward both stemmed from the same dark place in the human heart.

## CHAPTER TWO

# "A Relic of Barbarism":
# Cruelty, Civilization, and Social Order

Etta Wheeler's choice to contact the ASPCA may have been driven, in part, by her assumption that children and animals were similar beings, or that the methods of animal protection organizations could easily be applied to the cause of child protection. But she may also have shared the sentiment, expressed by many anticruelty reformers, that animal and child protection were logically linked because violence toward them was similar in spirit. Indeed, many reformers believed that a slippery slope of passionate violence connected cruelty toward animals with cruelty toward children. John Shortall gave voice to this in a speech delivered before the fourteenth annual meeting of the Illinois Humane Society, explaining that "he who is cruel to his beast will abuse even his own child."[1]

The notion that cruelty toward animals evinced an essentially evil nature that would eventually culminate in dastardly acts toward human beings was not an idea original to American humane societies. For several centuries moral reformers of all stripes had considered animals, because of their relative defenselessness, as a perfect object lesson in, on the one hand, passionate self-indulgence and, on the other hand, principled self-restraint. In an early expression of the sentiment, sixteenth-century author Michel de Montaigne claimed that "natures that are bloodthirsty towards animals show a native propensity towards cruelty," and pointed to the example of ancient Rome, where "after people had inured themselves to watching the slaughter of animals, they went on to men and gladiators."[2] With the indiscriminate slaughter of animals, then, Montaigne saw not only the expression of vicious spirits, but the seeds of the declension that later befell the entire Roman civilization. Foreshadowing the teleology of later moral reformers, he linked individual depravity and social ruination in a straightforward cause-and-effect relationship. Applying this trajectory to personal rather than social development, John Locke encouraged seventeenth-century parents to check all cruelty toward animals in their children, predicting that "the custom of tormenting and killing beasts will, by degrees, harden their minds even towards men."[3] Locke's admonition was given visual force by British artist William Hogarth's *Four Stages of Cruelty* in 1751, depicting a boy-cum-man's developmental "progress" from harming a dog to murdering his fiancée after forcing her to steal for him.[4] And, in Harriet Beecher Stowe's moral calculus, youthful horse-whipping both reflected and provided the training ground for a lifetime of hardhearted slave ownership.[5]

Like Locke, Hogarth, and Stowe, animal welfare reformers also depicted cruelty as a progressive, almost addictive, behavior that, if given license, would overtake a man's character and eventually unleash his inner despot on all of "the forms of life below him."[6] Employing a modified version of the oft-invoked argument against slavery—that it was as bad for the master as it was for the slave—anticruelty societies depicted acts of cruelty as degrading to both victims and perpetrators. For mankind, insisted the IHS's John Shortall, "loss of temper is self-degradation," leading men to become what the Wisconsin Humane Society termed "slaves to appetite and passion." Reverend Alfred Gooding made a similar point to his Portsmouth, New Hampshire, congregation when he noted that cruelty to animals and human beings stood equally in the path of "the cultivation of those high moral qualities" because they were animated by a similar passion.[7] And the consequences of this failure were not simply personal, or between a cruel man and his God. Rather, they spelled ruin to the cruelist, his victims, and the larger social body. *Our Dumb Animals* explained that children's cruelty to animals, "begun in levity and thoughtlessness," was actually quite pernicious, for it "hardens the heart, and the parents who, unmoved, behold a child torture a kitten or a bird, are really educating that child for cruelty and murder."[8]

As such dire predictions suggest, animal and child protectionists saw violence toward animals and children as linked in spirit and practice and they connected that violence to social disorder—domestic violence, murder, mayhem. Theirs was a slippery-slope theory of violence in two ways. First, as we have seen, anticruelty reformers believed that violence toward animals was on a continuum with cruelty toward human beings, particularly children. Second, they also believed that a slippery slope connected individual suffering with social disorder. Though an individual instance of cruelty manifested itself first in the pain experienced by an animal or child, acts of cruelty also ultimately harmed the larger social body. In connecting cruelty to animals with cruelty to children, and in linking both to disorder, protectionists made cruelty into a social problem and transformed private suffering into a matter of public concern.[9] Though protectionists believed that the behaviors they gathered under the rubric of "cruelty" were self-evidently problematic, in fact their slippery-slope theory of violence meant that the precise nature and harm of cruelty was quite ambiguous. Was an action "cruel" because it caused undue suffering or because it violated social norms and disturbed the peace? What did animal and child protectionists care more about—suffering or social order?

Some historians have been suspicious of the motives of animal and child protectionists and have tended to see them as less concerned with suffering than with condemning and controlling the behavior of working-class and immigrant populations. But anticruelty reformers would not likely have seen the need to choose between these potential motivations. Indeed, long before the first SPCA or SPCC was founded, cruel acts were understood to cause undue suffering, violate social norms, and degrade public morals. As a moral concept, then, cruelty traditionally did not separate but rather joined personal to social harm. Nineteenth-century anticruelty reformers carried this notion of cruelty forward as they argued not only that a continuum linked harm to animals with harm to children, but also that cruel behaviors injured their victims, perpetrators, and the social body. In the case of children, the link between individual suffering and social order expanded "cruelty" beyond physical suffering to include moral endangerment. For a child's immorality harmed not only him or her, but also society.

Animal and child protectionists hoped that fellow Americans would view violence toward helpless and dependent beings not simply as a fact of life, but rather as an unfortunate and preventable problem. In order for cruelty to become a moral and social problem, though, human violence and the experience of pain had to seem anomalous and offensive rather than inevitable and mundane. Cruelty only emerged as a social problem as ideas about human nature, the religious significance of suffering, and the medical ability to control pain shifted across Western Europe and the United States from the eighteenth century forward.

Some of the theological changes that underpinned new ideas about childhood also contributed to a wholesale reevaluation of human nature. While at one time most theologians, philosophers, and ordinary men and women might have subscribed to the idea that humans were by nature sinful, driven by animal passions and self-centered desires that could only be overcome by strenuous religious devotion, by the nineteenth century this dim view of human nature was challenged by a new, softer vision. These far-reaching shifts congealed in the doctrine of what historian Norman Fiering calls "irresistible compassion," a sense both that suffering is unnecessary and that man is innately moved to relieve the pain of others. Beginning in the eighteenth century, the Anglo-American world witnessed a series of challenges both to the notion that reason alone should serve as man's moral guide and to the Puritan and Hobbesian conceptions of human nature, which collectively portrayed man as depraved, motivated by passions, and singularly self-interested. This new view of human nature, attached to a realist epistemology, came to be known as the Scottish "common sense" school of philosophy. In place of an assessment of the passions as base, common sense philosophers rejected the notion that passions were self-interested. Instead, they harnessed emotion to the general welfare, claiming that human feelings naturally tend toward others and toward the public interest; all those that did not were deemed "unnatural," perversions rather than revelations of true human nature.[10] Indeed, Fiering argues, philosophers such as the Third Earl of Shaftesbury identified "fellow-feeling with the essence of true human nature," extending the reach of compassion to include even the nonrational and the nonhuman.[11] By midcentury, the notion that God gave man an innate "moral sense" exercised through compassion was well established in philosophical circles and began to be popularized throughout the Anglo-American world by William Wollaston and Frances Hutcheson. To the extent that evil existed in the world, men like Hutcheson believed that it resulted from a hardening of the moral sense that could be overcome.[12] Hutcheson's student, Adam Smith, continued to popularize his idea, and placed special emphasis on the "spectatorial nature of sympathy," assuming that the moral sense was activated through the sight of suffering and an instinctual, empathetic identification with the sufferer.[13]

Of course the idea that mankind was endowed by nature with a sixth sense for the detection of morals was not without its problems for the theologically orthodox view of original sin and human depravity. But in the nineteenth century, these theological problems were mitigated by the liberalization of mainline Protestant theology and the spread of evangelical Christianity. As American ministers during the first half of the nineteenth century replaced the powerful and awesome Calvinist God with a "maternal and affective" one, they reinterpreted Jesus's sacrifice as an expression of love for man, not a repudiation of sin, and deemphasized a painful and morally wrenching conversion experience in favor of nearly universal salvation and a gradual, but inevitable growth toward God. [14]

Liberal ministers also reinterpreted the meaning and value of suffering. Christian theologians had traditionally interpreted human suffering as a consequence of human sin and a form of punishment from God. Medieval clerics, for example, located the origins of suffering not in the body, but in the soul. Pain was not only inevitable for fallen humanity, but also it was just. In antebellum America, by contrast, evangelical ministers began to emphasize human goodness and Christ's love more than God's anger and to suggest that suffering was not inevitable. In an address before animal welfare reformers, the Reverend Phillips Brooks reflected these developments when he asserted that "pain is an evil which was never meant to exist, and which is a sign of disorder."[15] As pain and suffering lost their didactic and retributive significance, the importance of feeling others' pain was heightened. In the antebellum evangelical framework, the centrality of feeling in religious experience was heightened, and empathy became the glue holding men and women together in a common life.[16] Together, the rise of a humanitarian sensibility combined with the spread of liberalized and evangelical branches of Christianity created a moral calculus in which emotions, aroused through direct or fantastic contact with suffering, parsed right from wrong.

At the same time, physicians in the developing field of anesthetics endeavored to transform physical pain from a religious to a medical experience. Like ministers, they too suggested that far from being an inevitable fact of life in an impermanent body, or a just trial at the hand of a stern God, pain was a "treatable pathology," an avoidable inconvenience.[17] At the same time, scientists interested in treating pain continued to assume that not all creatures suffered equally. Vulnerability to pain was, many medical men believed, a benchmark distinguishing the relatively impervious, the brutish and animalistic (such as Africans, Indians, and the criminally inclined), from the more highly developed and civilized (such as whites, women, and the wealthy).[18] Thus, even as suffering lost its religious import and its medical inevitability, the *ability to suffer* was reinforced as a hallmark of humanity, a marker of one's place in the great chain of being.

As new ideas about human nature, God, and physical pain recast the notion that sin was innate and that pain was inevitable or just, tolerance for both violence and the suffering it wrought decreased. From the late eighteenth century onward, reformers sought to improve social order by eliminating the experience of pain, instilling greater self-control among individuals, and excluding passionate or violent behavior from the public square. In the new republic, the advent of such reforms is associated with the rise of the middle class and the dawn of market capitalism. The middle class prided itself on avoiding the excesses of either the aristocracy or the poor, and across the antebellum period, middle-class men and women devoured etiquette and advice manuals that taught, in the words of one historian, "bodily management" and "emotional control." At the same time, the new economic order rewarded those who could internalize self-discipline, delay gratification, and adhere to a more rationalized ordering of work and time.[19] As the urban and town-dwelling bourgeoise learned to exercise self-control in order to succeed, many were also attracted to reform movements that, in one way or another, sought to teach such internal restraint to others. These took the form of campaigns to expunge the nation of pain and violence as earnest organizers tried to eliminate corporal and capital punishment, abolish slavery, and end alcohol abuse. Across these somewhat disparate movements, reformers shared a belief in the perfectability of mankind and equated human progress with the elimination of both suffering and violence. Individual self-mastery, they believed, would lead to social harmony and earthly peace.[20]

In the United States, many linked the elimination of violence not only to personal and social improvement, but also to political progress. Beginning with the Revolution, Americans associated political tyranny with barbaric violence as they accused the British army of perpetrating "inhuman and worse than savage cruelty" in their fight against the rebels. By contrast, partisans depicted the forces for independence, and Washington in particular, as "benevolent and humane" even in wartime.[21] These sentiments rested on the belief that a republican government would depend on public virtue, the suppression of private passions, and would eschew force or physical punishment. If the social and political hierarchy expressed in monarchy produced cruelty, the egalitarianism of democracy would act as a solvent eroding tyrannical violence. Early national antigallows reformers, for example, believed that republican forms of government also demanded new attitudes toward both state and personal violence. As Louis Masur explains their point of view, "one issue seemed clear: if severe and excessive punishments marked monarchies, mild and benevolent ones would have to characterize republics." Hopes for a new, less violent order were not confined simply to relations between states and citizens; advocates for penal reform such as Benjamin Rush maintained that "our republican forms of government will in time beget republican opinions and manners." What began as a political revolution against tyranny and cruelty in public life might, in other words, end in the transformation of social and private life.[22]

Indeed, over the course of two centuries the charge of "cruelty" was applied first to protest oppressive government and then to renegotiate relations of power in the private sphere. In the American context, the prohibition of official "cruelty" was central to the establishment of a liberal political order. Made famous by the Eighth Amendment ban on "cruel and unusual punishment," this prohibition is repeated verbatim in most state constitutions. Derived from similar wording in the Massachusetts Bay Colony's 1641 Body of Liberties and in England's 1689 Bill of Rights, the amendment was intended to outlaw certain types of punishment common in Stuart England such as disemboweling, decapitation, pillorying, and drawing and quartering.[23] Coming as part of documents such as the Body of Liberties and the Bill of Rights, the ban on cruel state punishment is linked to the history of political agitation for greater civil and political rights and to the struggle for rule between crown and parliament.

While cruelty's legal existence historically regulated relationships between rulers and subjects, or citizens and the state, it also became a means to talk about personal violence in the private realm, a trend that accelerated in the nineteenth-century United States.[24] Historian Robert Griswold has demonstrated the increasing use and acceptability of cruelty as a ground for divorce in the second half of the nineteenth century. According to the English legal tradition adopted by the United States, cruelty was acknowledged as a cause for divorce, but until the 1840s judges on both sides of the Atlantic held that cruelty was constituted solely by extreme physical violence that caused considerable pain and suffering. By midcentury, however, American judges, influenced by reigning ideals of domesticity and companionate marriage, began to allow that actions short of violent beating may be cruel. They recognized a category of mental cruelty— psychological torment so great that it induced physical deterioration and harm. While the emphasis remained on somatic effects, cruelty was redefined to include verbal harm that had physical consequences. By century's end, marital cruelty was expanded even further to include purely mental suffering that need not have any physical effects. From purely physical to purely mental suffering, the widening concept of marital cruelty kept pace with the number of divorces filed on the ground of cruelty, which nearly doubled in the years between 1867 and 1906.[25]

Though revolutionary-era thinkers such as Rush, who linked the elimination of tyrannical cruelty to political and social progress, may not have envisioned divorce as the proper expression of "republican manners," they nonetheless contributed to an evergrowing sense that civilization demanded both the elimination of suffering and the improved status of dependents. This assumption both positively linked progress to the amelioration of suffering and negatively cast those who caused suffering as anachronistic, barbaric, even beyond the pale of common humanity. On the positive side, the opposition between pain and progress was exemplified by advocates of those causes who sought to eliminate violence and suffering. Antebellum arguments for the reform of the death penalty, for example, often deployed such a dichotomy. G. W. Peck, writing in the 1848 *American Review*, for example, argued for the use of chloroform in hanging because civilization demanded the elimination of pain from state punishment. Deliberate infliction of pain, Peck explained, is "unbecoming in civilized Christian people." Indeed, Peck went on, "the gradual abolition by our ancestors . . . of cruel modes of punishments, is a consequence of gradual progress in refinement; though the hearts of men be the same now as ever, we are certainly better acquainted with the laws of the universe than they were, and more delicately sensitive in our nervous organization."[26] Peck equated sensitivity with civilization, pain with backward barbarism, and its elimination with the forward historical movement that the "laws of the universe" seemed to require. On the negative side, the notion that mankind was naturally benevolent and sympathetic, and that history was a story of the progressive instantiation of this God-given nature, could lead to a decidedly unsympathetic view of those who perpetrated violence and suffering. As Karen Haltunnen has shown, this dynamic profoundly shaped changing responses to murderers between the colonial and antebellum eras. Once seen as exemplars of humanity's fallen state, by the mid-nineteenth century murderers were pathologized as people apart from ordinary humanity; rather than holding up a mirror to our common nature, those who would kill seemed to transgress it.[27] Men who deliberately inflict pain short of murder were likewise regarded as beyond the pale of humanity. In the words of Henry Bergh they were moral monsters with "sensibilities blunted almost to the degree of wild beasts."[28]

As Bergh's condemnation of cruelists suggests, during the last quarter of the nineteenth century anticruelty activists helped to cement the notion that the violent were not simply inhumane, but inhuman. Reformers merged their understanding of cruelty as a betrayal of human nature with the increasingly popular language of civilization and savagery, arguing that if the progress of civilization brought the amelioration of suffering, then violence was a kind of atavistic barbarism. Emerging from the incorporation of Darwinian evolutionary theory into protestant millennialism, scientists, social theorists, ministers, and midway hucksters alike all hewed to the belief that civilization, Christian to its core, was the natural product of the struggle for survival. Most nineteenth-century Americans could not digest the truly chaotic process at the heart of Darwin's theories, but they could accept a modified version of this theory. Man may have descended from animals, but evolution's trajectory was one that naturally pushed mankind away from his animal heritage and toward the natural end of Christian perfection.[29] At the 1893 World's Columbian Exposition in Chicago, for instance, the Congress on Evolution spent much of its time trying to reconcile evolution with Christianity, concluding, in the words of one clergyman, that "'evolution from lower to the higher, from the carnal to the spiritual, is not merely the path of man's past pilgrimage, but the destiny to which the future calls him.'"[30] Progress, in this scheme, was tantamount to the fulfillment of Christian morality, and was figured as inevitable and yet imperiled by the persistence of the less-evolved types of mankind that peopled the nether regions of the world and increasingly, it seemed to many, the cities of the United States.

According to this modified version of Darwinism, the persistence of savage, barbarian, or animalistic traits—so evident in such groups as American Indians, ex-slaves, Italian immigrants, and primitives from across the world—was a sort of evolutionary throwback, or what anthropologists and other social scientists termed "atavism." Such groups provided scientists and laypeople with ready material to study the process of evolution, and scientists busily measured, tested, and categorized savage and barbarian peoples, eventually reconstituting the hierarchical chain of being in the sanitized terms of scientific racism. Unsurprisingly, white Anglo-Saxons topped the chain, most nearly perfecting evolution's goal of civilization, while physical and cultural atavism were evidence not just of tardy evolution, but also of heathen immorality. Far from being the sole province of an educated elite, this "evolutionary millennialism" was the topic of widespread conversation in newspapers and magazines, and was dramatically illustrated in Smithsonian-arranged exhibits and midway spectacles at successive World's Fairs from Philadelphia's Centennial Exhibition (1876) forward.[31]

With the idea of progress at its heart, the discourse of civilization and savagery was also an ideal language of reform. Long linked with brutish and animalistic behavior on the part of man, cruelty was readily incorporated into the binary separating Christian from heathen and civilized

from savage. As the liberal sociologist Lester Frank Ward wrote in 1884,
"if nature progresses through the destruction of the weak, man progresses
through the *protection* of the weak." With some success, animal welfare
reformers argued that a society's treatment of animals, and the weak in
general, was a chief indicator of its progress toward millennial perfection.
In a series of articles in the *North American Review*, Rush C. Hawkins,
a lawyer, art collector, and Civil War colonel, and Robert Ingersoll, the
popular orator and outspoken freethinker, considered cruelty to animals
as evidence in their debate over whether the United States was experiencing moral decline. In his 1891 essay "Brutality and Avarice Triumphant,"
Hawkins lamented the state of the nation, arguing that its basic creed was
greed and deception. The national motto, he suggested, should be changed
to "Plundering Made Easy." Though he cited the land grant acts, stock
watering, railroad wrecking, the company store, and the treatment of Indians, Hawkins especially noted abuse to animals—the destruction and
slaughter of buffalo and bear populations in the West, the killing of songbirds for sport and fashion, the starving of stock on the Western range and
in the transport to market, and the overfishing of the seal—and argued
that it evinced the new national creed. And what, Hawkins asked, was the
church doing about all this? Nothing—and yet it goes forth to teach the
heathen "who do not know the A B C of dishonesty and cruelty practised
in Christian America." "The influence of these offences against civilization," he warned, "is far-reaching and destructive."[32]

In a fierce rebuttal of these charges, Robert Ingersoll claimed that
Hawkins had the trajectory all wrong: the last thirty years of American
history had experienced progress, not decline. Witness the end of slavery, urged Ingersoll, an avaricious system if there ever was one, and the
growing equality between men and women, the durability of our free institutions, and the hearty cry raised against cruelty to animals. Though
it might be true that many animals have been destroyed and ill treated,
he conceded, it was also true that "hundreds of lawmakers have not only
protested against cruelty to animals," but enough even to "secure the enactment of laws making cruelty towards animals a crime." And though he
was a freethinker, Ingersoll asserted that the church had not been an idle
partner in this progress, for when Henry Bergh began his campaign for animals, he "was seconded in his efforts by many of the Christian clergy not
only, but by hundreds and thousands of professing Christians—probably
millions."[33] Echoing the concerns of many moral reformers over national
declension, the debate between Hawkins and Ingersoll signaled both the

rising status of cruelty to animals as an index of moral progress and its link to concepts such as barbarism, violence, and greed that formed the staple vocabulary of the discourse of both civilization-savagery and of anticruelty reformers.

According to animal and child protectionists, cruelty was a relic of barbarism, what John Shortall called "a savage, animal remnant of heredity that speaks out in the race, here and there, in such conscienceless depravity" as humane society officers confronted in their daily rounds.[34] By contrast, the ability to suppress the passions and sublimate them in the service of Christian mercy was the route toward civilization. "As we look back into the shadow past," reported a local agent of the Wisconsin Humane Society, "when cruelty was at a premium, and man's inhumanity held the sway, our hearts thrill with rapture" to live in an age "in which humanity is taking the place of cruelty, and tender caresses and gentle words, that of blasphemous oaths and the whip."[35] An 1897 article in the WCTU's *Union Signal* echoed these sentiments, declaring that "the spirit of cruelty is the deadliest enemy to a high civilization," since "all history shows the relation between barbarism and cruelty." Calling cruelty the "salient feature of the barbaric state," the author offered the evidence that savage religions were "noticeably deficient in humane principles" and often "marked by absolute cruelty."[36] The work of defeating cruelty was, then, bound up with the "welfare of the race" and the progress of civilization. "There is no surer or truer indication of the advancement of a people," echoed the *Humane Journal*, "than the way in which they treat their voiceless and helpless fellow beings."[37]

Reformers also linked the suppression of cruelty to progress and the development of Christianity in their frequent invocation of the ancient Romans' love of blood sports. Writing in the *Ark*, one author reminded readers that Christianity began by opposing the gladiatorial games and "will never be content until it has conquered the last vestige of cruelty in the human heart," while another noted that both Christians and animals were tortured by Romans in the Coliseum's pit.[38] Henry Bergh, for his part, sent a letter to the governor of every state and territory in which he claimed that a civilization may be judged by how it treats animals, offering as proof the fact that Rome's fall was associated with "brutal exhibitions, at which wild animals were made to tear each other to pieces for the amusement" of all classes.[39] Bergh was no doubt doing more than reminding high government officials of a distant past—he was also using the specter of civilization's decline to scare his contemporaries into taking animal abuse more seriously. If the intertwined forces of Christianity and civilization had moved forward by opposing cruelty, then cruelty's continued existence threatened them both.

While examples of cruelty's peril could be found in Western civilization's distant past, contemporary examples linked cruelty to barbarism and kindness to civilization by highlighting the contrast between the Protestant West and the rest of the world. The WCTU's Mercy superintendent, Mary Lovell, repeatedly excoriated Spain for its bullfights in just such terms. It is difficult to believe, she wrote in 1896, that any "countries professing to be civilized" would persist in the goading and goring of bulls and horses in this manner. Any citizenry that can derive pleasure from witnessing "such a scene of butchery is not to be classed with enlightened nations." These acts of barbarism degraded the entire populace; Spain's masses were, Lovell claimed, uneducated, "illiterate and degraded," and its streets were filled with "filthy beggars." Cruelty not only morally degraded the Spaniards, but it was also linked to greed. Rather than spending money on education, Spain's government allowed the nation's treasury to be drained by the staging of such spectacles, letting private greed run amok over the public good. "Those who believe that cruelty is the salient feature of barbarism," and kindness the essence of civilization, "will not look for much progress among the Spanish people while bull fighting is regarded as heroism, and bull ring syndicates absorb money which should provide free education for the masses."[40] Doing her part to make up for the laxity of the Catholic Church and the Spanish government, Lovell declared her intention to have the WCTU's Mercy propaganda translated into Spanish.[41] At the outbreak of the Spanish-American war, Lovell connected Spanish aggression to its national pastime and declared that war was the highest form of cruelty, "a relic of barbarism" and "the great anachronism" of an otherwise progressive age.[42] Like the World's Fair exhibits replicating the stages of mankind's evolution, in reform language the continuum from savage to civilized proved to be as much an evaluative tool as it was a descriptive one.

Savagery and barbarism lurked in the midst of the United States as well. As reformers positioned kindness to human and animal dependents high on the civilizational scale, they often identified cruelty as a habit of the low—of immigrants, the poor, and of nonwhites. The racial or ethnic bias in the charge of cruelty could be oblique. One trope humanitarians consistently used was to play on the term "brute," depicting humans as more animalistic in their cruelty than the animals upon whom they vented their violent passions. Margaret Garvey, for example, in speaking before the Ladies' Humane Society of St. Louis in 1888 pointed out to her audience that Darwin had established that animals were "fellow creatures," composed of the same materials as humans save for "a few more or a few less convolutions of gray matter in the brain, or a greater or lesser number of cells" in the body. But having reminded her listeners that animals were much like humans, Garvey reversed the terms and pointed out that humans could be animalistic. "Think how often you see a horse on the street," she urged, "driven by something which gloried in the form of a man, but groveled in the lowest brute instinct. . . . Of the two, he who wore the human form was the brute." The image of the horse being better than the man driving it was a common refrain, echoed in complaints that too often a "brute [is] holding the reins" while "intelligence [is] drawing a heavy load."[43]

While such reversals clearly played on the assumption that humans were superior to animals, they also implied that the cruel were of low class or foreign origin. For in the years between the Civil War and the end of the century, to charge a person with being low on the civilizational scale was to invoke his low social origins as well. Though he was not formally associated with the humane cause, William Hosea Ballou's 1887 article in the anticruelty-friendly North American Review made this link quite clearly. Entitled "Are the Lower Animals Approaching Man?" Ballou's essay made the case that animals were so highly educable that with proper training they could learn most of the skills normally assumed to be the exclusive province of humans. To prove his point, Ballou claimed not simply that animal equality was a thing of the future, but a reality in the present. For "many species of lower animals of to-day possess a higher mentality than primeval man . . . [and] the lower classes of men of to-day." The trope of reversal used by protectionists was, for Ballou, literal—the horse might in fact exceed its driver in intelligence and civility. Indeed, he invoked the same image as protectionists, complaining that horses were often beaten "by a man-shaped brute, who can neither write his name nor mention the common decencies of life." Ballou then outlined his animal-human civilizational scale, grouping man and beast in ascending order. At the bottom he positioned "low and ignorant mankind," including "aborigines," alongside insects and many undomesticated and untrained animals. In the middle he put "trained lower animals" including pets and domesticated animals, and at the top he positioned "educated man." As Ballou's fantastical etho-anthropology suggests, the discourse of civilization could function not only to hierarchically rank human beings, but also to variegate the otherwise categorical distinction between humans and animals.

Targeting the drivers of horses as protectionists and Ballou did was often as not a clear signal that the cruel man in question was not only poor,
but also likely foreign-born. While such oblique references formed a staple
of many humane publications and speeches, many anticruelty reformers
were explicit about the greater cruelty of the poor and nonwhite. Animal
protectionists, for example, were as concerned to reach African Americans, Indians, and immigrants with humane education programs as they
were to proselytize humanity to the heathens of the Philippines, Cuba,
or other colonies.⁴⁴ One of the South's leading organs against animal cruelty, the *New Orleans Picayune*, intoned that "negroes, either as slaves
or freemen, have always been notorious for their cruelty to our most useful animals—horses, mules, work oxen and mulch cows." And, in a moment of class as well as racial antipathy, the paper admitted that "tens and
thousands of ignorant and brutal white men treat their work animals and
milch cows no better than the negroes treat theirs." ⁴⁵ Likewise, an address
on "Humane Work in the South" by Richard Reed of Natchez, Mississippi,
charged African Americans with being more cruel than whites. The "colored race," Reed explained, supplied the majority of the South's criminals,
and crimes against animals and children were no exception to the rule.
"It seems very difficult to educate the negroes to be gentle and kind in
their treatment of animals," Reed lamented, and "they often punish their
own children in an extremely cruel manner." Because of their impervious-
ness to education, Reed explained that African Americans would only be
reached by prosecution at the hands of the law. "They will be merciful because they fear the law; not from any moral motive or principle. We have
to command them to be humane." Reed ended by acknowledging that of
course many "negroes" were kind and humane, and explaining that most
did not mean to be cruel, but simply acted on "uncontrolled passion or
thoughtless neglect." But in order to impart self-control and civilization,
Reed urged the organization of special colored branch humane societies
among the South's black population.⁴⁶ Delivered in 1890 by a Mississip-
pian in Tennessee, Reed's speech drew on and reinforced the allegation
against African Americans prevalent in lynching discourse: inclined toward greater criminality by nature, subject to uncontrollable passions, African Americans could only be reached by force.⁴⁷

Child protectionists too used prevailing social hierarchies to form
their portrait of the cruel. The St. Paul, Minnesota, Society for the Prevention of Cruelty reported in 1896 that as the "foreign population" of
the city became Americanized "less cruelty is being practiced both upon
animals and human beings." Like early republican antiviolence crusad-

ers, St. Paul's humanitarians assumed that American democracy, civilization, and kindness were indissolubly linked. These assumptions were widely shared. The New York SPCC also identified immigration as one of the chief factors contributing to cruelty against children and particularly targeted Italian parents. In its tenth annual report, the society complained about garbage-picking children, who they assumed were forced to labor by their parents, and claimed that such children were almost exclusively Italian. "The Italian quarters which exist in several sections of the city menace the public health because of these practices," warned the report. And though no humane society recorded the race or ethnicity of either the perpetrators or victims of its cruelty cases, statistics from the NY-SPCC's annual reports indicate that a majority of children that the society removed from their homes were Catholic, thus likely either Irish or Italian. Gerry's annual address to the society in 1891 helps to explain why his organization might have targeted so many foreign-born. Complaining that "juvenile depravity" was still on the increase, Gerry attributed this unfortunate trend to continued "immense immigration from Europe." In particular, foreign parents were unfamiliar with American laws (such as those that the SPCC enforced) and had "views in regard to the treatment, education and care of children [that] are to say the least lax in many instances."[48] Like his colleagues in St. Paul and like so many other late-nineteenth-century observers, Gerry shared the view that the newest immigrants brought with them alien habits that threatened the stability of American institutions. To animal and child protectionists, "cruelty" was chief among these foreign traits.

Some animal and child protectionists took the perceived relationship between savagery, civilization, and cruelty to its logically conservative extreme. Henry Bergh, Elbridge Gerry, and John Shortall all joined a chorus of voices calling for a return to corporal punishments—specifically the whipping post—for certain crimes. Though corporal punishment had been abolished in nearly all states, many saw reason for its revival. Between 1876 and 1901, twelve states and the District of Columbia introduced legislation to bring back the whipping post as punishment for particular crimes. Advocates of this legislation were normally, like Gerry and Shortall and other protectionists, "eminently respectable" men interested in legal affairs and law enforcement.[49] In 1877, Bergh figured prominently in a debate in the *New York Times* about whether to revive the lash for criminals, arguing that for certain criminals, rehabilitation was impossible and only corporal punishment could reach them. He argued that the man who "steals, insults respectable women on the street, is cruel to his wife and children, and is reckless of the personal rights of his fellow-creatures" would not, as the old anticorporal punishment argument had it, be degraded by whipping since he had already sunk so low. Moreover, Bergh believed that whipping was a more efficient and effective form of punishment. Most men in the "criminal classes" did not, he argued, view time in the penitentiary as a punishment, but rather as a "devilishly attractive" place to while away some time. The lash, by contrast, held "terrors" for the criminal and would thus truly punish and, more important, prevent crime. Bergh knew that many believed that the lash was a potent symbol of both slavery and barbaric, premodern regimes. But he maintained that it was only a false sense of humanitarianism and "civilization" that opposed whipping criminals. For in Bergh's view, the alternative to effective law and order was social chaos and violence. In a true civilization, the machinery of justice would create order and peace through swift and effective punishment of those that abdicated their rights and their humanity by preying on the weak.[50]

Bergh tried to make his dream a reality when, in 1881, he urged the state's legislature to pass a law to punish wife-beaters by whipping them no fewer than twenty-five times on their bare backs.[51] The bill was not passed, but Bergh's idea was revived by Elbridge Gerry a little more than a decade later. Though Gerry had been instrumental during the 1880s in reforming New York State's death-penalty procedures, urging the adoption of death by electrocution, in the 1890s, he, along with the IHS's John Shortall, advocated the return of corporal punishment for violent crimes. Specifically, Gerry and the New York State Convention of Humane Societies urged that the lash be applied as a penalty in cases of "gross acts of cruelty to children." Like Bergh's earlier bill, Gerry's too went down to defeat, but much more narrowly this time.[52] In lawyerly fashion, Gerry explained that punishment had three basic goals: retribution, individual reform, and deterrence. The latter aspect, he claimed, was ill served by current sentencing for violent crimes, which could not handle the new type of criminal in the midst of America's cities. In the past few years, Gerry claimed, America had witnessed an influx of foreigners, whom he called the "offscourings of the criminal classes of Europe," and whose only intent was to perpetuate their Old World crimes on New World soil. In this assessment, Gerry was joined by hosts of American criminologists who declared that the crimes besetting the nation's urban areas were the product of alien invaders, those immigrants from Italy and other such climes who wreaked havoc with their atavistic behaviors.[53] Gerry thought that noncorporal punishments were designed for a different type of criminal—

for the "educated man"—and aimed, however nobly, at reformation alone. But these methods could only fail with the new type of criminal, for he "leads a purely animal existence; he has no fine feelings to be injured, no sensibilities to be crushed," and is concerned only with the basic physical facts of his existence: food, shelter, and rest. Because the lower type of criminals "instinctively dread" pain, corporal punishment is "an argument which they can appreciate, no matter how illiterate they are, or how debased by crime, or how besotted by indulgence in liquor."[54] In a strange twist on sentimentalism's universalist language of pain, Gerry asserted that physical suffering was a language that even the lower orders of humanity could understand. And though he believed that animals should be spared pain, the cruelist's link with savagery cast him below the beasts, whose helplessness elevated them to an unnaturally high position in the great chain of being's *moral* ranks.

The irony that a man who spent his life decrying cruelty and violence toward animals and children would end up by arguing that the barbaric animality of some criminals required that they be made to suffer pain was lost on Gerry, Shortall, and the other humane reformers who called for a return to the whipping post. Many of their compatriots disagreed with their arguments, but their tactics point to the problems presented both by the deep intermingling of the language of cruelty with that of civilization and savagery and by the conceptual paradoxes of cruelty itself.[55] For in the relentlessly hierarchical logic of "civilization," the cruel were thought to have renounced their place in the civilized world; betraying its moral and social norms, they lost its protections. By portraying cruelists as animalistic and immune to regular methods of reform, Gerry made their corporal punishment *reasonable* rather than excessive, the last choice left open to a society in need of self-protection. As a form of self-defense and an appropriate response to violated innocence, corporal punishment for violent crimes appeared neither ill motivated nor excessive. Far from violating civilized standards of decency, it upheld them.

Though identifying cruelty with savagery and humanity with civilization, Christianity, and progress often led animal and child protectionists to affirm racial and ethnic stereotypes—and to take a "law and order" line—anticruelty reform was not simply a case of outraged elites judging and punishing the marginal. As Gail Bederman has shown, the language of civilization was "protean in its applications" and could serve "to legitimize conservatism and change, male dominance and militant feminism, white racism and African American resistance."[56] Indeed, many reformers stressed that "respectable" habits and fashions often entailed considerable cruelty, particularly to animals. The anticruelty movement's widely publicized campaign against the use of bird feathers in millinery demonstrates the flexibility of the concepts of both cruelty and civilization. In attacking the fashionable use of bird feathers and stuffed birds on women's hats, anticruelty activists targeted their own ranks—the middle and upper classes—and charged them with cruelty in the language of barbarism, effectively using civilization's self-image against itself.

Published by the American Humane Education Society in 1898, the novel *Some of New York's 400* took aim at the bird-laden millinery that adorned the heads of New York's society ladies. Its principal character, Laura Burton, is a sensitive and ethical young woman born into New York's highest social circles, but under the thumb of a vain and self-serving mother, and surrounded by what she regards as rich hypocrites, the sort who piously attend church on Sundays while leaving their horses outside, overchecked, docked at the tail, and foaming at the mouth from poor bits. Though Laura spends many a night wandering the city streets admonishing cabmen who overload their horses and rescuing stray dogs and cats from harassment and starvation, she finally decides to address the moral blindness of her own class, realizing that "humane education among the rich is quite as necessary as among the poor." Because her callous mother has denied her a sufficient allowance to carry on her humane activities, Laura decides to strike two blows at once. By setting up a millinery shop that uses dried flowers instead of bird feathers, Laura aims both to stem cruelty among rich and fashionable women and to earn extra money to support her other rescue efforts. With a little help from a family friend, Laura soon opens the Floral Millinery Emporium.[57]

As New York's elite women wander into Laura's new shop on its opening day, Madame Dupont, the French woman whom Laura has hired to make the featherless hats and serve as the proprietress, explains that feathers were "losing favor" because "they were too suggestive of Indian adornments and savage-like relics to be permissible." Their procurement not only caused the death of millions of beautiful songbirds each year, but also left many baby birds abandoned to die of starvation as their mothers were snatched up and killed. Immediately the fashionable women in attendance regret that they have "unwittingly" contributed to such a cruel industry and follow the lead of a Mrs. Montague, who moved that "we denounce the custom as semi-barbaric."[58]

Many outside Clouston's pages would have agreed with Mrs. Montague. Indeed, one of the chief arguments against bird millinery was its connection to savagery. The editor of *Harper's*, a frequent supporter of humane causes, pointed out that while many women were revolted by things they consider vulgar or barbaric—the butcher, the rings savages wear in their ears, or the bound feet of Chinese women, for instance—they thought nothing of wearing birds on their hats. The woman who wears a bird hat, explained the editor, "encouraged the 'slarter' of the loveliest and sweetest of innocent song birds merely to gratify her vanity. The butcher, madam, may be vulgar, but at least he does not kill in order to wear the horns and tails of his victims." These hats are "memorials of heartless slaughter" and are "bought at a monstrous price." Will women continue to "make themselves accomplices in a crime against the innocent" or will they wake up to this "thoughtless wrong"?[59] Another writer wondered how women could sanction a practice that destroyed avian families. "The sufferings of the mother-bird must touch the mother-pity in woman, as she reads again and again the story—Torn from her nest, stripped of her beautiful plumage, thrown upon the ground to die in agony at the foot of the tree, where she can hear the cries of her starving little ones in the nest above. All this, for a tuft of feathers! What savages these mortals be."[60] Calling widespread practices savage, reformers left the civilized/savage hierarchy in place, but upended the Western world's place within its ranks and used the gap between sanctimonious ideals and sordid realities to demand change.

The contradiction between society's professed Christian civility and its actual barbaric practices was heightened here by its refraction through a gendered lens. Playing on two distinct images of women—as frivolous and indulgent slaves to fashion and as the nation's moral stewards—antimillinery language allied fashion with savagery and contrasted it with the latter, suggesting that women's moral transgressions were particularly egregious. A little inhumanity from men was disappointing but not shocking—from women it was an unsexing display. "We have been so accustomed to believe in tender sensibility to suffering as a grace of womanhood," wrote an anonymous author in *Our Animal Friends*, "that we have found it difficult to give credit to [the] many facts" proving that women have sustained the millinery trade and the fashionable docking and checking of horses as well.[61] In its campaigns against bird-based millinery, the WCTU sponsored, among other things, an essay contest. Its winner, Mrs. Velma Beebe, wrote that "a woman who will wear the body of a dead bird can hardly be credited with a woman's heart."[62] In betraying their natural role as the nation's moral guardians, women both unsexed themselves and heralded civilization's decline. If, as many believed, civilization was characterized not only by a benevolent and Christian moral code, but also

by gender differentiation, then women's acts of cruelty threatened both.[63]
By invoking the links and contrasts between moral womanhood, cruelty,
and savagery, humanitarians stretched hierarchical language to mount a
self-reflexive critique of their own classes, suggesting that the language of
cruelty enabled them to see more than just the iniquitous passions of the
immigrant and working classes.

Because the flexibility of civilizational language meant that cruelty could
be identified with the rich as well as the poor, many in the anticruelty
movement might have disagreed with Gerry and Shortall's view that cruelists deserved corporal punishment. Nevertheless, many likely would
have agreed that cruelty caused harm that redounded not simply on its
perpetrators and their victims, but on society as a whole. In this, as in
much else, animal and child protectionists operating after the Civil War
shared many assumptions with their predecessors. Like those in antebellum movements to stem violence and suffering, protectionists regarded
cruelty as a violation rather than an expression of human nature and as
an offense against history and civilization. Accordingly, they regarded the
"cruelist" with disdain. And like those involved in campaigns to abolish
corporal and capital punishment, end slavery, or stem alcohol abuse, animal and child protectionists regarded the problem with cruelty as social
rather than as simply moral. Cruelty was a problem not only because of
the suffering it caused individual animals or children, but also because
of the social disorder it wrought. This disorder stemmed from the ways
in which cruelty damaged both perpetrator and victim. As the ruined-
through-cruelty narratives discussed in the previous chapter revealed, protectionists believed that cruel treatment rendered animals and children
intractable and likely to cause disciplinary problems for those around
them. Perpetrators of cruelty thus damaged not only their victims, but
also themselves and the larger social fabric.

As a term for describing a moral and social problem, "cruelty" was both
a powerful and an ambiguous choice. The shifting and multiple meanings
of cruelty are best illustrated by the animal protection statutes passed at
the behest of SPCAs during the second half of the nineteenth century. Unlike those crimes that protectionists gathered under the rubric of cruelty
to children, the crimes constituting cruelty to animals were both more
novel and more likely to be consolidated under a single statute; they were
thus the object of more sustained discussion by both protectionists and jurists. Determining what kinds of behavior were "cruel" to animals proved
far from simple. In part this was due to the fact that cruelty denoted excess

rather than fixed behaviors. Someone was cruel when he caused "unnecessary suffering," but necessity, of course, could shift. Cruelty also proved
an ambiguous term because the nature of its harm was difficult to locate.
What, in short, was "wrong" with being cruel? According to some protectionists and contemporaries, cruelty was wrong because of the suffering it
caused its victims. To others, it was wrong because it ruined the character
of its perpetrator. To still others, cruelty was wrong because it violated
social norms and disturbed public peace and morals.

For animal protectionists, a large measure of cruelty's harm was the
pain it caused animals. Shortly after Henry Bergh founded the ASPCA, he
went before his state's legislature and successfully convinced the body to
pass a bill that both criminalized cruelty to animals and deputized Bergh's
society to enforce the provisions of the law. Bergh's organization and his
law became a model, and by 1900 every state in the nation had enacted
laws similar to those in New York.[64] The law adopted in New York was a
significant departure from common law understanding of animals' legal
status. Under the common law the crime of cruelty to animals did not
exist. As nineteenth-century legal commentator Joel Prentiss Bishop explained, "Man has always held in subjection the lower animals, to be used
or destroyed at will, for his advantage or pleasure." Man's right of property
in animals superseded all animal interest in being free from harm, Bishop
continued, and so "the common law recognizes as indictable no wrong,
and punishes no act of cruelty, which they may suffer, however wanton or
unnecessary."[65] Because property was understood as an instrument of its
owner's will, to be a victim of cruelty required a status above that of personal property. The identification of animals with property was, as Bishop
recognized, a longstanding one. Indeed, virtually every liberal theorist,
from Adam Smith and John Locke to William Blackstone, identified animals as the first form of property and suggested that their subordination
to man's will—that is, their domestication—was an essential component
of the human civilizing process, enabling man's progress from primitive
to more advanced states of social organization.[66]

In spite of their designated role as mankind's subordinates, animals,
like other forms of real and personal property, were subject to a variety of
protections and regulations.[67] Common law did offer animals what Bishop
called "indirect" protections. It was, for instance, a crime to injure or kill
a domestic animal belonging to another. The crime, however, was a form
of malicious mischief, a vengeful destruction of property, and the harm
was understood as directed against the animal's owner, not the animal
itself. In this respect, animals were treated like other household depen-

dents under coverture—they were unable to be directly harmed and were
without legal personhood. Moreover, since malicious mischief was a violation of property rights, this indirect protection of animals left a man
free to harm or kill his own animals as much as he liked—for they were
his possessions. In another form of indirect protection, the common law
also held that it was a crime to beat an animal in public, but as with malicious mischief, the crime was not against the animal, but instead against
the public peace and the public morals. It was a crime of nuisance, an offence against one's neighbors and the social order. In both instances, neither the suffering of animals nor the concept of cruelty guided the law's
sense of harm or culpability. Under such nuisance and mischief penalties,
explained Bishop, "protection to the creature as a sensitive being is not the
thing sought."[68]

Prior to the legislation adopted in New York in 1866, several states including New York had some positive law provisions regulating the treatment of animals. As early as 1641 the Massachusetts Bay Colony's legal
code, the Body of Liberties, had prohibited beating certain kinds of animals. In the 1820s, Maine outlawed beating cattle or horses, New York
banned maliciously killing another's livestock or maliciously beating
one's own, and in the 1850s Minnesota, Connecticut, and Vermont made it
a crime to kill livestock belonging to another person.[69] None of these ex-
tant laws, however, were truly anticruelty laws. Rather, they were akin to
the common law crimes of malicious mischief and public nuisance, concerned chiefly with property in animals and the public peace. Describing
this history, a *Scribner's* feature on Henry Bergh and the ASPCA recounted
that "up to 1865 no law for the protection of animals from cruelty could
be found on the statute book of any state in the Union. The common law
regarded animals simply as property, and their masters, in wanton cruelty,
or anger . . . might torture his sentient chattels without legal hindrance or
accountability."[70]

The innovation of the New York state and subsequent anticruelty laws
was that by isolating cruelty as the chief harm to be prevented and punished, they made the crime consist more clearly of violence against animals themselves rather than the violation of property rights or disruption
of the public order. Crucially, anticruelty laws were written such that cruelty was an offense no matter the relationship of ownership between the
man and animal—it could be perpetrated against "any living creature,"
and it was an offense whether it took place in the public square or in a
private home. Another distinctive feature of the new anticruelty laws was
that they sanctioned not just positive acts of violence against animals, but

also various kinds of neglect. Consistent with its concern for the public peace, common law had regulated the keeping of animals, requiring their owners to keep control of them and making owners liable for animals' mischievous behavior such as stealing food or injuring humans.[71] As with the prohibition on positive acts of cruelty to animals, the neglect provisions of post-1866 anticruelty laws were quite different from such common law assumptions and requirements. Instead of protecting the public from bothersome animals not well kept, the anticruelty concept of neglect entitled animals to sustenance, protecting them from their owners or caretakers. On the whole, the new anticruelty laws implied that animals had a specific identifiable interest in being free from pain, whether it resulted from the sharp sting of a blow or the protracted agony of starvation. Moreover, by removing property relations from the equation, anticruelty laws constituted the law's object as harm to animals, not their owners.

Not long confined to New York, the spread of this new form of legislation, and this new conception of the relationship governing man and animal, was rapid. By 1900 all forty-seven states had similar positive legislation on their books. Nineteenth-century jurists and legal scholars immediately detected the near-revolutionary character of these new laws. Writing in the *Central Law Journal*, Oscar Quinlan noted that "cruelty, as such, is punishable only by virtue of recent legislation," and was not indictable at common law. "This prohibition of cruelty," he went on, "is superior to the rights of ownership, and regardless of value, of the animal injured and of the privacy or publicity of the act."[72] Likewise, Bishop insisted that there was no common law basis for the crime of cruelty—it was a pure product of the nineteenth-century state, an attempt, as one Arkansas judge put it, "to transcend what had been thought, at common law, the practical limits of municipal government."[73] Interfering in the relations between owner and owned, and between man and animal, by interposing the mediating term of cruelty was indeed an innovation foisted on states by animal welfare reformers.

Happy to see themselves as revolutionaries on the side of right, animal protection activists generally heralded the groundbreaking nature of state anticruelty legislation. Charles Barnard, an attorney for the Massachusetts SPCA, declared that the new laws "differ from earlier enactments, and from the common law regarding this class of offences, in proceeding more clearly upon the principle that animals have *rights*," by which he meant that the law was concerned principally with animal suffering rather than with the protection of property or the public order.[74] The point of anticruelty laws differed from the indirect protections of the common law.

While the latter sought to protect property and preserve human morality and order, the former aimed to protect animals from undue suffering. The common law definition of guilt or harm was, in other words, amended by nineteenth-century SPCAs that sought to replace the old sense of harm—the destruction of property or the disturbance of public peace and morals—with a new harm: the suffering of animals themselves.

Nevertheless, though protectionists clearly understood cruelty in terms of animals' suffering, cruelty was still difficult to categorically define, even among humanitarians. Humane publications, from annual reports to didactic readers for children, often addressed themselves to defining cruelty in sections aptly titled "What Is Cruelty," or "The Nature of Cruelty."[75] Here they tried to draw the fine lines that distinguished ordinary pain from cruelty. For most animal protectionists, cruelty was "giving needless pain" or the "unnecessary ill usage of the animal." Thus it was not pain per se that either the concept of cruelty or the law itself prohibited since, as the MSPCA's Charles Barnard put it, "pain inflicted for a lawful purpose, and with a justifiable intent, though severe," is not cruel.[76] Thus, although protectionists sought to eliminate pain and suffering and identified their amelioration with progress, "cruelty" as a moral and legal term recognized as wrong only excessive or unnecessary pain.

As Barnard's reference to "justifiable intent" suggests, cruelty legally hinged on the balance between intention and outcome. As one lawyer in an anticruelty trial explained, "the intent and the act must concur to make the offence."[77] In turning from the outcome—animal suffering—to the intention, animal protection laws redefined the nature of cruelty's harm, moving from a focus on the body of the wounded animal to probing the mind of the perpetrator. For if cruelty hinged not on the severity of the pain but on its justifiability, then the legal focus shifted from animal suffering to the human mind, the seat of purpose and intent. Anticruelty laws were not novel in this respect, for all criminal laws require the combination of a harmful act and an evil intention—absent one of these elements, there is no crime.[78] As criminal codes, anticruelty statutes automatically built in the requirement for mens rea, or a criminal mind, and typically specified that the pain inflicted must be done wantonly, maliciously, or with reckless disregard for the animal's welfare. Likewise, very few actions were considered prima facie cruel, but instead cruelty was determined on a case-by-case basis that weighed, among other things, whether the actions in question were undertaken for a legitimate purpose and with the proper intent.[79] Castrating one's animal, for instance, might cause great pain but would not be, for that reason, considered cruel since the purpose, and thus the intention, was legitimate and the pain produced "necessary" to achieve a legitimate end.[80] Similarly, a man might whip or otherwise strike his animal in the process of training it without approaching cruelty—the distinction that courts drew was between chastisement undertaken for the purposes of training and that which "results from any bad or evil motive; as from cruelty of disposition, from violent passion, [or] a design to give pain to others."[81]

Establishing the intention behind actions that caused pain was not, however, a simple matter—nor was determining the relative importance of intention versus effect in a given case. On the one hand, intent was a critical element of the crime but, on the other hand, anticruelty statutes operated, as did all other criminal laws, on the assumption that "every man intends the natural, necessary, and even probable consequences of an act which he intentionally performs."[82] Courts, furthermore, disagreed about the importance of intent and how to define the necessity of certain human actions, like fox hunting and pigeon shooting.[83] Anticruelty activists, for their part, undertook public campaigns to redefine "necessity" and to argue that cruelty could result from thoughtlessness (the law's "reckless disregard") as well as from the overt desire to inflict pain on a helpless being. Generally speaking, SPCAs reserved prosecution for cases that they believed fell into the latter category, or those for which ignorance, whether of the law or of the suffering incurred, seemed an untenable excuse. In part, this reflected the difficulties encountered by SPCAs in prosecuting cases in which the intent to harm was less than clear.[84]

Even when state courts were willing, as they sometimes were, to grant that ill motive or intention could be "immaterial" to the question of whether the crime of cruelty had been committed, their understanding of cruelty's harm nonetheless focused not on animals, but on human morals. An Arkansas judge, for instance, noted anticruelty legislation's novel departure from the property and public nuisance protections of common law. However, he went on, to construe such statutes literally would result in their being a "dead letter" since, as written, the state "might drag to the criminal bar, every lady who might impale a butterfly, or every man who might drown a litter of kittens." To avoid such "absurdities" the judge admonished that the "laws must be rationally construed." "So construed," he assured, "this class of laws may be found useful in elevating humanity, by enlargement with all God's creatures, and thus society may be improved."[85] Unable to contemplate a legislative intent to protect animals from pain, the judge assumed that their intent must have been to forbid the *human* degradation accompanying indulgence in violence.

Six years later, the 1887 decision in *Commonwealth v. Turner*, a Massachusetts prosecution for fox hunting, affirmed the view of the Arkansas judge. The court declared that the offense of cruelty was against neither property nor animals' rights, but instead "is against the public morals, which the commission of cruel and barbarous acts tends to corrupt."[86] Indeed, cruelty laws were most often incorporated under the sections of state criminal code regulating the public welfare and morals.[87] Similarly, after an extensive review of state court decisions to date, an 1894 law review article concluded that anticruelty legislation did not establish animal rights but, rather, that the object of the laws was to stem "brutality in man," which is "destructive of that morality and humanity upon which all government is founded."[88] In cases such as this, nineteenth-century legal interpreters located the harm of cruelty not in animal suffering, but rather in the violation of public morals and order that violence toward animals could cause. Jurists shared anticruelty reformers' assumptions that pain and civilization were antithetical, and that the cruel are barbaric, but unlike reformers, judges tended to focus on cruelty's relationship to social disorder at the expense of attending to individual suffering.

Though animal protectionists were genuinely concerned with lessening animal suffering, and though they authored and promoted legislation that placed animals' interests more squarely before the law than ever before, the concept of cruelty, the laws that criminalized it, and the judges who interpreted and applied those laws all paid substantial attention to human morality. Because cruelty was constituted by an excess of pain and an evil intent, both interpreters and opponents of cruelty vacillated between locating its existence, on the one hand, in the sentient experience of animals and, on the other, in the mind of the criminal. This vacillation both reflected and contributed to the confusion over the harm of cruelty—and whether it lay in the criminal mind, the animal body, or the public morals. Writing in *Law Notes*, "J. H. L." honed in on "the fundamental question, why men should be restrained by law from acts of cruelty towards the lower animals." Is it, he wondered, because there is "a positive right sanctioned by the sovereign power, so that there is a bond of law between them and men? Or is it a right 'which derives its sanction from the human revolt against the mystery of pain'? Or, is it founded simply upon moral utilitarianism," prohibited because restraining men from such actions improves their character.[89] In the pages of humanitarian publications, appellate court cases, and legal commentaries, J. H. L. could easily have found support for each of his propositions, "moral utilitarianism" not least among these.

The law's focus on the content of the human mind and heart as an important constituent of cruelty was echoed in the words of animal and child protectionists who stressed that cruelty was a product of uncontrolled appetites. Understood as a war against human appetite, the anticruelty movement appears akin to the moral reform campaigns that received a boost from the union's victory in the Civil War, which many Christian reformers regarded as a victory over sin par excellence. Upset over what they saw as declining standards of personal behavior, postbellum moral reformers undertook campaigns to legally regulate the consumption of alcohol, tobacco, and other drugs, and sought to prohibit polygamy, "easy" divorces, delivery of the mail on Sundays, the lottery, distribution of obscene materials, prizefighting, and prostitution. What linked these diverse concerns was, according to historian Gaines Foster, a belief that all were rooted in a common source: the free reign of appetite and avarice, which signaled lack of self-control and submission to desire. In the view of such reformers, desire was the first step on the slippery slope toward moral depravity and evil deeds. For "appetite led to sin, and sin seemed especially dangerous" to them because "they considered sins interconnected and believed committing one led almost inevitably to others and, in the end, to total degradation." Though moral reformers involved in organizations such as the WCTU, the National Reform Association, and Anthony Comstock's Society for the Suppression of Vice sought legal changes at both the state and federal levels, their understanding of the problems besetting American society were framed in individual, moral terms. Unlike their counterparts under the banner of populism, the social gospel movement, or progressivism, moral reformers framed social disorder in individual rather than structural terms, insisting that moral regeneration—the victory over appetite—would transform society from the inside out.[90]

Anticruelty reforms shared many of the assumptions of moral reformers laboring in other fields, very often attributing cruelty to the twin demons of appetite and avarice. Though humane organizations frequently conceded that much cruelty was the result of ignorance and thoughtlessness rather than a truly evil spirit, they nonetheless stressed the basic depravity underlying acts of cruelty toward both animals and children and tended to stress individual rather than systemic transformation as the solution.

In addition to portraying cruelty as a problem of passionate indulgence in general, reformers often linked cruelty to specific vices like intemperance and greed. Not only were drunkards more likely to be abusive to animal and child alike, but also indulgence in passion was, like dipping into

drink, but another form of intemperance.[91] Caroline Earle White, the leader
of Philadelphia's Women's Branch of the PSPCA, wrote in the society's
1878 annual report that no doubt much cruelty is "owing to the drinking
of intoxicating liquors." She wondered if "ought we not then, in our desire
to ameliorate the sufferings of our dumb friends, to add our efforts to those
who are laboring for a reform in this manner?"[92] Henry Bergh too considered alcohol to be a "personal devil," and declared that "rum, or anything
else that steals away the human senses is the instigation of all crime."[93]
And though it would be nearly a decade more before any formal alliances
were made between humane and WCTU activists, White's organization
and others across the country busily erected water fountains in cities from
San Francisco to Boston, on the theory that they were "thus combining
temperance and mercy," by providing men and animals a place to get a
fresh drink aside from the saloon.[94]

Beginning in 1887, George Angell began to forge links with the WCTU,
sending its members accounts of the MSPCA's educational work and ply-
ing them with humane literature. Invited to speak at their 1887 annual
convention, Angell regretfully declined, but joked that the real name of
the MSPCA should be "How a Drunkard Treats His Horse."[95] A year later,
Mary Lovell, a member of the PSPCA's Woman's Branch and a cohort of
Caroline Earle White, successfully advocated for the incorporation of
the Band of Mercy movement into the WCTU. Lovell was appointed as the
WCTU superintendent in charge of forming Bands of Mercy within the
WCTU's youth branches, the Loyal Temperance Leagues. In 1889 Lovell
founded the Pennsylvania state WCTU's Department of Mercy and in
1890 became head of the National WCTU's newly formed department of
the same name. A year later she explained to the annual convention that
"cruelty being an effect of the drink vice, we have a department for the development of mercy, the Christ-virtue."[96] In 1895 the IHS and the WCTU
unveiled the Francis Willard fountain on the corner of Monroe and La-
Salle streets in Chicago. Named for the leader of the WCTU, the fountain's operation and maintenance were under the purview of the IHS.[97]
"It is certainly fitting," intoned WCTU president Lillian Stevens a decade later, that her organization "should have a Department of Mercy . . .
and it is even more important that every society whose object is the prevention of cruelty to animals should have a Total Abstinence Department." Citing the authority of George Angell, Stevens explained that "the
horse of the drunkard, like his wife and children, is overworked, underfed,
poorly housed, neglected and abused. It is but natural that in some places
children are included in the work of the humane society. If all the money

wasted for strong drink were spent to provide good homes and home comforts the child labor problem would more easily be solved."[98] Rather than suggesting that employers of children be held responsible, Stevens attributed blame to individual failings—children labored because their parents were drunkards.

No humane societies acted on Stevens's suggestion to establish abstinence departments, but many in the movement nonetheless agreed with her that alcohol and cruelty were basically similar problems. Tales of drunken men leaving horses outside saloons to freeze at night, or driving horses too hard and fast, were legion. Likewise, when they described their cases to the public, humane society officers very often described the perpetrators as inebriates or "confirmed drunkards."[99] Henry Bergh, addressing the fourth annual meeting of the ASPCA, summed up these points. "The man who gives unrestrained license to his violent passions must inevitably make a miserable end," he warned. Invoking the teleology of cruelty, Bergh predicted that "He that ill-treats his horse is insensibly led to ill-treat his wife and children." Having torn apart his home, the cruelist will then seek refuge and comfort in the local saloon, where he finds further stimulus for his violence among "companions as riotous and unprincipled as himself." "Drunkenness goes hand in hand with cruelty," Bergh concluded, "and with drunkenness loss of character, degradation, and the crimes which bring him at last within the reach of the law."[100] Bergh and others believed that stemming cruelty was effectively nipping other forms of violence and unlicensed behavior in the bud, thus concurring with the law's view that cruelty's harm lay in the criminal heart and its threat to the public welfare and morals.

The trope of drunkenness expressed protectionists' sense that cruelty was rooted in lack of restraint, and was thus destabilizing to the social order. Humane publications redrew the map of community around character rather than kind, referring to cruelists and drunkards as "beasts" or "brutes" as much, if not more, than they used such terms to describe the animals they sought to protect. Invoking the specter of wild and undomesticated animals, the term "beast" suggested that the drunken man, like even the sober cruelist, transported himself outside the bonds of the human community. In a story that simultaneously praised animals and cast aspersions on men, revealingly titled "Which Was the Brute," the *Humane Journal* told of a drunk man lying "utterly senseless on the stones" in Central Park. The city police, endeavoring to remove the man, were held at bay by his loyal dog, "a friend who stuck closer than a brother, in spite of the degradation and shame." Keeping a vigilant watch over the man's body, "The dog was at his best, and doing his best, with a more than human fidelity," while "the man, at his worst, degraded and disgusting, lay helpless, under the care of the brute."[101] Drunk beyond self-care and self-control, the man showed that animality did not, in fact, obey the species line.

Like intemperance, cruelty's relation to human greed was the subject of much humanitarian propaganda, and it similarly suggested that greed exemplified a failure to properly consider one's place in the human and moral community. The nation's first oration on animal rights, delivered by Herman Daggett in 1791, pointed to "the blind and criminal selfishness of the human heart" as the root of all crimes, including cruelty. Crimes against animals and humans share a motive, Daggett asserted, and whether one steals a bird's nest or a neighbor's property, the drive is "self gratification" all the same.[102] Writing nearly eighty years later in response to a reader who asserted that all cruelty was the result of intoxication, the editors of Our Dumb Animals replied that the situation was not so simple after all. "Much of the cruelty comes from love of money, much from loss of temper, and much from thoughtlessness," the magazine explained.[103] For all indulgence of the passions was related by the underlying property that greed encapsulated most clearly: self-concern and self-interest. Rather than consider beings outside himself, the greedy man thought only of his own desires and needs—he was the perfect inversion of the sympathetic man of feeling. This self-indulgence, quite surely, could lead to cruelty. The Illinois Humane Society's Humane Journal explained it this way: "self-devotion has narrowness, and further on, meanness and cruelty attendant upon it."[104]

For many nineteenth-century animal protectionists the tight relation between greed and cruelty was exemplified by the overloading, overworking, and abandonment of horses, practices that might not entail overt violence, but which they nonetheless characterized as forms of "diabolical cruelty."[105] Most of the complaints received by SPCAs—and most of the cases pursued—involved such practices.[106] Henry Bergh was legendary for patrolling horse-driven streetcar lines and often stopping overloaded cars and forcing passengers to get off and wait for another, less burdened car to come along. As a result, the ASPCA prosecuted a number of cases against New York City's horse-driven railway companies, successfully proving in one case that the cars were constantly packed to the brim "simply for the gain and cupidity of railroad directors."[107] George Angell and the MSPCA likewise endeavored to prove that overloading a horse fit the crime of cruelty. "Demanding of animals a service which they are unable to perform," intoned *Our Dumb Animals*, "is a cruel act, and punishable by law." Angell went further, publishing a treatise on how to detect the signs of overloading in a horse in the hopes that it would convince jurists and horse drivers alike that the practice was indeed a form of cruelty. Angell's interpretation of overloading was adopted by the legal profession when Joel Prentiss Bishop incorporated it into his own 1873 *Commentaries on the Law of Statutory Crimes.*[108]

Reformers also protested the sale of old horses at horse markets, a practice that often led to the use of painful if not lethal substances that would, at least temporarily, make a decrepit horse appear fatter, more agile, and more lively.[109] A Wisconsin Humane Society publication imagined a horse, speaking in verse, asking his master, "Do you think I'm a creature with feelings, / Deserving your sympathy / And thought for my better protection? / Or is it money in me? / Do you do anything for my profit / Unless you believe there will be / A bigger return on my labor / Than you've ever divided with me? / Do you ever stop to consider / Me at all, but what I cost to you?"[110] In this protest against the sale of old horses, Wisconsin's animal protectionists suggested that the greedy man was the inverse of the ideal humanitarian, the person for whom "love does not mean love of me or you, but it means love always and for all."[111] Unable to imagine that animals might have feelings, the greedy man, for mere "mercenary motives," would inflict as much pain and suffering through overwork and miserly neglect as would the man who beat his horse to gratify his passion for violence.

The argument that cruelty stood at the beginning of a slippery slope of violence and debauchery evinced protectionists' belief that all antisocial behavior was of a piece. Reformers' sense that acts of cruelty were linked by the way in which they allowed perpetrators to selfishly indulge their passions betrayed their concern not merely for those who suffered, but also for the mind and heart of the cruelist. Concern for the cruelists' moral state was linked, in turn, to protectionists' desire to stanch cruelty in order to defend social order. For, as leaders like George Angell warned, cruelty and criminal behavior were connected not just logically but also empirically. In a speech before the 1876 meeting of the American Social Science Association entitled "Prevention of Crime by Moral and Educational Instrumentalities," Angell reported that a study of two thousand prisoners in the United States revealed that only twelve had grown up with pets.[112] Here Angell implied that if, as antebellum moralists and postbellum humane educators argued, the care of pets could serve as a child's moral foundation, the converse was also true—the failure to de-

velop tenderhearted relations with animals would blunt the moral sense
and lead to crime. Others in the anticruelty movement echoed these sentiments. Speaking on "Humane Education" at the fourteenth annual meeting of the AHA in 1890, Mrs. Mary L. Schaffter reminded her audience
that "crime is on the increase, blotting this fair land of ours." Rather than
search for the best method of rehabilitating criminals, Schaffter suggested
that Americans would do better to search for means of *preventing* crime.
According to Schaffter, humane education was the answer, for it would
"nourish the moral and mental powers of a man" by rooting out the causes
of crime, "revenge, covetousness, anger and all the deviltry" that lay
buried in man's heart. But inculcating principles of sympathy, kindness,
and humanity in each child and adult would "have our prisons empty,"
Schaffter predicted.[113] Suggesting that the prevention and prosecution of
cruelty would eliminate crime from the social fabric, Schaffter and Angell sounded much like the state jurists who interpreted cruelty's harm
as against the public health and welfare, not as a violation of the rights of
animals.

In taking up the banner of animal and child protection, the WCTU
also stressed the close relation of cruelty to crime, even claiming that
"it was the study of criminal conditions that gave birth to the humane
idea."[114] In a speech before the International Council of Women, superintendent of Mercy Mary Lovell identified cruelty as a "necessary constituent" of the "worst vices." She contended that "it is a well-established fact
that some of the worst criminals began their evil careers by cruelty to
animals in youth," and gave the example of a Philadelphia man, arrested
for murdering his wife, who had been charged a few years prior for "revolt-
ing cruelty to a poor little mare."[115] She claimed further that the success of
her Department of Mercy would be measured by the "decrease in crime"
in the nation, and advocated humane education as the means toward that
end, proudly citing the opinion of the general superintendent of the Detective Association of America that "'in searching for the cases of crime, we
find that the lack of humane education is the principle one.'" At Lovell's
urging, the twenty-ninth annual convention of the WCTU adopted a reso-
lution recognizing the link between cruelty and crime on the one hand,
and the salve of humane education on the other. "Whereas, Almost all
crime contains the element of cruelty," it read, "and whereas the systematic teaching of the law of kindness to every living creature has proved to
be a sure preventative of crime, therefore, Resolved, that we recognize the
fundamental need of such teaching."[116] Like the jurists who interpreted
animal protection laws in terms of public morals, anticruelty reformers

who argued for the connection between cruelty and crime also understood cruelty's harm as social disorder rather than individual suffering.

Though antivice and moral reformers declared themselves most interested in individual self-control and social order, anticruelty organizations claimed to be concerned, first and foremost, with ending the suffering of animals and children. Yet when they identified cruelty as a species of vice akin to greed and debauchery, and when they warned that cruelty led to crime, they shifted the locus of the problem to order rather than suffering. The ambiguity of "cruelty" as it applied to animals—the uncertainty over whether its chief harm lay in the suffering it caused its victims, in the evil heart of its perpetrator, or in the ways it could perturb social order and public morals—was compounded when protectionists turned their attention to children. For though anticruelty reformers explained the link between animal and child protection in part through their slippery-slope theory of violence, in reality "cruelty" as applied to children was an even more diffuse term. To begin with, the legal changes wrought by anticruelty reform were somewhat more complex for children than for animals. Generally speaking, it was not necessary for humane organizations to secure specific legislation to combat the physical abuse of children. Such had been, historically, and continued to be prosecuted under general assault and battery laws. But by the second half of the nineteenth century, courts, particularly in the North, were challenging the presumptive right of fathers to their children's earnings, labor, and person. In cases arising from divorce, adoption, and indenture disputes, for example, judges began to substitute the standard of the "best interests of the child" for that of father-right. Unlike the legal history of animal protection, for children the problem was largely one of enforcement. Toward the end of the nineteenth century, however, some humane societies instigated a successful movement to make cruelty and neglect of children into specific statutory crimes.[117]

So long as cruelty and neglect were narrowly construed, anticruelty activists could largely rely on common law and changing judicial regard for children's interests to help them combat these social vices; but they quickly began to define cruelty and neglect in more expansive terms that required they seek specific legal remedies. As humane society leaders and agents saw the matter, their mission was not only to protect the bodies of children, but also to protect their moral development. Humane societies were thus as concerned with the moral as they were with the physical environment of children's rearing. According to the prevailing wisdom in Gilded Age charity circles, poverty and vice were a problem of mind rather than matter. Reformers were fearful that the children of the "laboring classes"—with whom they largely dealt—would, through no fault of their own, absorb the bad habits of their parents or their vice-ridden neighborhoods. Reared in vice, the children would become vicious. Hence humane societies sometimes sought, in the words of Elbridge Gerry, to remove children "from local scenes of crime and misery and plac[e] them in a purer atmosphere." SPCCs and humane societies were not alone in believing that sometimes children were best separated from their parents or guardians. Under the direction of Charles Loring Brace, the New York–based Children's Aid Society sent thousands of poor children packing west to be placed with "good" families away from the iniquity of urban America.[118]

Humane societies joined these efforts. Within a quarter of a century after the founding of the first SPCC, anticruelty reformers lobbied for and enforced legislation prohibiting the employment of children in entertainment, in street trades, and, in some states, manufacturing. They sought to keep children out of saloons, dance halls, and houses of "ill fame"; they kept children from buying tobacco and alcohol, and otherwise attended to their morals. They investigated complaints of bastardy, of truancy, of disorderly youth. "In the new laws" enacted and enforced by anticruelty organizations, explained Illinois Humane Society attorney George Scott, "children were protected from evil by removing them from contact with the immoral and the vicious. . . . What was considered to be prejudicial to the interests of the child was deemed contrary to the policy of the state to permit." Those activities they saw as likely to corrupt the morals of children, humane societies defined as "cruel." Thanks to this work, wrote the superintendent of the Wisconsin Humane Society, "it has been established that inoffending young children shall not be raised for unquestionably vicious ends."[119]

Anticruelty reformers defined the moral endangerment of children as "cruel" in no small part because they relied on a developmental view of childhood in determining how both children and the broader public might be harmed by such ill treatment. Child protectionists believed that early experiences and associations formed a child's character and habits in ways that would shape him or her for life. If domestic ideals held that children were innately innocent, the flip side was that they were malleable, a trait that made them easily susceptible to evil influences. But because children were powerless to control the circumstances in which they were raised, the adults around them were responsible for ensuring that they grew up in an environment conducive to good morals and habits. Indeed, child protectionists spent much of their time on a range of problems that can best be described as efforts to control the circumstances and the manner in which children were raised. Children, reformers worried, could succumb to moral ruination through no fault of their own—they could, in other words, have their life chances endangered by their parents and other guardians in relation to whom they were dependent and helpless. Child protectionists believed that this unfortunate fate—the moral ruination of an otherwise innocent child—was a form of cruelty. In Baltimore, humanitarians went so far as to call their organization the Society for the Protection of Children from Cruelty and Immorality.[120]

The kind of physical abuse that Mary Ellen Wilson suffered was, as we have seen, characteristic of a minority of cases of cruelty to children investigated by humane societies and SPCCs. Instead, anticruelty reformers concentrated much time and energy on segregating children from environments they believed would lead them astray for a variety of reasons. Because reformers shared the view that the ideal environment for a child was a two-parent household supported by the labor and wages of the father, they often pursued cases of nonsupport or desertion.[121] Children who were not financially supported by their fathers were likely to grow up in poverty, have working mothers, and be unsupervised—all circumstances that might cause children to begin traveling down a wayward path.

Writing in the August 1881 edition of the Illinois Humane Society's *Humane Journal*, author O. C. Gibbs explained this logic in his essay "Neglected Childhood." According to Gibbs, children who were "victims of cruelty and neglect" were likely to end up as members of the "criminal and dangerous classes" upon reaching adulthood. As Gibbs explained, "the child left to follow its own inclinations, and especially if living in the midst of surroundings and influences that are demoralizing and degrading, gravitates as naturally to evil courses as water runs down hill." Among the "demoralizing and degrading" influences that a child might be subject to, Gibbs included growing up with parents who failed to support their offspring. These parents, "vicious and dissolute," failed in their duties and taught their children bad habits by forcing them to "beg and steal." In spite of his dire prediction about how readily the children of such parents would swell the ranks of paupers and criminals, Gibbs was confident that poor children could be saved by simply removing them from their parents and placing them in adoptive homes. The "natural family home" was the best place for children, and the task of child-savers was to ensure that every child was reared in one.[122] Gibbs's diagnosis of the problems facing child protectionists was typical—he linked cruelty and neglect as species of the same, larger social malady: the failure to provide a proper home, to properly respect the nature of childhood and the purpose of the family. His sense of how children were formed, too, was typical: he believed that children were good unless made bad by their parents, and that the ruin of children's character was a kind of cruelty because it violated children's dependence and helplessness as much as did physical abuse.

The conflation of cruelty with neglect and abandonment of middle-class family norms helps to explain why humane societies so frequently investigated cases in which husbands failed to support their wives and children. In many such cases, husbands were physically present but were "habitual drunkards" who refused to work or who spent their wages on themselves rather than on their families. In one such case from 1895, Mrs. Digby sent a postcard to the IHS asking an agent to come visit her at home. "I have a sick baby and three other children, my husband won't work and drinks all the money he can get," she explained. Agent Little called on Mrs. Digby, who told him that Mr. Digby "has been drinking for the last several months & has done nothing for the support of his family but comes home nights & abuses her & the children." Mrs. Digby explained that in the recent past her husband had been in the "Washingtonian Home" for one week "& for a long time afterwards was all right." The Washingtonian Society was a temperance organization run by and directed toward working-class men. Mrs. Digby wanted Little to help her force her husband to go to the organization's home again to sober up. Little arranged to meet Mrs. Digby at the police station the following day so that she could take out a warrant for the arrest of her husband. When officers from the IHS went to serve Digby his warrant, however, they found him sober and promising "to go to work & care for his family." At Mrs. Digby's request, "the warrant was not served as she wants to give him another trial."[123] Though the Digby case involved allegations both of abuse and nonsupport, officers of the IHS seemed to agree with Mrs. Digby that the source of the family's problems lay in intemperance and that the chief manifestation of this was Mr. Digby's refusal to work in order to properly support his family. The abuse, which only Agent Little mentioned as a problem, was secondary to the more fundamental problem of a disordered home and family structure.

From the late nineteenth to the early twentieth century, SPCCs and humane societies were instrumental in strengthening and enforcing laws against desertion and nonsupport. In part, anticruelty organizations' efforts to have fathers support their families were in keeping with the tenor of the late-nineteenth-century charity movement, which grew increasingly suspicious of indiscriminate philanthropy and increasingly interested in forcing "able-bodied" men to support themselves. Internally, charities instituted "scientific" new methods to distinguish between the deserving and the undeserving poor. Among the deserving were those who were helpless to prevent their own poverty—widows and children, for example. The undeserving were those who were physically able to work but "chose" not to. But in the midst of intermittent panics and depressions from the end of the Civil War to the turn of the century, even the best efforts of charities to rigorously prevent pauperism and dependence among the poor could not stem the tide of poverty. Often at the behest of charity officials, states across the nation passed harsh laws against beggary and vagrancy, essentially making it a crime for a man to refuse work.[124] By forcing fathers to support their families, anticruelty organizations fell in line with the more general trend to narrow the relief roles to the truly "deserving," for whom no other possible sources of support were available. Though anticruelty organizations' casework thus dovetailed with the assumptions and aims of the practitioners of "scientific charity," they also departed from them in considering such nonsupport a form of cruelty to children. The problem, in their minds, was not simply that relief pauperized its adult recipients, but rather that the family disorder that necessitated relief was likely to ruin a child's life in ways beyond his or her control.

Besides attempting to resurrect proper family structures and relationships through reform of the private home, protectionists also understood the campaign against cruelty to encompass the segregation of children from immoral public spaces. In essence they sought to more strictly delineate the boundaries of childhood by carving up urban space into separate zones for adults and children. Keeping children out of saloons, pool halls, dance halls, and houses of "ill repute" were some of the ways that reformers sought to accomplish this. Officers of the Minneapolis Humane Society, for example, scoured the city's dance halls seeking to enforce the provisions of the state law that forbade minors under the age of twenty-one from entering. Prosecutions were often successful, and in one case, repeated violations of the law led a dance hall proprietor to shutter his doors.[125] Reformers promoted the middle-class notion that childhood was, by nature, a time of innocence, and they sought to physically impose this vision through the regulation of children's movement. Bounding the space of the city, protectionists hoped, would create an environment conducive to the growth of good character and increased life chances.

In seeking to more strictly separate children and adults through spatial and other forms of regulation, anticruelty activists joined a host of other late-nineteenth- and early-twentieth-century reformers who sought to stanch what they saw as a tide of immoral influences likely to envelop children and cause their downfall. Anthony Comstock and his Society for the Suppression of Vice's efforts to regulate the distribution of obscene literature are among the most well-known examples. But the SSV worked in a crowded field. Alongside its temperance and anticruelty activities, the WCTU, for example, ran an extremely active Department for the Suppression of Impure Literature (later called the Department for Purity in Art and Literature). Under its aegis, the WCTU sought to restrict the sale of sensational publications such as the *Police Gazette* and, later, to regulate children's access to moving pictures and other forms of media. Historian Allison Parker has shown that the WCTU, acting in the name of protecting vulnerable children, was joined in its censorship efforts not only by the SSV, but also by a host of other prominent national organizations including the YMCA, the American Library Association, the League of American Mothers, the National Congress of Mothers, the General Federation of Women's Clubs, the Watch and Ward Society, and the National Association of Colored Women.[126]

Even reformers who might not have supported censorship (though this was the mainstream middle-class position for most of the nineteenth and twentieth centuries) agreed that the promiscuous mixing of adult and child space was likely to negatively impact the latter. When Jacob Riis, for example, collected many of his reports on New York City together into his book *Children of the Poor*, he identified poverty's problems in part by showing how tenement-dwelling children could easily cross into adult—and immoral—realms. "The tenement and the saloon, with the street that does not always divide them, form the environment that is to make or unmake the child," Riis warned his readers. He urged fellow Americans to try to insulate children from "evil" influences—not simply the street and the saloon, but also "trashy novels and cheap shows," cigarettes, and gambling. And though Riis regarded the tenements and their mostly immigrant inhabitants as a danger, he also regarded the problem as environmental and viewed child-saving as a matter of remaking the city into a place with safe, morally conducive spaces for children. It was the job of reformers and government officials to clearly separate adult from child spaces by providing playgrounds and other wholesome, child-specific places in the city.[127] According to all these reformers, from the SPCCs to the WCTU and muckrakers like Riis, exposing children to immoral influences was a social problem both because it injured the child him or herself, and also because the child's ruination negatively impacted the social body as a whole. When SPCCs and humane societies called this moral ruination "cruelty," they simply gave a particular name to the more widely accepted notion that harming a child's character was as pernicious as harming his or her body.

Perhaps the best example of this interpretation of cruelty as moral endangerment rather than physical abuse is the campaign to prohibit child performers working in a variety of entertainment venues. Although children's performances might not seem akin to the other acts that more squarely fit under the rubric of cruelty, such as the flogging or starvation of children, the plight of child performers was part of the public's understanding of cruelty from the beginning. Indeed, the concern for child acrobats performing in Massachusetts was among the first cases of cruelty to children called to the attention of an existing SPCA. But it was not until the formation of the New York SPCC that any anticruelty organization officially made children's performances central to its definition of cruelty. In 1876, Elbridge Gerry was instrumental in persuading the New York state legislature to make it illegal for any adult to exhibit a child "singing, playing on musical instruments, rope or wire dancing, begging or peddling, or as a gymnast, contortionist, rider or acrobat." Simple stage acting was not banned, but could be prosecuted if proven injurious in a particular case. Though the details of the law varied from state to state, by and large other SPCCs and humane societies also tried to restrict the work of child performers. Gerry and other child protectionists insisted that they were but a less obvious form of the same evil. In the work of child performers, physical harm and moral degradation went hand in hand. First, Gerry claimed, such performances were "physically injurious to children" because they overworked the children, depriving them of natural rest and making them more susceptible to disease. Second, time spent on stage was time stolen from education, thus denying young thespians "the best capital in this country to inspire success in life." Finally, Gerry warned that theatrical life was immoral and degraded its young participants before they knew better. "The associations are bad for children," he claimed, because they are always around "persons about whose morality or virtue the less said the better." A childhood in the theater was a sure path to an adulthood filled with debauchery and sin, particularly for its vulnerable female participants. Defending his organization's crackdown on theaters, Gerry invoked "the recorded instances of female ruin and criminal acts, originating in the miscellaneous companies and evil associations connected with these performances."[128]

Gerry's dire predictions seemed to be confirmed by the experiences of the Wisconsin Humane Society, which also tried to regulate child per-

formances. In its *First Biennial Report* from 1881, the WHS reported rescuing "an unusually bright and intelligent" girl from "one of the lowest
dens of infamy and crime." In this bawdy house, "her sweet childish voice
had been trained to sing lewd and vicious songs" and to tell "foul" stories. Shockingly, the girl "was in fact, the star attraction of a house fre-
quented by the lowest characters." This ruin of body, mind, and morals
was, furthermore, motivated "by the avarice and cupidity of their parents,"
who assume that the child is their property and thus can "be starved, ill
treated, or forced to do whatever the parent may see fit to compel."[129] Like
the man who overloaded his horse to earn a little more money, parents'
greed was objectionable because it took an instrumental view of a living
being, bringing about its ruination for little more than "self-gratification."
Far from contributing a necessary wage to a poor family, children's theatrical labor should, protectionists insisted, be framed solely in terms of the
wrongs of parental greed and the threat of the child's impending slide into
the world of vice, the very seat of cruelty itself.

Rather than being an idiosyncratic reaction to child performers—or
one that simply expressed an outdated, Victorian suspicion of the theater—
anticruelty reformers' objections were shared by other child-savers, including those who would come to be called "progressives." In the early
twentieth century, the Chicago-based Juvenile Protective Association and
the National Child Labor Committee also railed against the use of child
actors in terms similar to those laid out by Gerry. A. J. McKelway, the
chief organizer for the NCLC in the Southern states, who explained in
1912 that his organization opposed child performers because "the vast majority of children who entered upon a stage career . . . have become so
much human waste." The toleration of child actors was, he concluded, tantamount to the "sacrifice of childhood." Likewise, another spokesman for
the NCLC explained that theatrical performances were bad for children
because they were physically exacting, exploitative, and involved children
in "moral hazard." Formed in 1907 to prevent juvenile delinquency, the
Juvenile Protective Association was founded and run by many of Chicago's leading progressives, including many of the women instrumental in
running Hull House. Like humane societies and the NCLC, the JPA also
considered child performers as victims of adult greed, exploitation, and
as subject to demoralization. The head of the JPA's Juvenile Occupations
Department, F. Zeta Youmans, led the organization's charge against child
actors. According to Youmans, time on stage was "detrimental to both
[the] health and morals" of children and was largely the product of parents'
and theatrical companies' desire to earn money from the public's natural

desire to see children perform.[130] Like the anticruelty reformers who came before them, progressives in the JPA and NCLC regarded childhood as a time of innocence and feared that exposure to the stage—with its exhausting work requirements and dubious moral connections—endangered this innocence for little more than adult greed.

Though little might seem to connect the plight of the overworked horse and the child performer, anticruelty reformers believed that such problems existed on a continuum. In the slippery-slope theory of violence they promoted, abuse of animals would lead to the abuse of children. For what would stop a man who would vent his passions on one species of dependent from unleashing them on another? And since reformers believed that cruelty was a form of intemperate indulgence, they believed that cruelty lay at the root of many crimes and social problems. The man who was cruel thus harmed not only his victim, but also himself by losing his self-control, and he harmed the social fabric by disturbing the peace, degrading public morals, and ruining the character of his victims. The same chain of violence that connected animals and children also connected their suffering to social disorder.

Reformers connected cruelty to animals and children not just negatively, but also positively. If violence against animals and children stemmed from the same, evil source in man, the elimination of cruelty against both was also part and parcel of the same forward historical movement. As protectionists and their contemporaries saw it, civilization and suffering were opposed; the amelioration of pain and the elimination of violence were inexorably linked to progress. This view led anticruelty reformers not only to villainize the cruelist and cast him among the savage and barbarian, but also led to the view that the elimination of cruelty was central to the realization of the American liberal project. Complaining about a bullfight that took place on July 4, 1884, in Kansas, Henry Bergh declared not only that it was an "assassination of civilization" but also that it was an act of "national hate" that betrayed the "civilizing policy and patriotism taught by the noble founders of the Republic."[131] Like Benjamin Rush, who had declared some one hundred years earlier that republican institutions would require republican manners, Bergh too assumed that democratic principles would find their instantiation not simply in laws and legislatures, but also in everyday acts. For anticruelty reformers, their project was not simply civilizational or Christian, but it was also liberal—for, as they believed, to end cruelty was also to establish rights.

## CHAPTER THREE

# "The Rights of Whatever Can Suffer": Reconciling Liberalism and Dependence

B oth sentimental discourses of domesticity and the slippery slope theory of violence created important cultural connections that underlie the institutional link between animal and child protection. But as the rhetoric surrounding the rescue of Mary Ellen Wilson suggests, anticruelty reformers relied on liberal as well as sentimental tropes. To men like Henry Bergh and Elbridge Gerry, Mary Ellen's story was not simply a tale of suffering that demanded sympathy, but her plight—and their reaction to it—also seemed to demonstrate the unfolding of natural rights in historical time. As Henry Bergh insisted at the first meeting of the New York SPCC in 1875, "there is a providence in the affairs of men." In Bergh's mind, providence dictated progress, for "the slaves were first freed from bondage; next came the emancipation of the brute creation, and next the emancipation of the little children was about to take place."[1] Linking Mary Ellen's rescue to the cause of the Civil War, Bergh implied that just as the end of slavery had secured rights for former slaves, so too the advent of animal, and now child, protection was ensuring rights for other former dependents.

But what did it mean to say that animals and children had rights just as former slaves did? Though he equated the former status and present progress of slaves, animals, and children, Bergh elided important differences between them. For even as he declared himself an agent of animals' and children's "emancipation," Bergh did not mean to alter their status as dependents. What Bergh and Gerry wanted for Mary Ellen was her liberation from a particularly bad and unnatural household, but they did not seek an end to parent-child relations and they did not critique the household as a fundamentally inegalitarian and flawed institution. To the contrary, they celebrated Mary Ellen's subsequent assimilation into a properly functioning household, implying that "emancipation" could take place within the family circle and that rights might be consistent with certain kinds of status inequality. Late-nineteenth- and early-twentieth-century child welfare reformers equated children's rights with protection rather than with liberation, developing what one scholar has called a "paternalistic strain of rights talk" designed to prolong childhood and increase children's dependence on adults.[2]

Unlike the radical dismantling of the system of slavery that characterized abolitionist versions of "emancipation," Bergh and others in the postbellum anticruelty movement sought to reconcile a liberal language of rights with the persistent hierarchies, and forms of dependence, that characterized human-animal and household relations. Indeed, far from destroying the dependence of animals and children, anticruelty activists sought to protect it. The problem with Mary Ellen's guardians was not, in other words, that they kept her in a state of dependence, but rather that they exploited her natural dependence. In so doing, Bergh and Gerry believed, they violated her rights. Insisting that children had rights in dependence, Bergh and Gerry employed a logic they had developed in the cause of animal protection.

The rhetoric of children's rights and the practices of child protection that developed in the wake of Mary Ellen's rescue owed much to a sentimental rights discourse developed by American SPCAs. From the beginning of his crusade, Bergh enveloped animal protection in liberal symbols and language. In 1865, when he returned home to New York City from his post as diplomat in Russia, Bergh delivered a lecture at New York's Clinton Hall entitled "Statistics Relating to the Cruelties Practiced upon Animals." He drew his audience's attention to the daily suffering of the city's draught horses, its butchered animals, and its harassed dogs and cats. Having aroused the sympathies of his listeners with a plea to exercise Godlike mercy and abolish these practices, he asked them to stand and sign a document he had penned, the "Declaration of the Rights of Animals." Many of those present obliged, including the ex-governor and mayor, John Hoffman, the Harper brothers of publishing fame, John Jacob Astor, and two of the Roosevelts. Carrying such eminent names with him, Bergh took his appeal to Albany and secured a charter for an organization that would enforce the tenets of his declaration. In issuing a declaration of rights, Bergh obviously sought to associate his cause with cherished liberal values and with a stream of similar documents—from the Declaration of Independence to the Declaration of Sentiments in 1848—that seemed to propel history forward. And like these other manifestos, Bergh's Declaration of

Rights was framed in terms of grievances, rights enumerated by detailed attention to wrongs. But there was also a crucial difference. Unlike the colonial petitioners against the depredations of King George III or the women's rights advocates who gathered at Seneca Falls, the animals to whose rights this declaration referred did not act on their own behalf. The act of claiming rights for animals neither evinced, nor did it depend, on animals' own capacity for independent thought, speech, or action.

In February of 1869, an article in *Our Dumb Animals* exemplified the same conundrum. Written by Harriet Beecher Stowe and entitled "Rights of Dumb Animals," the text, like Bergh's speech, explored animals' rights largely by enumerating human wrongs. Stowe not only lambasted the hunting of wild animals as a "savage" practice but also lamented that humans had such a "very imperfect sense of right and wrong" in regard to domestic animals. Old horses, cats, and dogs, for instance, were routinely sold off or abandoned when they became even slightly inconvenient to their owners. Fortunately, she reported, societies for the prevention of cruelty to animals were being formed across the country. For "if there be any oppressed class that ought to have a convention and pass resolutions asserting their share in the general forward movement going on in this world," then surely it must be the animals, "that hapless class" that "can neither speak, read, nor write."[3] Stowe, like Bergh, imagined that animals' rights would be recognized through traditional political means—in this case, conventions and resolutions instead of declarations—and she too imagined that this would form part of the natural unfolding of historical progress ("the general forward movement"). But at the same time as Stowe suggested that animals should engage in such acts of self-representation, she also dubbed them "hapless" because they could not represent themselves. They were mute, or *dumb*, as suggested by the title of the magazine in which Stowe's essay appeared. In this sense, they were not only hapless, but helpless. But Stowe, like Bergh, did not suggest that these incapacities negated animals' rights; rather, they both agreed that animals' rights would depend on the existence of intermediaries.

In drawing on the rights-infused language of American liberalism, Bergh and Stowe were typical of the animal protection movement that swept across the urban centers of the Northeast in the years following the Civil War. Frequently, the reformers of the newly founded SPCAs voiced their concerns in the language and logic of the dominant American political, ideological, and religious traditions. At the same time, Stowe's focus on the suffering of animals was also typical. For in addition to animals' rights, reformers focused on animals' feelings. The men and women of the SPCAs imported the techniques of the sentimental appeal that Stowe herself had perfected some years earlier in *Uncle Tom's Cabin*, encouraging humans to recognize animal suffering and experience it as their own. Freely mixing the language of traditional liberalism with that of sentimentalism, animal welfare reformers groped toward a newer, more expansive vision of the rights-bearing community that would include, as had Stowe, the helpless and dependent. Combining the language of rights with that of feeling, suffering, and dependence, reformers hoped that their hybrid discourse would one day lead to a world in which all might "respect the right of harmless things to life, liberty and the pursuit of happiness."[4]

For animal protectionists, framing their claims in rights language was not only a strategic choice to deploy a dominant idiom, but also a way of intervening in the postbellum debate about the grounding and the content of rights. By abolishing slavery, the Civil War lent a renewed vigor to the language of rights and reopened questions about the entailments of many of the keywords in the American political lexicon: "freedom," "rights," "independence," and "citizenship." In the wake of emancipation, it was by no means clear what "freedom" would mean, nor what "rights" might consist of, for former slaves. Nor was it clear that freedpeople, congressional Republicans, and former Confederates would be able to agree on the shape of things to come. Moreover, the end of slavery impacted both practical politics and political language not just for freedpeople and the South, but also for the nation as a whole. Because the Fourteenth Amendment incorporated the Bill of Rights to the states, all Americans experienced a profound transformation in the nature of citizenship and the role and reach of the federal government. Because the war disrupted one of the most obvious forms of dependency in the country's history, it called into question other relations of inequality and dependency: between husbands and wives, employers and employees, parents and children.[5]

Many animal welfare reformers claimed that the lesson of the war was clear and simple: the Civil War had awakened the nation's conscience to the "rights of the defenseless." By this logic, protecting the "lower races" of animals was simply the logical outcome of the battles that had so recently torn the country in two.[6] Linking the status of animals with the cause of the Civil War was grandiose, but not illogical. Postbellum liberals widely shared the belief that the Civil War had turned the world-historical tide in favor of progress, freedom, and democracy. Moroever, even those who opposed both Bergh and his ilk drew connections between the fate of freed slaves and animals. Just after Bergh founded the ASPCA, New York's

*Sunday Mercury* sarcastically accused him of trying to replace natural instincts with millennial dreams. "Nature, that permits the hawk to pluck alive the gentle sparrow, and inspires pussy with a taste for harmless mice," the paper jeered, "will be rectified as soon as the new millennium is realized, and Negro-suffrage and the rights of pigs and poultry to life, liberty, and the pursuit of happiness, is established."[7] For the *Mercury*, granting citizenship rights to African Americans was of a piece with animal protection; both were an assault on natural hierarchy. By contrast, when Bergh argued that the war established a precedent for protecting the "rights of the defenseless," he did not mean that slaves and animals occupied the same rung on nature's ladder. Rather, Bergh and other animal protectionists believed that their mutual defenselessness described a social rather than a natural status; further, they believed that if defenselessness—the condition of slaves—were no longer a barrier to the recognition of natural rights, then rights could also flow to another defenseless class: animals.

But it was not as easy as Bergh and his fellow workers imagined to incorporate the defenseless into liberal categories. For one thing, defenselessness implied *dependence*, and the status of dependents in both republican and liberal political theory, and in the history of democratic politics, has been problematic. As an ideological term, the designation of "dependence" has worked to mark the boundaries of citizenship, individual rights, and claims on the state under both feudal and liberal, premodern and modern, political regimes. Though the population of those deemed dependent has changed over time, the notion that the dependent lack the basic capacities required for claiming rights has remained remarkably stable. In the United States, even as the specific meanings of freedom and *in*dependence changed in the years between the Revolution and the end of Reconstruction, the equation of citizenship with independence did not. Even after the Civil War, the metaphor of slavery—the core of which described a dependent relationship of subordination—continued to serve as freedom's rhetorical opposite.

For centuries in Europe and the British American colonies, legal and political status were defined by one's position in the patriarchial household. While the male head of the household was independent, the members of his household—including his wife, children, servants, and, later, slaves, were dependent. In the preindustrial and premodern household, dependence was at once an economic, a sociolegal, and a political condition. Dependents were not only economically bound to the patriarch, but also they had no separate legal identity and no direct relationship with the state.

Most dependents existed in a state of partial or complete coverture, their legal and political identity literally subsumed by that of another. To the extent that dependents, whether wives, children, servants, or slaves, could demand legal attention or redress, it was not as rights-bearing individuals but in and through the head of the household. Dependents were not without legal protections, but these protections did not take the form of rights. Instead, protections, or obligations on the part of the patriarch, flowed to dependents by virtue of their status—their membership in a household and in a community, the orderly maintenance of which were important legal goals. And though dependents were disadvantaged by these rules, dependence was not considered deviant. Indeed, in the early modern West, household and political hierarchy were not only normal but normative. Patriarchy was practical policy and political theory. In patriarchalist political thought, authority in the family mirrored that of the state, and the family served as a metaphor for the monarchical state. Just as a king ruled his country, so too a father ruled his wife, children, and servants.[8]

To the extent that the emergence of republican and liberal political theory was a repudiation of patriarchalist political theory, it made the state of individual dependence politically problematic without necessarily eliminating the social, economic, or legal conditions of dependence. Long important to liberal theorists like John Locke, individual independence became an important criterion for citizenship following the American Revolution. At the beginning of the new republic, unpropertied white men were largely excluded from voting on the grounds that, as John Adams put the matter, those "destitute of property. . . . are too dependent upon other men to have a will of their own." Adams, like many others in the Revolutionary generation, had imbibed republican ideals, including the notion that dependent men might not have sufficient freedom of mind and will to act with disinterested virtue on behalf of the common good. Thomas Jefferson's fantasy that the new nation might be composed of yeomen farmers was guided by the same logic; he hoped for a maximal number of independent, property-owning men to sustain the republican experiment. In addition, transforming the colonies from part of a monarchy into a republic changed the valence of dependence. As subjects, all colonials had been dependents of one sort or another. In a republic, however, the citizen rather than the subject was idealized as the norm. The dependent became not only theoretically troublesome and potentially corrupting, but also deviant. Besides worrying that poor men could not be trusted to form independent opinions, Adams worried about creating a slippery slope, for propertyless men were "to all intents and purposes as much dependent on others who will please to feed, clothe, and employ them, as women are upon their husbands, or children upon their parents." In keeping with patriarchalism, Adams located dependence in the household and defined all those who were subordinate to the head as beyond the ken of political participation and representation. Most legislators in the new United States agreed with Adams, and restricted the suffrage through property and tax requirements.[9] Alongside a regime of individual rights for "independent" men, American legal and political institutions maintained a "feudal" regime based on a hierarchical model of the household.

Though in the half century after the Revolution, citizenship rights did expand to encompass poor, propertyless men, the ideological equation of independence with citizenship remained in place. But the substance of "independence" changed as the market revolution transformed more and more Northern men into wage laborers with no prospect of ever owning their own shop, farm, or house. The tension between wage labor and democratic citizenship was not lost on the nation's new wage workers. Many working-class men relied on the equation of freedom with independence to protest the wage system. Rather than providing a means to future economic independence, as the artisanal apprentice and journeyman system did formerly, the wage system appeared to offer nothing but a life of permanent dependence upon the will, and the money, of other men. Tellingly, Northern wage workers protested by calling themselves "slaves," suggesting that they had, forcefully and without consent, been abjectified. In the context of sectional tension generated by the antebellum expansion of slavery into new territories, it was the *opponents* of slavery and its spread who helped to defang the critique of wage labor as a form of dependency. Southern apologists for slavery never tired of reminding their Northern neighbors that chattel slavery, if paternalistic and hierarchical, was at least benevolent. In defense of Northern society, antislavery activists argued that "free" labor was not only more efficient and productive, but also was more moral. Henry Clay expressed such views in a speech before the Kentucky Colonization Society. While "as a mere laborer, the slave feels that he toils for his master and not himself," the free laborer "knows that he will derive the profits of his industry" in the form of wages, and that "if he is treated badly, he can exchange his employer" for another. "In a word," Clay went on, "he feels that he is a free agent, with rights, and privileges, and sensibilities." In asserting that slavery was an immoral usurpation of natural liberty, abolitionists and free-labor advocates argued that every man had property in his body. Property was not external to the self, but originated with the body in labor. Working for wages was thus not a form of slavery, but an equal exchange of property: labor for money. Slavery, based on theft rather than consensual exchange, was perforce a violation of liberty. Thus even as white male suffrage and wage labor expanded, the importance of independence to citizenship was not undermined; instead, in free-labor thought independence was redefined as self-ownership.[10]

But like the transition from subjecthood to citizenship after the Revolution, the inclusion of the mass of wage-earning white men inside the categories of "independent" and "citizen" also changed dependency's valence. As men in dozens of Jacksonian-era state constitutional conventions met to rewrite their state's rules on fundamental issues from suffrage access to property rights, they considered whether free blacks and women should be granted these basic civil and political rights. The answer, of course, was a resounding no. This exclusion was justified owing to the dependence—often coded as "degradation," natural servitude, or inherent domesticity—of blacks and women. Delegates to Wisconsin's constitutional convention in the late 1840s, for example, worried that some slave owner might decamp in their new state and free his slaves; though nominally free men, the former slaves would still undoubtedly feel tied to their former master and, as one delegate put it, "having long been accustomed to his command, he might control their votes, and carry an election by it." A half century after the Revolution, this Wisconsin delegate still explained political exclusion in terms that would have made sense to John Adams: it was not race or class or gender per se, but dependence that defined the boundaries of the polity. Though the definition of "independence," and with it citizenship rights, expanded in the years before the Civil War, dependence, now explicitly racialized and feminized, remained an important grounds for exclusion.[11]

By linking self-ownership to the doctrine of contract, abolitionists, apologists for capitalism, and even some workingmen's advocates reconciled the spread of waged labor with the longstanding assumption that in a democratic republic, rights and citizenship rested on individual economic independence. And because the northern victory in the Civil War enshrined free-labor ideology as the national creed, the substance of postbellum politics was refracted through a particular political language. From the end of the war until the end of the century, claims about freedom, rights, and citizenship would be framed in terms provided by the metaphor that stood at the heart of free labor: contract. In the postbellum years, this rather narrow definition of "independence" influenced the course of Reconstruction policy, charity reform, the women's rights movement, and labor activism. In the wake of slavery's end, Republicans were sure that the route to former slaves' freedom—and to Southern economic rehabilitation—lay in labor rather than government handouts. As a Tennessee Freedman's Bureau official opined, "a man can scarcely be called free who is the recipient of public charity." After the war, as before, citizenship and freedom were identified with independence as defined by free labor ideology. Though freedmen and women had an expansive vision of freedom that encompassed, but went beyond, traditional civil and political rights and included support for a strong state, this vision was largely ignored. Instead of land and an opportunity to experience the independence of Jeffersonian yeomen, freedmen and women got the 1866 Civil Rights legislation, which guaranteed that their rights of contract would not be abridged. And by the 1870s, even the Republican Party was backing away from its support for federal intervention in the South. Republicans, claiming that blacks wanted too much from the state, voiced a fear of black dependence. Having defined freedom as contract and waged labor, officials of the federal Freedman's Bureau reviewed and enforced labor contracts and did little to stop the rise of the Southern Black Codes that criminalized nonlabor as vagrancy and beggary. For if poverty was a form of dependence, then any measures designed to ensure economic independence through labor pointed down the path to freedom. Similar thinking shaped the approach of postbellum charity refomers in the North. Like Freedman's Bureau officials, charity reformers were, as Amy Dru Stanley points out, "heir to an intellectual tradition that dissociated relations of personal dependence from transactions based on free contract." Seeing almsgiving as a paternalistic relic of the feudal order that the war had made obsolete, northern charity reformers too criminalized the dependence of ablebodied men through statutes against vagrancy and beggary. Violators could be punished by fines, imprisonment, or compulsory labor. Where poverty and alms made men dependent, compulsory labor made them free.[12]

Postbellum women's rights advocates likewise identified independence with self-ownership and dependence with unfreedom. From the point of view of this largely middle-class cohort, the problem was not so much waged work as it was the forced dependence created by the laws of coverture. Unlike wage labor, which theoretically had been removed from the hierarchical sphere of the household, marriage was still legally understood to create a relationship of dominance and subordination. Indeed, it was the act of subordination that brought the household as such into being. Even when female activists began to argue for women's rights to property and political participation, they argued essentially for women's right to own themselves, enforcing the equation of freedom with independence and self-ownership.[13]

But in the midst of postbellum industrialization and of periodic depressions stretching from the panic of 1873 through the depression that began in 1893, wage laborers and their advocates continued to question whether waged work and independence were really compatible. But no matter what side of the "labor question" they stood on, all agreed that dependence was an unacceptable status for adult, white men. As labor activism mounted, complete with strikes and countermeasures on the part of employers—from ironclad contracts to the use of strikebreakers—the "labor problem" came to dominate national politics. At issue was the presumed equality of employers and employees, and hence the legitimacy of contract as a description of workplace relations. In an 1883 congressional investigation of what was termed the "labor problem," a spokesman for the Knights of Labor told the committee that "the working people feel they are under a system of forced slavery."[14] As it had before the war, the claim of dependence (and slavery) provided a language of protest. For workingmen, the problem was not that freedom was defined in terms of independence; rather, the problem was that wage labor precluded independence, and hence freedom. Indeed, many union leaders proffered the ideal of a "family wage" that would allow every male wage laborer to act as the head of household by supporting a dependent wife and children. Like the men who gathered in antebellum constitutional conventions, such labor leaders reviled their own dependence even as they accepted that some relations of dependence—chiefly those of the household—were natural and normal.[15]

The belief that dependence was a form of unfreedom not only provided a basic language of political protest in the United States, but it also has informed the plot structure of many historical narratives of both liberalism and the family. Such accounts differ little from the teleologies of "providence" and "general forward movement" to which Bergh and Stowe referred in their attempts to situate animal and child protection within the unfolding of liberalism. The plotline of decreasing dependence and increasing rights was famously outlined by Englishman Sir Henry Maine in his 1861 treatise, *Ancient Law*, about the evolution of "progressive societies" from, as he put it, "Status to Contract." Maine based his succinct teleology on a rough kind of anthropology—he undertook a survey of "primitive" societies and their laws. In spite of surface variation, Maine argued, all societies that evolved (that were not, in other words, hopelessly mired in savagery and barbarism) were characterized by "the gradual dissolution of family dependency and the growth of individual obligation in its place."

In this schematic, Maine equated dependency with unfreedom, if not outright slavery, which he in turn located in the illiberal space of the household. Over time, he believed, the individual rather than the family came
to be regarded as the proper legal and political unit, and the legitimacy of
relationships came to rest on their having been freely chosen. In Maine's
telling, contract was central to a new and improved stage of human history; it was the end toward which historical relationships and legal forms
evolved; and, most important, it was the essence of freedom.[16]

Though he was British, Maine expressed ideas with transatlantic currency. Writing in 1883, the Yale sociologist William Graham Sumner
echoed Maine's central points. As one of the chief spokesmen for laissez-
faire economic policy, Sumner regarded the transition to a society based
on contract as an unalloyed good. It represented a movement away from
"feudal ties" of personal dependence and toward a society expressive of
human equality. Like Maine, Sumner deplored relations of dependence,
which he identified with the feudal past, as inconsistent with freedom,
equality, and personal independence. Significantly, Sumner differentiated
the feudal from the modern order in affective terms. In his telling, the
feudal society of status was composed of ties forged between men based
on their lifelong membership in a certain order, such as a guild or a rank,
within the social structure. "Consequently," Sumner wrote, "society was
dependent, throughout all its details, on status, and the tie, or bond, was
sentimental." By contrast, the "modern state," of which Sumner took the
United States to be the apogee, was based on relations of contract. "Contract, however," Sumner wrote, "is rational. . . . realistic, cold, and matter-
of-fact." The ties created by contract were consensual rather than customary or prescribed, lasted only as long as the parties agreed, and involved no
affect. "In a state based on contract, sentiment is out of place in any public
or common affairs." The only proper place for sentiment was, not surprisingly, the domestic sphere. But here, Sumner was quick to point out, sentiments developed not out of status-based relationships—for this would
make the beloved home, and the marriage relation upon which it stood,
into a relic of feudalism—but out of relations of "personal acquaintance
and personal estimates." Certain kinds of sentiment, and certain kinds of
dependence, were apparently safe for the liberal order of contract. It was
understandable, Sumner admitted, that some might lament the passing of
this older, more sentimental age, and might cling to its linaements, but in
reality there was, he advised, no turning back from the march of progress.
While the sense of obligation and interdependence born of feudal hierarchy
might be lost, this was more than made up for by the fact that "a society

based on contract is a society of free and independent men. . . . [and] gives the utmost room and chance for individual development."[17] To be embedded in a set of specific, historical, and familial relations was, for Sumner, to be dependent, unfree, thwarted, bound by birth, time, and place to a life not of one's own choosing. But abstracted from affective ties of dependence, the individual American stood outside of the domestic sphere, outside of history, and faced other similarly abstracted individuals, each ready to realize his freedom in a series of temporary, consensual contracts. Because "status" was identified with the household, and hence with feudal relations, theorists such as Maine and Summer counterpoised rights and contract to dependence and status.

The dissolution of dependence is also the story told by most historians of the American family, who chart a decline in the power of the patriarch and the demise of the hierarchal household. And, like the emergence of the rights of the "common man," the end of slavery, and the birth of women's rights, the story is largely a nineteenth-century one. Most historians agree that between the Revolution and the end of Reconstruction, former dependents entered into a more direct relationship with the state and were acknowledged to have interests that could not be adequately represented by the head himself. No longer understood by legislators and jurists to be an individisible unit represented by the patriarch, the household was instead increasingly understood as a collection of individuals, each with his or her own separate interests. The law of master and servant was replaced by modern employment law. Married women gained rights of property and contract, the right to divorce and obtain custody of their children. Children were governed by the doctrine of their "best interests" rather than by the rules of property. The Civil War ended slavery and marked the beginning of the end of the South's lingering patriarchalism.[18] In most historical accounts, then, as in both liberal political theory and nineteenth-century historical tracts, the end of dependence marks the beginning of rights.

Against the tide of both longstanding liberal assumptions and more immediate Gilded Age contractualism, anticruelty reformers sought to reconcile dependence with rights. As a species of property, animals clearly failed to qualify as independent beings worthy of rights and capable of citizenship; rather, they were instrumental beings, necessary for labor, food, and other supplies. In political and reformist discourse, animals served figuratively, like slaves, as among the paradigmatic dependent beings. Hence for abolitionists, slavery's violation of natural liberty was often framed as a problem of putting persons "on a par with brutes." Slaves were denied their individuality, their sentience, and their humanity. According to one abolitionist, slavery stole the enslaved from their rightful place as members of God's family and instead "yokes them with the beasts of the field, physically, intellectually, socially, morally, and religiously." Abolitionists regarded it as a problem that, like animals, slaves were regarded as mere instruments of their owners' will, and thus that a master's regard for his slave was strictly economic, guided by the profit motive and little else. "The steam engine is fed with wood, the horse with hay, the slave with hominy, and all for the same object—to create the power of action." It was partly this comparison of slaves with animals that informed some abolitionists' commitment to free wage labor as a morally and economically superior form of organizing work. William Lloyd Garrison contrasted the volition of the free wage laborer with that of the "domestic animal" that was little more than an extension of its owner's will. Of the free laborer, Garrison asked, "Are his movements dependent on the will and pleasure of another?" Garrison clearly believed they were not. Wage labor, unlike slavery, did not reduce man to a condition of dependence; it did not, in other words, treat man as a domesticated animal. As a trope of dependence, the animal stood below even the slave. Though some abolitionists extended their compassion to animals as well as slaves, more often than not, animals were invoked analogically to suggest the degraded dependency of the slave system. If wage laborers protested that they were treated like slaves, abolitionists protested that slaves were treated like animals.[19]

Like most heirs to the Enlightenment, Garrison and other abolitionists likely assumed animal subjection was a natural outgrowth of animal irrationality. Reason, long the basis for the fundamental distinction between humans and animals, also often served as the grounding for natural human rights. In classic works such as John Locke's *Second Treatise of Government*, human reason was the foundation of human liberty and, in subsequent centuries, reason was the grounds for both exclusion from and inclusion in the moral and political community.[20] And in their propaganda, animal protectionists often argued against such assumptions, claiming that animals could and did display reason. But the argument for animal rights from animal reason formed only one portion of protectionists' larger rights discourse. As much as reformers and their organs such as *Our Dumb Animals* focused on animal reason, they were just as likely to portray animals as beings capable of suffering equally with humans. In contrast to the argument from reason, when humanitarians drew attention to animals' capacity for suffering they tapped into more recent developments within Anglo-American liberalism and they helped to shift the ground underneath the rights-bearing community by arguing that rights may also rest on capacities such as feeling and sentience, and that, on this basis, rights might also extend to the weak, the dependent, and the helpless. In calling attention to pain and suffering, animal protectionists often highlighted rather than denied animal dependence.

And though abolitionists like Garrison might assume a natural hierarchy between man and beast, animal protectionists used abolitionists' own methods to establish commonality across the species line. For it was abolitionists, as Elizabeth Clark has shown, who had established the conceptual and cultural links between suffering, sentience, and rights. During the years leading up to the Civil War, abolitionists began to ground their claims for slaves' rights less in the reasoning capacities of slaves and more in their capacity for suffering. They promulgated these ideas in what Clark calls "cruelty narratives," which relied on the "trope of the suffering slave" as a critical component of abolitionist strategy. Publications relating the "gruesome tribulations" of the slave body began to appear in the 1830s. By 1838, Lydia Maria Child had published her *Authentic Anecdotes of American Slavery*, and the next year Theodore Dwight Weld attempted to arouse the country's sleeping moral sense with *American Slavery as It Is: Testimony of a Thousand Witnesses*. The 1840s and 1850s witnessed modifications in the genre of such cruelty narratives, with the rise of slave autobiographies and sentimental fiction such as *Uncle Tom's Cabin*, but certain stock scenes of corporal punishment and confinement persisted.[21] In such tracts, depictions of pain served a dual purpose: they proved the wickedness of those who would inflict suffering and the humanity of the wounded.

In addition to highlighting the tyranny manifest in slaves' bodily pain, abolitionists focused their fellow Americans' attention on the emotional pain caused by the breakup of slave families through sale. The emotional trauma of broken households was, of course, a central structuring device in Harriet Beecher Stowe's 1852 *Uncle Tom's Cabin*, but the trope was by then decades old. An 1832 letter to the "Ladies Department" of the *Liberator* exemplifies the genre. After asserting that slaves "have the same tender emotions" as free white men and women, this female abolitionist called her "sisters" to gaze on an imagined slave market. As she guided her readers through this market, she asked them to imagine themselves undergoing the different forms of family separation she described. First, the writer conjured the separation of mother and child: "See her tender suckling torn from her maternal bosom, carried away by ruffian hands! Never again shall her eyes behold it!" Next she turned to the separation of husband and

wife: "Husbands torn from their shrieking companions, yet smarting under the blood-stained lash!" Combining both physical and emotional pain
together in one image, the author suggested that "hearts must bleed" at
such trauma. Being taken away from one's family was like being wounded
in the seat of feeling: the heart. Lydia Maria Child's 1833 tract, *An Appeal
in Favor of Americans Called Africans*, likewise described the devastation
wrought by the procurement of slaves on the African coast as beginning
with a scene of family violation. "Houses are broken open in the night,"
and "Husbands are torn from wives, children from their parents, while the
air is filled with the shrieks and lamentations of the bereaved." In spite
of possessing genuine family feelings equal to those of whites, "the poor
negro," lamented Child, "is considered as having no right in his wife and
children." The emotional pain caused by family separation was here deployed as an argument for slaves' inherent humanity and, hence, for their
natural rights, expressed in the bosom of the family.[22] Although abolitionists often emphasized the economic and moral advantages of free labor,
and hence stressed the link between freedom and independence, by list-
ing family separation as chief among slavery's wrongs, they also suggested
that some relations of dependence—those figured as natural and domestic,
rather than imposed—were a source for, and manifestation of, rather than
a barrier to, human rights.

By insisting that slaves suffered, abolitionists relied on the body and the
emotions rather than the mind as the grounding for the equality of master and slave. Abolitionists were, by the same token, using the emphasis
on empathy and suffering within contemporary liberal, evangelical Prot-
estantism to communicate the "notions of individual integrity critical to
liberal political theory."[23] The abolitionists' focus on the pains of body and
soul drew on the spread of a liberalized and evangelical branch of Christianity to create a moral calculus in which emotions, aroused through direct or fantastic contact with suffering, parsed right from wrong.

Antislavery discourse, in turn, formed part of what Clark calls a lay
rights tradition that equated moral right with political and civil rights,
and that grounded an expanded vision of individual rights and government
intervention in sentient experience. The significance of this lay conception is not just that it served as a viable argument for the extension of
rights to new groups, but also that its vision of rights went far beyond
the essentially negative liberties guaranteed by the Constitution. Empathy, the ability to imagine that someone else is like oneself, Clark argues,
had been critical to the spread of rights. The image of the suffering slave

helped to forge new moral and legal norms such as the right to bodily integrity and the right to be free from avoidable pain.[24]

Abolitionists thus provided a model congruent with the sentimental
humanitarian assumptions of animal protectionists: to prove your object
worthy of attention, prove that it feels pain. To prove rights, in other words,
one need only establish wrongs. In depictions of suffering slaves, animals,
and children, sentimentalism and liberalism converged at the site of violation. Because individual rights are typically imagined as imposing duties
of omission rather than active responsibilities, their existence, and their
exercise, often remains invisible except in the moment of infraction. It is
the negation of rights that calls attention to their existence, making the
language of rights hardwired as a language of wrongs. Likewise, in sentimentalism, wrongs provide the opportunity for sympathetic identification,
for the activation of the moral sense, and for the relief of suffering. Wrongs
are the moments when both the corruption and the blooming of the moral
sense are respectively evinced in the perpetrator and the observer of abuse.
As with rights, fellow feeling is conjured into existence at the moment of
violation since such acts provoke feelings that might otherwise lay dormant. Though both sentimentalism and liberalism cherish a set of positive values, at the center of each is an instance of trespass—a moment of
rupture that reminds its observers of the sentience, the humanity, and the
individuality of the wounded.[25]

Depictions of suffering that called attention to the pains of the individual body defied the logic of coverture and its denial of legal personhood to the dependent. Historically, household dependents were unable
not only to independently own property, make contracts, or otherwise
represent themselves economically, politically, and legally, but they were
also unable to suffer direct harm under the law. In legal terms, harm to
dependents was understood to redound not on them directly, but instead
on the public order or on the head of household. Under common law, a
married woman, a child, a servant, or a slave could not sue in court for
bodily injuries suffered at the hand of another. Instead, courts recognized
only claims made by the household head for the "loss of services" he suffered as a result of being denied the labor of the injured. Tapping Reeve,
author of *The Law of Baron and Femme* and the antebellum era's foremost
expert on domestic law, explained that "the husband may bring an action
in his own name, to recover damages which he sustained" as a result of
a third party's "battery" of his wife. A similar logic applied in cases of
injury to children, servants, and, in the South, slaves.[26] Though the harm

was bodily, its consequences were construed as economic and the injured party was thus the head, the only one with the legal ability to transact property. Just as scientists saw the ability to suffer as a sign of humanity, courts also linked the capacity to be harmed to personhood. In arguing that the consequences of bodily pain and injury were deeply felt by the individuals directly wounded rather than by their masters and keepers, abolitionists' sentimental techniques asserted the personhood of slaves in terms that had legal and political as well as moral consequences. Far from a merely technical issue in the law, the ability to suffer direct harm was an index of personhood in a liberal order. Depictions of suffering were, then, linked to a call both for sympathy and for rights; and though sympathy may not be intrinsically bound to the recognition of rights, recent American history provided postbellum protectionists with a language for connecting the two.

As we have seen, both opponents and adherents of animal protection sought to link the cause to abolition. To press their case for the positive links between the two, anticruelty reformers circulated anecdotes about Abe Lincoln's boyhood kindness to animals, certain that his early moral logic was identical with the impulse that had made him the great slave liberator. One writer saw clearly that "we owe the Emancipation Act, first of all under God, to Abraham Lincoln's early pity for [animals]. The same tender heart felt to the quick the injuries he afterward saw inflicted upon the slaves at New Orleans; and in the fullness of his mature kindness, the boy, who began by protecting a worm, ended by rescuing three millions of his fellow-man from bondage."[27] Writers likewise compared the railroad transport of sheep, pigs, and cows across the country to "the 'middle passage,' as full of horrors to [these animals] as it was to the negro slave." When feeling besieged, they reminded one another that because their work was "akin in magnitude to the overthrow of slavery," they should not find it surprising that "the great mass of people" considered them nothing but "sentimentalists, or 'long-haired come-outers,'" as they looked upon the abolitionists in the days of slavery."[28] Even after more than thirty years of organized effort on behalf of animals, the founder of Boston's Animal Rescue League complained that "I cannot help comparing the attitude of mankind toward the lower animals with that of the majority of men and women fifty years ago toward the negro, before the civilized world awoke to the true knowledge and realization of the cruelty of slavery." That is, she protested, an "astonishing" number of men and women still "regard the lower animals as less than machines," as a convenient if expendable means to an end.[29]

In the early days of animal protection, just following the Civil War, some activists did indeed move from abolition to animal protection, or came from abolitionist families, but more important was the way in which animal advocates imported the rhetoric and the cultural symbols of abolitionist discourse nearly wholesale into their work. Like abolitionists, animal protectionists centered their claims for animals' sentience on their experience of physical pain and their capacity for tender, domestic affections. Leaders such as Henry Bergh repeatedly stressed the helplessness of animals, their physical suffering, and their capacity to experience pain. "The sufferings of the lower animals are really felt by them," he explained to the men of the Putnam County Agricultural Society. "Theirs is the unequivocal physiognomy of pain," for they are incapable of dissembling as man is, and do not pretend to sickness and lameness except when it really affects them. Even to the untrained eye, Bergh went on, their suffering is visible, for they "give forth the very indications of agony that we do," a fact verified by the very vivisectionists who cut them open in the name of science. "When the scalpel of the physiologist lays open the secret recesses of their system," he said, "there stands forth to view the same sentient apparatus, furnished with the same conductors for the transmission of feeling, to every pore upon the surface."[30] By emphasizing animals' capacity for suffering, reformers pushed them ever upward in the chain of being.

For those without access to the theaters of surgery where they might, like Henry Bergh, see animals' "sentient apparatus" laid bare before their eyes, the publications of SPCAs trained ordinary eyes to detect the bodily clues of animal suffering. Frequently they did this through use of illustration. For the first ten years of their existence, many animal protection societies labored to eliminate the use of the checkrein on horses. Used by the fashionable and designed to force horses' heads to remain erect and upright at all times, the reins prevented horses from using the full strength of their bodies to pull heavy loads, transferring the stress and strain of draught work from the larger muscles of the body to the neck, head, and mouth. Protectionists insisted that, while fanciers of the checkrein saw only tidy-looking horses who kept their heads up and looked the part of the proud and noble steed, those trained in the detection of animal suffering could see the expressions of pain emitted by the horse in check. As one article in Our Dumb Animals put it, the average carriage driver or rider would look upon such creatures "with admiration, to see how 'handsome' his horse appears, and imagines that the tossing head, open mouth, and gnashing teeth are signs of game and strength." To the humane eye, however, the very same gestures were marks not of nobility but instead were

**Figure 5.** Learning to see suffering. *Our Dumb Animals* 1, no. 6 (November 3, 1868): 44.

"the most unequivocal evidences of distress and agony." To fix permanently the signs of the equine body, the magazine provided what it called "infallible proof" of the cruelties of the checkrein: a before-and-after illustration of a horse in checkrein and accompanying text that described the difference in appearance between a comfortable and a suffering animal (fig. 5). In the "before" picture the viewer was instructed to note that "the corners of [the horse's] mouth become *raw, inflame, fester*, and eventually the *mouth* becomes *enlarged on each side*, in some cases to the extent of *two* inches." In contrast to the grotesqueries of enlargement and inflammation caused by the checkrein, the horse who was allowed to "have his head" would exhibit a normal mouth, be able to stretch out his neck, and would carry his load up hills without strain or collapse. Having illustrated the physiological signs of pain and comfort, the magazine expected its readers to remember them. "Let this be a sign," it warned, "to every master and servant."[31]

Humanitarian reformers extended this strategy of reinscribing the everyday with marks of suffering and pain by challenging readers to imagine themselves in the position of animals. Continuing the campaign on behalf of horses, the Massachusetts SPCA instructed horse drivers to ask "are these dumb creatures, like ourselves, subject to a variety of pains" and "are they, like ourselves, sensible of acute pain from blows and whipping, from the galling and agonizing pain of blisters produced by tight collars and other harnesses" and do they not, therefore, deserve kinder treatment?[32] About the checkrein in particular, it asked drivers: "if you were working would you like to have your head buckled up in that manner"?[33] An illustration entitled "Is Turn About Fair-Play?" drove the point home (fig. 6). Two men, chained in harness and straining with bits in their mouths, struggled to pull a loaded cart while being whipped by their driver, an ox in human clothing. Well-dressed oxen and mules stood and watched while the cart's human cargo, hands and legs tied together and bodies piled one on top of the other, bore the signs of pain and discomfort on their faces. Beneath the illustration a caption asked its viewers "How do you like this?" and explained that *Our Dumb Animals* had purchased this print and several others to induce people to consider how they would react if treated like animals. Imagine the animals asking you "How do you like check-reins now?" the magazine instructed. If it doesn't look comfortable or fair, it continued, then your animal friends would probably tell you that "If you don't like it for yourselves, don't do it to us!"[34]

Reversing the position of humans and animals remained a favorite tactic of the animal protection movement throughout the nineteenth century. In the months that followed the publication of "How do you like this?" more illustrations of a topsy-turvy world appeared: birds stole young children from their homes, frogs stoned young boys as they tried to swim, and men screamed in pain as they were plucked alive by geese (fig. 6).[35] Likewise, year after year, humane publications featured stories of human-animal reversal. In such stories, children suddenly found themselves, like butterflies, captured and pinned to boards by a race of giants; boys were turned into fish, only to find their mouths gored by large hooks; men became caught in the traps they laid to catch fox or mink; and women dreamed they were ducks, helplessly watching their children being plucked and skinned alive to make fashionable muffs and bed coverings.[36] These visual and imaginary depictions inserted pain where mere sport, labor, or fashion had been before, reinscribing common human practices with the taint of cruelty. Likewise, such strategies depended upon the assumption that human and animal suffering were substantially alike, if not identical. For cruelty, explained William Alger at an MSPCA annual meeting, is always the result of "a lack of imaginative sensibility," always a failure of empathy.[37] Animals' rights, on the other hand, spread as far as the bounds of human sympathy would permit.

Besides a common capacity to suffer physical pain, anticruelty reformers also argued that animals shared with humans the positive feelings, such as love and affection, associated with family life and domesticity. "Almost all domestic animals are naturally affectionate," explained one writer.[38] This general affection flowed toward both other animals and humans. An article reprinted from the *Exchange* told the story of a sick horse and his canine nurse. The stable dog, upon seeing that one of the horses had fallen ill, became quite upset and "commenced fawning around him,

**Figure 6.** Humans suffer animal treatment. *Is Turn About Fair-Play?: Our Dumb Animals* 4, no. 1 (June 1871):110; *Dive, Boys, Dive: Our Dumb Animals* 4, no. 4 (September 1871): 134; *Birds Robbing Child's Nests!!: Our Dumb Animals* 4, no. 2 (July 1871): 118; *Geese Plucking!: Our Dumb Animals* 4, no. 6 (November 1871): 150.

BIRDS ROBBING CHILD'S NESTS!!

GEESE. PLUCKING!

licking the poor animal's face, and in various other ways manifesting his sympathy with the sufferer." The dog even went so far as to fetch their common master each time the horse groaned in pain, and stayed by his side, continuing to tend to and lick him until he recovered.[39] Even cats, long assumed to be selfish and aloof, were proved to be loving creatures. In Lydia Maria Child's story of the two cats Pussy Malta and Grizzly Tom, the two formerly antagonistic housemates were transformed into friends by the former's suffering. Grizzly Tom, Child explained, was a generally grumpy old cat who looked with almost uninterrupted disdain upon Pussy Malta—until the day she entered the house howling in pain. Old Tom was instantly by Pussy's side, inspecting and tending to her. "I never," Child reported, "saw any dumb creature express sympathy so humanly as he did." Pussy Malta, it turned out, had been pregnant, and though she died giving birth, Grizzly Tom demonstrated another form of affection by becoming the protector of her orphaned kittens. Indeed, the old cat's sympathetic and paternal urges took physical, and supranatural, form as, to the wonder of all in the neighborhood, Tom nursed Pussy's kittens from his own breast.[40]

As often as the affective bond among animals was stressed, so too was that between humans and animals. Known as a beast of supreme loyalty and intelligence, the dog was a favorite exemplar of emotional excellence, and few dogs were more revered in this respect than "Greyfriar's Bobby," whose story was told and retold in numerous animal welfare publications. Bobby first surfaced in the United States as the subject of the Pennsylvania SPCA's handbill, *Strange Story of a Dog* (fig. 7). In the late 1850s, Bobby's story went, a very poor man died in Edinburgh and was buried in Grey Friar's Churchyard. Few mourners attended the burial of the poor man, save for his little Scotch Terrier, Bobby. The gravekeeper drove the dog out after the ceremony, but Bobby devotedly returned each day to his dead master's grave to keep watch over it. After many attempts to ban the dog, he was finally allowed to make his permanent home in the cemetery, where he kept his vigil faithfully until he himself died in 1872, his limp body flung on top of the spot where his decaying master lay.[41] Some years after Bobby's death, a patron of Britain's Royal SPCA, Baroness Burdett Coutts, had a statue of the dog erected in the Edinburgh cemetery where he had spent his final years.[42]

Bobby's dedication to his master argued so forcefully not just for animals' emotional capacities but also for the tendency of these capacities toward all that was noble and good that his life was regarded as inherent proof of animals' worthiness and their close connection to human beings.

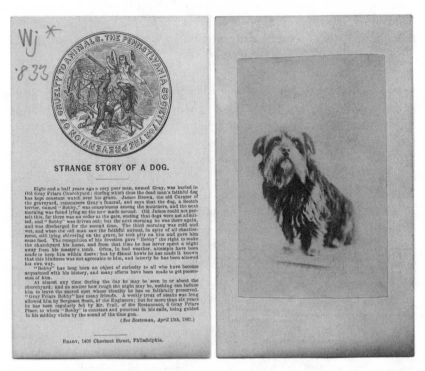

**Figure 7.** Animal sentience: Greyfriar's Bobby. Pennsylvania Society for the Prevention of Cruelty to Animals, *Strange Story of a Dog* (Philadelphia: Brady, [1867]).

After rehearsing Bobby's story, the Reverend Dr. Putnam remarked that it showed "what affectionate friendships sometimes exist between brute and human creatures, and how important a part of the home-bound circles animals often are." In actions such as Bobby's, and by their communicative countenances, concluded Dr. Putnam, animals show that "they are often capable of a depth and tenderness in the eyes, and of a wistfulness of look, and of cries and motions, that should plead with us with more than the power and pathos of any proxied appeal from man's stammer lips in their behalf."[43] Animals, dumb though they may be, could, protectionists repeatedly suggested, communicate a whole range of complex and highly valued emotions with their bodies.

As Putnam's use of Bobby's story suggests, animal affection was meant to serve as a proxy for their sympathetic tendencies, which should, in turn, arouse human sympathy. Proof of animals' innate moral sense could, of course, take many forms, and, as the stories of Grizzly Tom, Pussy Malta, and Greyfriar's Bobby suggest, reformers' portraits of animal affection often drew on the same sentimentalized visions of domestic emotions that had structured the appeals of antislavery works such as *Uncle Tom's Cabin*. Writer Dara Dormoore, for instance, asked readers to consider "how very much like animals we are" and listed as proof, alongside a common ability to remember, communicate, and reason, "the moral sentiments of maternal love."[44] The "Children's Department" of *Our Dumb Animals* showed that maternal love was not just a source of, but also a cause of, moral behavior. Alongside a placid scene of a mother cow and her calf (fig. 8), the magazine included a brief text that instructed young viewers in how to read the scene before them. Look at how the mother cow lays her head on her baby's back, it noted, and see how she does this "as tenderly as a human mother folds her arms about her baby." See how she looks proud of her offspring, for "this, too, is very like a human mother." Taking its readers beyond the scene at hand, the magazine asked them to imagine what would happen if the mother and child were torn from one another. Would the cow suffer? "We know that she does," was the confident reply. To assure that children reached the proper conclusions from the evidence at hand, the moral entailments of maternal affection were drawn out in bold lines: "If, then, the animal creation is bound to us by that strongest and sweetest element of our nature, which we call affection, shall we do not well" to act as Saint Francis did and consider all animals as "part of the great brotherhood of earth?"[45]

That such appeals to animals' maternal instincts drew on embedded assumptions about the relationship between familial affections and rights was made clear by "H. J. P." in her protest against the Massachusetts SPCA's efforts. The organization, she complained, had paid too much attention to "starved dogs and overworked horses" when the real tragedy lay elsewhere—not in the cities where most SPCA officers patrolled, but in the country, where folks like herself were daily witness to the "evil" of mother animals being separated from their children. It has long been thought, she wrote, that "animals do not care much for their young," but she had seen cows run wildly after calves being led away, and ewes follow carts full of their lambs, bleating plaintively all the while. Lest these anecdotes be dismissed or explained away, H. J. P. reminded her readers that it was not so long ago when many said of the "poor black mother" that she did not care for her children, or that she could get used to the ordeal of having them taken away. To the notion that animals should or could just "get used to it" as slave women had been forced to do, she retorted that this process would be "a kind of dumb submission, a blotting of all hope, just as it would be in the case of a human being under like circumstances."[46]

**Figure 8.** Animal domesticity. *Our Dumb Animals* 7, no. 5 (October 1874): 38.

Having established that animals possessed deeply rooted maternal instincts, H. J. P. assumed that their existence would, as in the case of slavery, force a recognition of commonality that would, in turn, render the
customary suddenly strange and immoral. The hardening of animals'
maternal feelings would be as counter to their natures as it had been for
Cassy, Harriet Beecher Stowe's embittered mulatto mother, stripped of her
children only to satisfy the demands of the market in human flesh.

In addition to using the domestic logic of abolitionist texts, animal
welfare reformers also traded on the success of first-person slave narratives and fictional slave protagonists. By seeking to establish the identity
of man and beast through animal narrators and characters, animal protectionists relied on the empathetic structures of fiction to make readers live animal lives and feel animal pain. Works of fiction, which forced
readers to identify with their protagonists—and which had long been critical to the cultural production of empathy—were an ideal form through
which to incorporate animals into the family of rights-bearing beings. In
essence, they took the subjectivity-swapping logic of the role reversal a
step further.[47] By contrasting the sentience of the animal narrator with
his commodification in the marketplace and his brutal treatment at the
hands of men, first-person animal stories created a structural discord between the protagonist's internal subjectivity and his external treatment
that served, in effect, to establish animals' rights through highlighting
human wrongs.

The most famous of the first-person animal narrations is, of course,
Englishwoman Anna Sewell's 1877 novel *Black Beauty*, subtitled "The
Autobiography of a Horse." We have already seen how the reception and
marketing of Sewell's novel in the United States revealed the assumption
that animals and children shared a space of subjectivity. Beyond that, anticruelty reformers framed *Black Beauty* in ways that demonstrate the intellectual debt the animal protection movement owed to the sentience-
based rights discourse of abolitionism. For years before he encountered
*Black Beauty*, MSPCA president George Angell had been casting about for
a book that "shall be as widely read as 'Uncle Tom's Cabin,' and shall have
as widespread and powerful [an] influence in abolishing cruelty to horses
as 'Uncle Tom's Cabin' had on the abolition of human slavery."[48] Angell
wanted, in other words, a book that would make its readers see the world
anew by forcing them to acknowledge their likeness with, and hence to
assume the subjectivity of, the oppressed. It was not until 1890, however,
that an American actress forwarded a copy of *Black Beauty* to Angell. He
was thrilled. Here at last, he proclaimed, was a worthy successor to *Uncle*

*Tom's Cabin.* Under Angell's direction, the American Humane Education Society (AHES) immediately printed several hundred thousand copies of the novel, which they christened with a new subtitle: the "Uncle Tom's Cabin of the Horse," a moniker that several of the novel's subsequent commercial publishers also adopted.[49] In the years following *Black Beauty's* initial American publication, Angell and others in the humane education movement attempted to stretch the novel's reach by translating it into other languages, offering prizes for the best adaptation of the novel for the stage, and for the best sequel.[50] By presenting audiences with the same stock scenes that had animated abolitionist propaganda (of family separation, physical abuse, and degenerating fortunes at the hands of cruel and powerful men), humanitarians hoped that horses too would be seen as, like the meek and deserving, man's "faithful slaves."[51]

Despite Angell's thrill at finding the true successor to *Uncle Tom's Cabin,* Sewell's work was, as other scholars have rightly pointed out, a culmination of the transatlantic genre of animal autobiography rather than its originator.[52] In fact, long before Black Beauty made his direct appeal to British cabbies and grooms, horses in the pages of *Our Dumb Animals* and other publications had voiced many of the same concerns and plotted their lives along the same course that Beauty's would eventually take.[53] An early example of the protectionist use of this genre, "The Story of a Good and Faithful Horse, Told by Himself," appeared in 1868. Structured as a bildungsroman, the installments of the tale tell of a colt's introduction into the ways of the human and adult world and of a slow descent from innocent bliss into worldly experience, from tranquility into pain and servitude. From the outset of the story, the horse looks back to his earliest days, fondly remembering the time before he worked for man, the days when he roamed free in a large pasture with his mother, drinking her sweet milk, munching dewy grass, and growing into his body by prancing and running through the fields. The horse's utter naiveté is established by his inability to understand human language and his reliance on his mother, "an animal of large experience," to explain the words and ways of the boys and men who came and leaned against the pasture fence, idly observing the horses and casually tossing stones at the birds.

The young horse identifies the world of animals in general with this early innocence and harmony, whereas he remembers the human world as a disruption and an intrusion. He recalls, for instance, how flocks of birds used to occupy the trees of his pasture and he describes their domestic bliss in terms that mirror his own. "Many happy hours we spent in familiar association" with the local birds, "watching the building of their cosy little nests; their joy over their newly hatched young; the care with which they fed and sheltered them, and their efforts to instruct them." Shattering this tranquility, a human hunter would inevitably come and "break the sweet silence of meadow and grove with the report of his murderous gun." What appeared to humans as custom and sport was transformed, when seen through the eyes of an animal, into needless bloodshed. Having asked the reader to assume his perspective, the horse confidently appealed to his audience to "imagine our feelings when, after watching our charming young friends from the very egg" they were "maimed and wounded" and "the happiness of their brief life was over." Voicing the "naïve reason" of the uninitiated, a position often granted to children in similar stories, the horse observed how strange it was "that idle men should seem to take pleasure in killing and wounding these harmless creatures."[54] Seen from the vantage point of the meadow, how strange indeed!

Soon, however, the inexplicable violence of men turned toward the young horse himself as he moved from an observer of to an initiate into human society. Taken from the prelapsarian pasture into the dark and dank stables for winter, the colt found himself separated from his mother and subjected to the process of being "broken in." "It seemed," he recounted, "as if my heart would break." After neighing his goodbyes to his mother he was tied up and made to suffer the pain and humiliation of having his tail docked; his owner and grooms "cut through flesh and bone and all, and as if this pain was not enough, they brought a red hot iron and seared the bleeding stump and put me in such agony as I cannot describe." The rest of the story details the colt's further immersion into the world of man: he learns to take the cold, hard metal of the bit into his mouth; to be combed with a brush to satisfy human vanity; to draw a sleigh and a carriage with passengers; and he receives his first pair of shoes from a smith. Abruptly, the story ends after this installment, with the horse having just begun to experience the ways of the world. He leaves his readers after musing about the smith who shoes him, wondering if "the man realized that although it was a hoof it was a living thing he was filing away." Thus, although the young horse of this story is introduced to man's ways and largely accepts human expectations of a horse's lot in the world (even feeling pride at how well he can pull his master and children in carriage), the tension between the perspective of horse and that of human being is never fully reconciled. Having assumed a humanlike subjectivity, the horse narrator nevertheless forces the reader to remain, to the end, an animal and an outsider like himself.

The ultimate consequences of the progressive incorporation of the animal into human society were explored by Rob, an elderly horse who also told his life story to the readers of *Our Dumb Animals*. Rob's story, like that of the "good and faithful horse," is one of decline and increasing cruelty at the hands of man. His entrance into human society is charted along an axis that begins in the country and ends in the city—the heart of the world man has made for himself. Rob's life begins happily in a pasture, with his mother by his side and a good master in the house. Forced to squelch his feelings about losing his mother and to learn his duties as a carriage horse, Rob is sold for $500 in one of Boston's horse markets. From this first sale forward, the plot revolves around the erosion of Rob's status, his health, his treatment, and his declining value—as each slide downhill is marked by another sale at market. Given a shoddy pair of shoes by his second master, Rob develops a limp and is sold for a mere $75 to a horse railroad company, the owners of which want nothing more than to maximize their profits. After depleting Rob's poor injured legs of what little life they had left, the company sells him again, this time for $15 to a man who sees in the old horse a chance to make a quick dollar. At the hands of this man the horse experiences what he described as "my greatest and last misery from the cruelty of men." Reduced to a mere commodity, Rob is given a "poisonous substance" that makes him appear fatter and healthier than he really is, and his shoes are painfully rigged so that he cannot limp. "I was taken out every day," he recalled, "and in this agony made to show off before buyers." As luck would have it, Rob's first and kindest master attends the market one day and recognizes Rob by the white spot on his forehead. The fate of man and animal are momentarily parallel as Rob notes that "[his former master], too, had grown old in the time." Perhaps recognizing himself in the horse, the man buys his old horse back. But, as Rob notes at the story's end, age was where their similarities ended, for "the world had been kind to him, whilst it had been cruel to me."[55] Although Rob's story is resolved through his reunion with a kind master, the moral of the story is not that good horses will be rewarded, but instead that horses' fates arbitrarily diverge from man's, and that being "good and faithful" is no insurance against ill treatment. Throughout the story, Rob remains entirely dependent on the whims of the humans who treat him ill or well according to their moral character.

A letter from a horse named Caesar made the implications of Rob's story clear. Complaining that he was misunderstood and mistreated by his master and mistress, Caesar confided that he often conferred with his stable- and field-mates about making a "revolt from slavery forever." But, realizing their relative helplessness in the face of a human-controlled world, he and his friends inevitably stayed where they were, resigned to the fact that "it is the destiny of horses to be driven by people." Torn between his resignation and his desire for better treatment, Caesar ended on a more defiant note. "I will only add in conclusion," he wrote, "that horses have rights, as well as people, and feelings as well as people."[56] Equine feelings seemed, indeed, to be the basis for equine rights.

More often than not, animal protectionists made the link between animal feelings and animal rights indirectly, by suggesting, for example, that a humane curriculum in the schools would "help to educate the rising generation into sympathy with animals, and into an appreciation of their rights."[57] Only occasionally did reformers explore their own assumptions or ideas systematically. In one such treatise, James Macaulay placed sentience at the center of his moral argument against experimentation on live animals. "You might operate on human subjects with no higher intelligence, and of no higher moral condition, and certainly with no more sensitive frame, than the poor brutes that are carried to the vivisector's laboratory. It is the infliction of pain and injury that cannot be justified," he wrote, "whether the victim be an imbecile human idiot, or a docile dog."[58] By placing dogs in the same category as mentally impaired humans, Macaulay steered the argument for animals' rights from reason to feeling and positioned rights on a ground that transcended species. He followed the line of thinking—that "evidently the reason why it is wicked to torture a man is not because he has an immortal soul, but because he has a highly sensitive body"—through to its conclusion that "if we have no moral right to torture a man, neither have we a moral right to torture a dog."[59] (For the next half century, American and British activists would attempt, with very limited success, to give Macaulay's "moral right" the force of a legal one.) In granting rights to man and animals alike based on the "highly sensitive body," Macaulay had traveled far from the terms of classical liberalism to a new philosophical framework.

Like Macaulay, the liberal clergyman and Social Gospeler T. T. Munger also believed that cruelty was wrong not just because it was a failure of the moral sense, but also because "animals themselves have rights which we are bound to respect." Thus, he wrote, an act of cruelty also "becomes an act of injustice."[60] To defend this view, Munger began by examining the qualities of animals that recommend their inclusion in the moral community. First, Munger suggested, animals earn their rights through their labor. In the Bible, he noted, we find Jewish law prescribing that "thou shalt not muzzle the ox when he treadeth out the corn." This, he went on, is "grounded in a sentiment and a right"; it conveys the sense that the oxen have a right to the corn because they have labored to produce it. Echoing the Lockean argument that labor creates the first right of property, Munger explained that "when one puts labor into anything one acquires a certain right in it; or, at least, has a right to a return for his labor." This ancient law was, he concluded, "intended to teach the Jews that animals have rights which men are bound to respect." Employing a quasi-contractual logic, Munger argued that we owe respect and kind treatment to the animals that serve us, making human life more convenient, more productive, and more enjoyable.[61]

Second, Munger continued, we share this world with animals and must recognize that "they have just as much right here as we have, and their home is here just as ours is." Animals were, in fact, here on earth before we humans were, and lived free of us in a state of nature—that is, until God made man the ruler of earth. But this dominion does not thereby lessen the duty to recognize that we have "dispossessed" our animal friends and that they have "ancient rights" stemming from first possession of the land. This becomes even more binding, Munger elaborated, when we realize that animals were better off before the dawn of man. Wild animals, for instance, "have only an enemy in man and the only thing they have learned from him is to fear and avoid him." Domestic animals, likewise, have sacrificed their natural freedom to man's control and been made to forfeit a "happy, natural order." Echoing the voices of horses like Rob, Caesar, and the "good and faithful horse," Munger recognized that animals' movement from nature to society had been nonconsensual—and he reasoned that humans must therefore accept "a duty of the most stringent character" toward them.[62] Were humans to obey the reciprocal logic of contract, they would have to admit that animals, having given over something of not just their labor but also their liberty, were *owed* kind treatment as a matter of *right*.[63]

Those animals that humans have appropriated for their use are, Munger went on, not mere machines, but have "very nearly the same nervous organization that we have," and they suffer as we do. "Their suffering is, furthermore, not just a matter of body, as is sometimes thought, but also of mind, for they suffer keenly in their minds and hearts, or as we usually say, in their feelings." We now know, thanks to much scientific discovery, he explained, that animals are like us, and we are like them—that, for instance, horses and dogs can understand communication, have moral instincts, and a "wide range of intelligence." Many people who violate animals' rights must do so, then, only because "they know so little about animals and enter so little into their thoughts and feelings." Here

Munger assumed, as did many others in the animal welfare movement, a straightforward equivalence between heartfelt mercy and principled moral order, between love and justice, and between sympathy and the recognition of rights. Suggesting that empathy was the mechanism by which rights would be extended, Munger concluded confidently that signs of its progress were all around. Someday soon, he ventured, "the rights of whatever can suffer" would be universally recognized.[64]

Protectionists hoped that a sentimental emphasis on suffering would work to incorporate animals into the liberal logic of rights. And, as we have seen, they relied on changing definitions of humanity that emphasized emotion rather than reason as the source of commonality and natural rights. To the extent that suffering could prove sentience and expand the circle of rights-bearing beings, sentimentalism and liberalism were congruent. But, as many historians and literary critics have pointed out, sentimentalist representations of suffering were often problematic and complex. While their avowed purpose was egalitarian and humanitarian, portrayals of degraded and abject bodies were also, as Marcus Wood succinctly puts it, "semiotically contaminated by pornography." In antebellum abolitionist tracts, the wounded and suffering body could signify degradation, dependence, and difference as easily as it could boundary-crossing equality.[65] Indeed, the logic of sympathy, critics argue, relies not on equality between the sufferer and the witness, but on the "dispossession" and inequality of the wounded. To the extent that sentimentalism asks those who witness suffering to act on behalf of those in pain, it replicates the hierarchical, vertical logic of benevolence rather than the egalitarian, horizontal logic of democracy or equal rights. Rather than recognizing equality, a focus on pain and suffering could easily reinforce the difference, dependence, and ultimate helplessness of those who suffer.[66]

    While much criticism of sentimentalism has focused on the politics of representing slave pain in abolitionist propaganda, the same contradiction between equality and helplessness beset postbellum animal protectionists. Indeed, even as anticruelty reformers insisted that animals' ability to suffer connected them in morally relevant ways to human beings, and even as they crafted laws that would recognize animals' suffering directly, they also stressed that animals were, in critical respects, helpless and dependent. "The truth is," wrote one reformer in 1871, "the humane disposition is ever touched more deeply by the picture of perfect dependence than by almost any other."[67] If arguing that animals suffered equally with humans served to incorporate them within a certain strand of liberal rights discourse, SPCAs' focus on animal helplessness placed both the organizations and their clients inside the logic of organized benevolence.

Bergh and likeminded animal protectionists in other cities did not claim to engage in benevolence or charity work, and indeed they often made a point of differentiating the methods and objects of humane organizations from those of other local charities. But anticruelty organizations saw their job as offering relief to animal suffering and they highlighted animal defenselessness. Protectionists often emphasized animal confinement as proof of their incapacities. Depictions of confinement had been a central theme in many abolitionist tracts as well, and they suggested both helplessness and the denial of liberal values like bodily integrity and self-direction.[68] Animal welfare reformers called attention to everyday instances of restraint and confinement in their protests against the check-rein and the practice of tying livestock legs together while transporting them to market. The former, they claimed, not only caused pain but also denied horses the ability to exercise their natural strength and abilities. The check, wrote one humanitarian, destroys the horse's natural beauty, "the grandeur of the animal's bearing and noble poise of head are all destroyed by this peculiar method of checking."[69] Cramped and pinched by the checkrein, a horse was denied his natural horse-hood by being unable to control his body. Tying livestock legs together turned animals into things, also suggesting that physical restraint was a means of denying sentience, rendering animals helpless to use their bodies as they pleased. The Illinois Humane Society complained of visiting the Chicago stockyards and seeing calves, "their four legs drawn together with a stout rope, and the animals gasping and struggling fearfully," while others complained that animals so restrained were treated like mere "stones" or "cords of wood."[70] Complaining that animals were treated as objects indicted humans rather than animals, but nonetheless figured animals as helpless and in need of human protection.

In another instance of confinement that circulated widely in humane circles, the Wisconsin Humane Society rescued a horse from nine years of isolation in his stable. Locked away as punishment for trying to escape, during his confinement the "once beautiful sorrel horse . . . with intelligence like a man" was "reduced to nothing but skin and bones." Most grotesque of all, humane society officers believed, were the horse's overgrown hooves, which "long and rocker-shaped" were a denial of the horse's natural movements as much as was his locked stall. When released by the society's superintendent, R. D. Whitehead, the horse "hobbled out into the sunshine to nibble the green grass, and showed his gratitude by a low whinny." First featured in the Wisconsin Humane Society's annual reports, the story eventually made its way into the spotlight on the back cover of the American Humane Association's 1890 annual report.[71] As with the checkrein and leg tying, confinement in the stable not only interfered with the natural ability to move—the animal equivalent of free will—but also demonstrated what reformers referred to as animals' "helpless dependence, their faithful service, [and] their patient endurance."[72] Checked, tied, and locked away, animals seemed to many to be "dumb and defenseless," subject to man's will and whim.[73]

In addition to confinement, depictions of animal helplessness centered on the issue of language. Animals were literally confined by humans, but even when not physically restricted, they were trapped by their own bodies, doomed to a life of silent suffering. In a remarkable passage, one anticruelty activist, Mrs. Emma Rood Tuttle, wove together the themes of suffering and helplessness with the imagery of slavery. "We are constantly in sight of numbers of dumb and helpless animals which cannot speak for themselves, although their needs and nervous sensibility are scarcely less than our own," she said. Mrs. Tuttle went on: "They feel acutely the pangs of want, but cannot tell their needs in articulate language. They suffer and die, but cannot accuse their destroyers, nor tell their wrongs." While they cannot speak, Tuttle claimed that animals' bodies and groans spoke a "pathetic language . . . of the indescribable irritations to which slaves, whether man or beast, are subject."[74] As in other anticruelty texts, Tuttle placed animals' capacity to experience pain at the center of her claims for animals' equality with humans. But in focusing on animals' incapacity for language, Tuttle also equated silence with helplessness and stressed animals' difference from human beings. Like Harriet Beecher Stowe, Mrs. Tuttle suggested that in addition to animal suffering, their helplessness was a primary reason for their inclusion within the circle of human moral concern. Even as suffering made animals equal, the trope of silence made them dependent and granted agency to humans. Ironically, humans' moral responsibility toward animals reinforced human superiority. The proper relationship between animal inarticulateness and human charity was summed up by the title of the MSPCA's journal—*Our Dumb Animals*. Dumb, yes, but also "ours"—dependents and our wards.

The primacy of protectionists' insistence on animal muteness is striking given the centrality of language to the defense or denial of animal sentience. For centuries Western philosophers had taken animals' lack of language as proof that they had no consciousness. Speaking within a rights discourse, animal protectionists rejected this reasoning by stressing that animals spoke a corporeal language of pains and pleasures that human beings could learn to speak if only they tried. Emma Tuttle's description of animal silence suggests this tack—she refers to animals' "pathetic language" even as she insists that they cannot "tell their wrongs." Rights-inflected discourse encouraged anticruelty activists to emphasize animal capacities—the capacity for communication, the capacity for suffering—in order to establish their sentience. The language of obligation and benevolence, by contrast, which wanted to move humans from sympathy to action, encouraged a stress on *incapacity*, chiefly the inability to defend or help oneself. Though protectionists intended benevolent and liberal justifications for attention to animal welfare to be mutually reinforcing, the changing valence of animal speech shows both the fusion of, and the tensions between, sentimentalism and liberalism. Focusing on animals' helplessness, protectionists positioned them as dependent beings. And, as we have seen, dependence was more often the grounds for exclusion rather than inclusion from the imagined community of rights-bearing beings.

In basing rights on sentience rather than reason or independence, and in attempting to reconcile rights with dependence, anticruelty reformers developed a vision of rights based on protection rather than liberty. This vision accommodated both animals and children equally well, for it did not require claims of equal capacity. In promoting rights without equality, anticruelty reformers seemed to not only embrace a contradiction, but also to step outside their own time and cast one eye back to the "feudal" world of hierarchical, status-based relationships that contemporaries like Maine and Sumner saw as rapidly retreating in the face of a regime of contract. But anticruelty reformers did not simply act on anachronistic assumptions. For even as anticruelty reformers' focus on animals' and children's dependence seemed to anchor them in a world defined by the status hierarchies of the household, reformers also shared in emergent understandings of the individual in the modern world. Though the late nineteenth century was a period when independent, freely contracting individuals were idealized, it was also the moment when such liberal fictions were undermined by a growing chorus of social scientists, psychologists, and legal professionals. Together, they insisted that the modern, industrialized world was a complex, interdependent social organism whose constituent parts were connected whether they intended—or contracted—to be or not. In such a world, the possibility of traditional "independence" seemed to be undermined, and the meaning of notions such as liberty and individual rights changed accordingly. Structural changes underlay this new perception. Technologies of transportation and communication—the telegraph and the railroad—together with industrialization, urbanization, and the growth of large, vertically and horizontally integrated corporations eroded America's "island communities" and bound the fortunes of individuals and regions together across space and through time.[75]

Though the causes of postbellum integration were largely material, many of its important consequences were perceptual and ideological. Traditional understandings of individualism, freedom, liberty, and independence were challenged by a complex world in which it was increasingly unclear how much control individuals could exercise over their own lives. For many Americans, postwar economic changes were experienced both as a loss of personal control and a growing sense of national disorder. When, for example, Knights of Labor leader George McNeill protested in 1887 that the modern industrial system "makes the employer a despot, and the employee a slave," he not only recycled a familiar language of protest, but also expressed a conviction that modern forms of economic organization rendered men dependent. Unable to effectively control the terms of their labor, workingmen were, McNeill claimed, also helpless to stanch a cascade of negative consequences. The enslaved wage laborer experienced not just loss of control at work, but also ill health, reduced intellectual and moral capacity, and, importantly, loss of control over his family—his poverty meant that "his wife is forced from home, and his children from school." McNeill thus argued not only that an industrial economy rendered wage-earning men dependent, but also that the conditions of labor were inextricably bound to a host of other personal, and ultimately social, ills. What impacted the individual also, he argued, redounded socially. Though McNeill's protest acknowledged that lost control and enforced dependence were at the heart of the modern order, his protest hewed to an older, normative sense of liberty. As citizens in a republic, men *should* control their bodies, their labor, and their families—the problem, and not simply the condition, of modern life was that they did not. And while McNeill located the source of workingmen's problems precisely, in the system of wage labor and the greed of capitalists, for many other Americans, modernity brought with it a confused and loosened sense of causation. As Thomas Haskell has argued, for late-nineteenth-century Americans "unambiguous causality was difficult to attribute confidently anywhere" as increasingly distant forces and actors seemed to control even local events. Accustomed to thinking of themselves as independent individuals possessed of free will, the exigencies of an interdependent world called into question the ability of ordinary citizens to comprehend, much less control, the circumstances of their lives.[76]

Crucially, experiences—and representations—of suffering and injury formed a critical part both of Americans' dawning awareness of modern interdependence and of the reevaluation of core liberal ideals. As Barabara Welke has argued, "injury became both catalyst and text in prompting recognition that modern life had made Americans something less than 'free men.'" Increasing mechanization, especially the emergence of new technologies of labor and transportation, was a harbinger not simply of modernization or progress, but also of accident and injury on an unprecedented scale. Injuries sustained by workers and by railroad and streetcar passengers were accompanied by a flood of personal-injury lawsuits in which men and women told courts of grievous pain and bodily damage. Like abolitionists had done for slaves, litigants in personal-injury lawsuits made their wounded bodies into public spectacles that told a story of power, here lost by the individual and abused by the corporation. And like abolitionists had, litigants assumed that a right to bodily integrity was both entailed by and foundational to other rights. Initially, courts responded by applying common-law doctrines of personal injury, which had often assigned liability and responsibility to the injured party. Responsibility for one's own injuries was, courts reasoned, a condition and consequence of freedom. But the tide of injury lawsuits from 1870 forward prompted not only new legislative and regulatory regimes to prevent and compensate accidents, but also new understandings of personal responsibility, liberty, and independence. Like McNeill, personal-injury litigants protested their dependence even as they insisted upon it, arguing that they were helpless in the hands of corporate and mechanized power. As Welke demonstrates, new legal rules increasing corporate responsibility for injury were initially crafted in response to female litigants, who, as women, were not expected to assume responsibility for themselves. Eventually, however, rules made for women were applied to men as litigants, courts, and state agencies designed to regulate modern industries came to believe that modern liberty entailed not autonomy, but protection. Through stories of suffering and attention to the pains of the body, both litigants and courts reshaped the relationship between dependence and rights and argued that rights entailed, rather than limited, state protection. In short, Americans came to realize that "dependence rather than autonomy was a hallmark of modern life," and they came to expect their wounds would be both publicly recognized and compensated. When one railroad company executive protested that new tort laws "reduced all individuals to the level of prattling babe," he recognized a simple truth. In an interdependent world, the meanings of liberal keywords would have to change. So too might the model citizen. No longer the independent man of free-labor mythology, the paradigmatic American might as easily be the helpless dependent, the woman, the child, even the suffering brute.[77]

Anticruelty reformers' discourse of rights, which stressed that rights might be based in sentience, consistent with dependence, and consonant with protection, was, then, neither merely contradictory nor simply anachronistic. Rather, it expressed the profound transformations in liberalism characteristic of the second half of the nineteenth century. Even as the Civil War heralded the triumph of a version of liberalism that linked citizenship and rights to individual independence, self-ownership, and free labor, the conditions unleashed by the war—national economic integration, industrialization, and growing state power—undermined the conditions under which the war's version of citizenship might be realized. Anticruelty reformers, heralding the progressive "emancipation" of slaves, animals, and children, participated in enshrining a static, liberal teleology even as they, too, helped to reshape some of liberalism's fundamental terms.

## CHAPTER FOUR

# "The Dove Has Claws":
# Sympathy and State Power

By the time Etta Wheeler turned to Henry Bergh, she was a desperate woman. She lived in a city crowded with charities designed for the benefit of children—places such as the Institution of Mercy, the American Female Guardian Society, the Home for the Friendless, and the Children's Aid Society—yet none could help her rescue the little girl, Mary Ellen. As the city's charities likely told Wheeler as they turned her away, they could care only for those children who had legally and voluntarily been placed in their custody by parents or guardians.[1]

It was not just desperation, however, that dictated Wheeler's course. Wheeler believed that Bergh's kindness to animals represented not just a particular fondness for dogs and cats, but a more total sensibility, a general disposition to protect the weak from needless pain and suffering—it was that "natural instinct of humanity" she herself possessed.[2] And what Etta Wheeler and Henry Bergh recognized in Mary Ellen Wilson was chiefly a case of helpless suffering, a life story that, in the words of the *New York Times*, "no one can read without emotion."[3] In sympathizing with all sufferers, no matter their species, Henry Bergh affirmed longstanding tropes about humanitarian benevolence. As Etta Wheeler believed, Bergh was a modern version of the "man of feeling," a sympathetic man with a finely honed moral sense, a man whose mercy overflowed conventional boundaries.

But Bergh and his fellow anticruelty workers did more than embody a static ideal. And this, too, was part of Bergh's appeal to Wheeler. For Bergh's fame rested not just on his feelings, but also on his actions: his sympathy with suffering prompted him to decisive action. Combining moral suasion with police work, anticruelty societies were willing to arrest recalcitrant cruelists. Humane societies thus reshaped humanitarianism by creating a hybrid: the private charity endowed with public powers. By advocating law enforcement as the appropriate response to sympathy with suffering, anticruelty organizations went beyond the existing charity tradition and the antebellum humanitarian ideal to create an active, masculinized vision of the humanitarian. Crucially, they associated this with the wielding not just of moral authority but also of state power. In welding sympathy to the state and public powers to their private organizations, anticruelty organizations stood at the crossroads of postbellum transformations in governance.

By the 1870s, Etta Wheeler's assumption that one who cared for animals would naturally care for children, as well as Bergh's assurance that something like progress inexorably linked solicitude for slaves, animals, and children, was underpinned by changes in theology, science, and political philosophy. As we have seen, new ideas about pain and sympathy, rooted in the spread of common sense philosophy, evangelical Christianity, and antebellum reform, underlay the emergence of animal and child protection. By the 1860s, such ideas formed part of a popular sensibility. Even the more abstract ideas of common sense moral philosophy found a large and eager audience and were widely distributed in the antebellum United States through children's books, standard school curriculum, reform propaganda, and moral handbooks designed for a popular audience. Bergh and many of the other men who were instrumental in fostering organized anticruelty would have encountered the ideas of men like Shaftesbury, Hutcheson, and Smith as a part of a standard college education. In part because it seemed to affirm traditional Christian pieties, and in part because it avoided a number of troubling epistemological quandaries, the Scottish common sense school dominated the philosophy curriculum of American universities and theological seminaries from before the Revolution until after the Civil War. In both structure and content, college curricula were remarkably uniform. No matter whether he attended Dartmouth (as did the MSPCA founder George Angell), Columbia (as did Bergh and Elbridge Gerry), or Brown (as did longtime Minneapolis Humane Society president John Day Smith), virtually every male college graduate during the nineteenth century took a course in moral philosophy during his senior year. Typically taught by the college president, this course was presented as the culmination of a young man's education and it promised to integrate the findings of natural science with the teachings of scripture to provide both the principles of morality and the practical resources for living a moral life.[4]

Most commonly, young men did not encounter the Scottish philosophers directly, but read redacted versions of them available in textbooks
such as the widely popular *Elements of Moral Science*, first prepared by
Brown University president Francis Wayland in 1835. During his senior
year at Dartmouth, George Angell was assigned this text as part of the
course in moral philosophy. Divided into sections on "theoretical" and
"practical" ethics, Wayland's text proved not only that morality was composed of fixed laws, but also that each human being had a *"distinct and
separate faculty"* capable of discerning right from wrong—the moral sense.
In practical terms, Wayland outlined man's specific duties to God, to family, to fellow creatures, and to the government. Finally, in a note appended
to the end of his text, Wayland specified "our duty to brutes," another
"class" of "fellow creatures." Reciting arguments that would become standard in anticruelty circles, Wayland reminded his pupils that animals, like
humans, were not only creatures of God but also "sensitive beings, capable
of, probably, as great degrees of physical pleasure and pain as ourselves."
And while this alone did not make animals equal to humans, Wayland
argued that God permitted man to use animals only if they did so kindly,
minimizing their pains in labor and death, and maximizing their happiness in labor and companionship. Excoriating those who would deliberately inflict pain on animals, or who regard the destruction of animals
as mere sport, Wayland voiced the maxim that would later be repeated by
Bergh, Angell, and other anticruelty leaders: "there can be no clearer indication of a degraded and ferocious temper, than cruelty to animals."[5]

Even those who did not attend college were likely to encounter some
version of common sense philosophy. As a young pupil being tutored at
home, Harriet Beecher Stowe, for example, studied the work of Archibald
Alison and Hugh Blair, both important and popular American interpreters of Scottish ideas. Trained at theological seminaries such as Andover,
Princeton, and Yale, freshly ordained preachers also carried common sense
philosophy westward on their mission to save the unredeemed new territories. And, as philosopher and psychologist G. Stanley Hall surmised in a
review of nineteenth-century college textbooks, Americans were unparal-
leled producers of guides to ethical living; these included not only dozens
of formal texts such as Wayland's, but also "scores of printed sermons, lecture courses, letters, guides, manuals and 'own books' addressed to young
men and or young women," all of which reflected the orthodox common
sense view.[6]

Publications praising sympathy and benevolence had become so numerous that, in the same year that Wayland published the first edition of

his influential textbook, two men in upstate New York issued a compendium of such teachings, which they aptly titled *The Spirit of Humanity and Essence of Morality*. We are, they wrote in the book's introduction, "literally deluged" in this "book making age" with a flood of works touching on moral topics; their aim was to bring together the essential writings and topics in one volume. "Its theme," they continued, "possesses an all-absorbing importance, an interest, which every sense and every nerve of man must perceive." Their theme was "Humanity . . . the substance of Morality, of which it is the more intelligible and expressive name." Alongside extracts decrying the evils of slavery, intemperance, gambling, seduction, pugilism, and prison conditions, the authors included extensive writings arguing for kind treatment of animals. To the persistent problem that mankind regarded the "brute creation" as morally irrelevant, the authors suggested that "we should avail ourselves of the close alliance that obtains between the regards of his attention, and those of his sympathy. For this purpose, we should importunately ply him with the objects of suffering, and thus call up its respondent emotions of sympathy." Like Adam Smith, these authors assumed that sympathy was "spectatorial" in nature; like Wayland, they too assumed that animals were proper objects of sympathy. Antebellum children's books made essentially the same point—that kindness to animals reflected a good character and a reverence for God. One parental advisor placed teaching humanity to animals alongside instruction in "the cardinal principles, obedience, a sense of justice, a love of truth and hatred of falsehood."[7] Sunday-school primers likewise instructed children in kindness, making sympathy with animals a supporting plank in the edifice of Christian character.[8]

As the conflict over slavery intensified, abolitionists also relied on the assumption that kindness to animals was an important moral indicator. Lydia Maria Child's 1854 biography of Quaker abolitionist Isaac T. Hopper is a case in point. It illustrates how the idea of a God-given moral sense could not only link humanitarianism and Christianity, but also could serve as a trope structuring the narrative of a life. Child begins her story in Hopper's early years, during which his concern for animals serves as a turning point in his development. At her story's beginning, Hopper is a little prankster who disobeys his mother, misbehaves at school, and goads the family cow into kicking the milkmaid. Hopper's mischief begins to slacken, however, when his father presents the boy with a pet lamb. Isaac quickly becomes devoted to his new pet and in return, the lamb "trotted about after him like a dog." From this moment forward, Child's story is a narrative of humanitarian awakening, of the flowering of Isaac's true "tenderness of spirit." Generalizing outward from the love he felt for his pet lamb, Isaac next saves several squirrels and birds from being hunted by a gang of boys in the forest. After this episode, little Isaac's affections quite naturally became attached to "an old colored man named Mingo." According to Child, Hopper's "sympathizing heart" felt for the man because he knew Mingo had been stolen from his home in Africa and torn apart from his family, just as Isaac feared that the forest animals had been by the gang of boys that had tortured them. He was, Child concludes, "precocious in love." From animals to slaves, the path was a straight and logical one laid by the inner light of Christian love. What began as solicitude for a pet lamb ended with Hopper's dedication to his newspaper column, "Tales of Oppression," which recounted the lives of fugitive slaves.[9] Without arguing that slaves were animalistic, abolitionists linked animals and slaves through a bond of mutual suffering that only compassion could answer.

An 1879 sermon preached by the Reverend David Swing, the Presbyterian minister of Chicago's Central Church, demonstrates both the rejection of pain and the equation of feeling with Christian morality that held sway in postrevival America. Swing's sermon was a pointed call to both the church and his flock to recognize the value of the American Humane Association's work. Asserting that Christianity is theoretically limitless in its love, Swing lamented that in practice it had been too slow to recognize its duties toward "helpless inferiors" such as slaves, children, and animals. Perhaps, he reasoned, this was justified in the past, since "Pains of all kinds were once thought to be very natural," but there was currently no reason for the church to place limits on its benevolence. "When a religion founds itself upon love," he gently chided, "it cannot specify all the cases whither that kindness is to go. . . . for the sublime general term embraces all things in the universe which might possibly suffer." Thus, not only is pain unnecessary, but also the limits of love are unbounded.

Echoing the philosophers of the moral sense school, Swing assured his listeners that if they would confront "those details of cruelty which so abound in the history of man," they would be unable to resist humanitarian action, for "out of information comes emotion; out of emotion comes action." Swing identified both morality and religion so wholly with emotion that he suggested that feeling was more important and powerful even than the institution of the church. For if the church, Swing predicted, should fail to engender unbounded love of the sort that the American Humane Association embodied, congregations would nonetheless transfer their energies and loyalties to the *true* churches, those ostensibly secular institutions of benevolence. The minister, watching his flock flood out the doors of the church, would merely be left behind to contemplate "one more gem lost from the crown of religion." Swing concluded by urging the church to help craft the "perfect manhood," describing this as "a place where many tears and sorrows have met and mingled." It is precisely the capacity of humane work to "regenerate the heart," to awaken the capacity for tears and sorrow, that made it, for Swing, the perfect expression of "the deep stream of Christianity and civilization."[10]

The humanitarian, the embodiment of Swing's tearstained "perfect manhood," would, like Henry Bergh, link kindness to an animal with kindness to a child because both creatures suffered and thus qualified for love. In keeping with the notion that consistent compassion was unbounded, animal protectionists positioned kindness to animals as an index of character in general. Fond of quoting religious texts, they never tired of the biblical maxim "a righteous man regardeth the life of his beast." Not a narrow, specialized concern, concern for animals was, reformers suggested, part of a moral constellation that included Christian virtues such as benevolence, kindness, and sympathy and liberal values of justice, freedom, and liberty. Following such amalgamated logic, the ASPCA's headquarters had the slogan "Justice, Humanity, Compassion" engraved on its façade.[11]

Both Bergh and his supporters took pains to try to fit his unlikely life and personality into the figure of loving humanitarian, fashioning his life so that it might look like Isaac Hopper's. This fashioning seems to have been all the more necessary in Bergh's case since, prior to founding the ASPCA in 1866, he had showed no real signs of a humane sensibility other than the glimmer of sensitivity that perhaps flashed forth when he chose to study literature instead of business at Columbia. The son of wealthy shipbuilder Christian Bergh, Henry lived on his inheritance, attending, but not finishing, college, and rambling around Europe for several years. After returning to the United States and marrying, Bergh went back to Europe, where he lived for many years and where he eventually served as a diplomat in St. Petersburg under Lincoln, a post from which he resigned after two years. Known less for this work and more for his travels, his inheritance, his literary aspirations, and his penchant for wearing a top hat and tails, Bergh, for much of his life, cut the figure of a dandy better than he did that of a humanitarian.[12]

Nonetheless, Bergh and his biographers managed to fit the details of this rather aimless life into the proper emotional trajectory. His chief biographer, for instance, opens her book with a chapter entitled "Friend of Every Friendless Beast," meant to convey the quintessence of Bergh as a man of feeling. Press reports of Bergh likewise emphasized his "large and generous heart."[13] *Harper's* suggested that there was "no truer benefactor" than Bergh, while *Scribner's* crowed that he was "a man of refined sensibilities and tender feelings."[14] In his 1882 moral handbook, *Traits of Representative Men*, author George Bungay included Bergh alongside such luminaries as Ralph Waldo Emerson, Frederick Douglass, Henry Ward Beecher, and Henry Wadsworth Longfellow. A mere look at Bergh's countenance, Bungay claimed, would reveal his unique combination of sympathy and strength. "His portrait has the indefinable look of a gentleman, in which benevolence has the ascendency over the lower and baser faculties. The head is high in the region of the moral and intellectual organization. His face is serious, thoughtful, sympathetic, and shows an earnestness that will not yield to trifling, and a will-power that overcomes obstacles that would appall an ordinary man."[15] Like Bungay, many considered Bergh not just a model humanitarian but also a model human being. More than one publication held up Bergh as an exemplar for other wealthy young men— instead of leading dissipated lives of idleness and indulgence, they could choose, as Bergh had, to dedicate themselves to a benevolent and public-spirited cause.[16]

At the same time as Bergh's admirers in the press were praising his heart, they also frequently claimed that he was motivated by what might seem a more abstract concern: the love of justice.[17] The same biographer who termed Bergh a "friend to friendless beasts" also asserted that "not affection for animals, but a revelation of injustice seems to be the keynote" of his work.[18] Much was also made of the fact that Bergh received no money for his efforts, even though he did the same work as paid SPCA agents, patrolling the streets and bringing cases to court. As one admirer said, "he is working for God, without profit or early reward except the reward of his own noble heart."[19] At the ASPCA's first annual meeting, Bergh explained that only the secretary and detectives received any salary; he worked gratis, and "would continue as long as he lived without other reward than the consciousness that he was doing his duty to his fellow-creatures."[20] Bergh portrayed himself as unsullied by the taint of money or reward and impervious to any influence other than his conviction to serve the right. The claim that Bergh acted on behalf of animals to serve justice functioned in two ways. It firmly located Bergh's actions within the *general disposition* to act kindly, but it also equated kindness with justice, locating the repository of liberal values in the culture of sentiment. His convictions, said one contemporary admirer, were both "just and tender."[21]

In the United States, the fusion of common sense assumptions with

Christian values like those expressed by Bergh and Swing produced a code not just of morals, but also of politics. American proponents of moral sense philosophy believed that the spirit of humanity was expressed not only in the emotion of sympathy, but also in the institutions of liberal democracy. Revolutionary Americans, Gordon Wood has argued, believed that they could build a new society by replacing the patriarchal, monarchical ties of feudal society with other—more affective, more emotional, more natural—ties. Compassion, the gravitational pull of humans toward one another, would facilitate the formal separation of private relations of dependence from political relations of equality by promising a new, universal foundation for social bonds and moral behavior. "The natural feelings of love and benevolence between people," Wood writes, "could become republican substitutes for the artificial monarchical connectives of family, patronage, and dependency and the arrogance, mortification and fear that they had bred."[22] For the Revolutionary generation, sentiment and liberty were linked in a vision of the new nation as defending the identical virtues of humanity and freedom. Sympathetic identification with others, many early Americans believed, would temper the dangers that unchecked self-interest posed to any polity, binding citizens together and strengthening the nation. In American political discourse, then, sympathy was identified with key liberal values of justice, freedom, and liberty—feeling right would make one a natural defender of such values.[23]

Bergh himself explained his career with the assertion that "I always had a natural feeling of tenderness for creatures that suffer."[24] In his frequent communications with the public, Bergh portrayed his desire to defend the "brute creation" as an entirely instinctual, but wholly Christian response to obvious suffering. A speech he delivered on February 8, 1866, in New York City's Clinton Hall, just months before organizing the ASPCA, claimed that his interest in helping animals was founded on his desire to seek justice for those "creatures committed to our care by the Most High."[25] Not only had God given man special custodial duties with regard to animals, but he had also implanted the moral sense necessary to carry out the charge. Kindness to animals was, according to Bergh, "a solemn recognition of that greatest attribute of the Almighty Ruler of the universe, mercy." A few months later, Bergh accepted his post as the president of the ASPCA by calling the organization "the creation of warm hearts—of just generous men, whose cornerstone is Mercy and Humanity to the brute creation." Thus, Bergh himself took fondness for animals as a sign of a love that stretched over all of the earth's creatures and upward to heaven. Bergh's public persona merged sentimentalism, Christianity, and liberalism into an undifferentiated whole: the man who felt right was a true Christian, a defender both of the right and of rights, a man likely to bring heavenly and earthly justice closer together. In an apt pairing, one New Yorker said of Bergh that he "is the law and the gospel in this city."[26]

A well-established vision of the humanitarian informed Etta Wheeler's assumption that Henry Bergh would be interested in the plight of a suffering child. But sympathy with suffering was not the only trait that recommended Bergh to Wheeler. Rather than just reproducing the "man of feeling," Bergh transformed the type: he fused feeling with action. He represented not just the gospel, but also the law. Other New York City institutions—the church, the police, the orphan asylums—may have agreed with Wheeler that Mary Ellen's was a pathetic case, but none were willing, or able, to take ameliorative action. Wheeler's appeal to Bergh was founded on not just the recognition that Bergh felt sympathy, but also on the hope that his sympathy was allied with the willingness and the power to intervene.

Indeed, the transformation of sympathy into action was central to anticruelty organizations' self-conception. At the unveiling of a fountain built by Milwaukee humanitarians to honor Henry Bergh, David Swing remarked that many others before Bergh had professed their outrage at crimes against animals and children, but few had done anything. "The enlightened nations have talked about mercy ever since the days of Christ," Swing said. But Bergh's special genius was that he realized that the time had come "for us to behold in action some part of this mercy. . . . We are rallying today around the name of a man who turned divine thoughts into divine deeds."[27] What Swing identified as Bergh's contribution was the same as that recognized by Wheeler: he went beyond mere sympathy and mercy to "interpose the strong hand of law and justice" between cruelists and their victims.[28] This transformation of the man of feeling into the man of action was both rhetorical and institutional. Anticruelty societies forged a masculinized rhetoric of sympathy and created new organizations endowed with police powers.

Though David Swing clearly believed that Henry Bergh's mercy made him into a man worthy of admiration, the men who organized anticruelty societies struggled to make sympathy consistent with vigorous manhood. However much he was praised, Bergh was not universally canonized. Even those who penned homages to him frequently mention the ridicule that Bergh suffered. George Bungay noted that Bergh had been ridiculed by the press and "from the bar." Others recalled that he was "at first jeered as a

sentimentalist" and regarded by "not a few men of sense" as "a mere en-
thusiast" or as a "fanatic, a visionary, and a follower of Don Quixote."[29]

To feel sympathy for suffering may have been regarded as ideal in college textbooks, but the relationship between sympathetic humanitarianism and manhood was a vexed one. Though the man of feeling was, from
the mid-eighteenth century forward, revered in popular and scholarly
works alike, the emphasis on male feeling fit awkwardly alongside older
gender conventions that identified men with reason, women with feeling.
Even as many late-eighteenth-century men embraced the language of humanitarianism and fellow feeling, and took pride in acts of personal and
organized benevolence, the embrace of emotion required what historian
Bruce Dorsey has described as an elaborate balancing act. "The key for
men of refinement and gentility was to be feeling and sympathetic without falling into the trap of effeminacy." Men involved in Garrisonian abolition, for example, were particularly susceptible to the charge that their
activism, grounded in a language of sympathy with slaves, was unmanly.
In a culture that associated an excess of feeling (what one critic of anticruelty reform called "super humanity") largely with women, a man with
too much feeling could seem irrational rather than evenhanded and just.
Worse, he might become burdened by a distinctly feminine form of excessive emotion—hysteria.[30]

And what was true of the late eighteenth century was even more pronounced by the mid- to late nineteenth century. Though popular fiction,
school curricula, textbooks, and conduct guides continued to distill and
disseminate the basic assumptions and ideals of moral sense philosophy
well after the Civil War, the gendering of sympathy and benevolence as
female proceeded apace. Alongside the feminization and privatization of
Revolutionary-era virtue, the development of a market economy gave rise
to an ideology of domesticity that emphasized women's natural religios-
ity and morality. As a number of historians have shown, this "cult of true
womanhood" identified womanly feeling with transcendent morality,
consolidated middle-class identity, and justified women's benevolent la-
bors outside the home. Endowed with a sense of moral purpose, middle-
class women in the first half of the nineteenth century organized missionary societies, aid to the poor, orphan asylums, and involved themselves
in temperance, abolition, and other reform causes. Whether its aims were
conservative or radical, women's activism nearly always rested on the assumption, or at least the rationalization, that benevolence was not merely
consistent with womanhood, but was its highest and most perfect expression. Thus, although for most mid-nineteenth-century Americans of the

middle class, ideal manhood included traits of virtue, self-restraint, and protection of the weaker members of his household, it was still women who were chiefly identified with the tender feelings of the heart. Indeed, by the turn of the century, male reformers found themselves increasingly susceptible to the charge that they were effeminate meddlers. As Kristin Hoganson has shown, for example, men who supported the international arbitration treaty in the 1890s were derided as womanly and susceptible to "'sentimental gabble.'"[31] In the post–Civil War years, middle-class men responded to the "crisis of masculinity" engendered by bureaucratization, immigration, and the close of the frontier by embracing an aggressive, "muscular" version of masculinity—a far cry from the tenderhearted man of feeling.[32]

While some reform-minded men responded by challenging prevailing definitions of masculinity, others simply tried to make their activities consistent with conventional manhood.[33] Well before this, however, male anticruelty leaders tried to obviate their ridicule as weepy sentimentalists by emphasizing the heroic and manly aspects of their enterprise. In so doing, they reaffirmed that sympathy and self-control were equally masculine and they presented protection of animals and children as a form of knightly chivalry. "What is the oath of gentle blood and knighthood?" asked Illinois Humane Society president John Shortall. "It is to protect the weak and lowly against the strong oppressor."[34] The language of chivalry frequently shaded into outright militarism. Elbridge Gerry, for example, portrayed his organization as confronting a state of war. Calling the cruelists that the NY-SPCC prosecuted the "enemies of children," Gerry enumerated the available "weapons of war": "legal enactments and the support of the Press, with the cooperation of the Judiciary and the supplies for maintaining the fight through the liberality of the Public."[35] In such a context, neither mere relief nor moral suasion could adequately meet the demands of true sympathy. In a state of war, it was not talk but action that was needed. As a later NY-SPCC president put it, "our work is not a missionary or charitable nature. We are . . . 'engaged in the stern task of making war upon crime and vice in peculiar forms.'"[36]

The emphasis on humanitarian work as a form of chivalry was quite pronounced in the organized Bands of Mercy that protectionists formed across the continent. Like the Salvation Army, a contemporary organization that relied on military metaphors and structures, the Band of Mercy movement began in England. In 1882 the movement was brought to the United States by English minister Thomas Timmins and the Massachusetts SPCA leader, George Angell, to serve as a means of humane education for children.[37] Efforts to organize children had begun before 1882, chiefly in the MSPCA's Legions of Honor and the Women's Branch of the Pennsylvania SPCA's Boys' SPCA.[38] By the turn of the century, however, the nationwide Band of Mercy movement had produced over twenty-seven thousand branches with more than eight hundred thousand members.[39] Reformers typically founded groups through existing channels, like Sunday schools, public-school classrooms, and the youth-oriented Loyal Temperance Legions of the WCTU.[40] Organized into small groups, each band consisted of children who agreed to take a pledge promising that "I will try to be kind to all harmless living creatures, and try to protect them from cruel usage." Band of Mercy advocates suggested that groups meet once a month to "study the subject of kindness to all living creatures" through reading and discussion, recitation, speeches, and songs. Several books and articles detailing Band of Mercy songs and lesson plans were published and available for use.[41]

Humane educators were unabashed in declaring that "the American Bands of Mercy make for the Heart, the centre of life." The point of inculcating kindness in children was so that they would "enter into loving sympathy with all life" and grow into moral adults. Emphasizing feeling and sympathy as the basis of morality, the clubs represented another vehicle for the dissemination of a popularized moral sense philosophy. But as much as the bands were depicted as schools for "heart training," they were also presented as schools of Christian knighthood that taught "the Order of Chivalry, of the Golden Rule." Speaking before the New England Assembly, George Angell explained that, like the knights of old, these new knights fought for Christianity, "but for a living Christianity; a Christianity which shall abolish cruelty, and crime, and wars, and every form of violence, and usher in that millennial age, sung by poets, foretold by prophets, and heard by shepherds on the plains of Judea."[42] What transformed mere sympathy into chivalry, then, was the willingness to take action and make mercy a "living" precept. In the ASPCA's Band of Mercy organization called the Young Defender's League, child members were given badges and training as miniature agents of the society in order to report acts of cruelty.[43] Bands of Mercy transformed sympathy into protection and assimilated a tender, feminine heart with masculine aggression through the medium of chivalry.

The transformation of sympathy into action was what anticruelty leaders considered the greatest innovation of their movement and its organizational model. Frances Rowley, secretary of the American Humane Association in 1897, likewise contrasted mere sympathy "and bland pity"

**Figure 9.** A dual nature: the American Humane Association Seal. AHA,
*Report of the Proceedings, Twenty-Third Annual Convention of the American
Humane Association* (Fall River, MA.: s.n., 1899). Oberlin College Library.

with true humanity, which he deemed "armed, aggressive, and alert, never
slumbering and never wearying, moving like an ancient hero over the
land to slay monsters."[44] Protectionist organizations consistently stressed
that they served both sentiment and action, mercy and justice, Christianity and the law. Far from departing from Christian teachings, animal and
child protectionists believed that aggressive action to stop cruelty merely
insured that earthly and heavenly justice would finally merge. The corporate seal of the societies that protected both animals and children reflected this duality (fig. 9). Designed by the secretary of the Columbus,
Ohio, Humane Society, the *Humane Journal* explained the seal's iconog-
raphy. "On one side of the shield an angel of mercy outstretches her arm
in behalf of the dumb beast against its cruel driver, and on the other justice and law interpose their authority in protecting little children from
the brutal treatment to which they are subjected by an inhuman parent.
These illustrations," the *Journal* continued, "are very suggestive and elo-
quently typify and illustrate the work of the humane societies."[45] Both the
angel and Minerva, the female protector, represent moments of clear and
decisive intervention, and their appearance side by side suggests that the
sources of this action may lie equally in Christian or liberal visions of
justice.[46]

The experience and subsequent image of the Civil War helped North-
erners to link sympathy with stern, even militaristic, protection. Between
1869 and 1870 a series of stories entitled "The Judge's Pets" appeared in
the juvenile *Riverside Magazine*. In the story's principal male figures, the
Judge and his son George, their affection for animals indexes their general
goodness. In the person of the Judge, humane sympathy is fused with justice and with the administration of the law. Readers immediately learn
that "Everything loved the Judge." This was especially true of children
and animals, since he was so kind to both, a fact they immediately recognized. "Children made him their chief playfellow" and "no dog or cat ever
failed to know him for a friend at the first meeting." The Judge's "Christian and philanthropic" nature warranted the immediate and instinctual
trust of all whom he met, a trait that proved useful as he rounded up er-
rant pigs and led his children safely through the fields full of cows, whom
he was teaching them to love.[47] It must have come as no surprise, then, for
readers to learn in the next installment of the tale that this kind Judge had
harbored a runaway slave who was now, as a free but faithful servant, like
a member of the family.[48]

Where the Judge assimilated humanity with the law, his eldest son
George embodied the combination of humanity with military valor. A soldier for the North in the Civil War, George is described as a valiant fighter
in battle, a true man who balanced bravery and compassion so well that
even his enemies "never feared injury to their women and children from
his command." Taking a bullet in the "heart that had beaten so warmly
with the love of all God's creatures," George dies on the battlefield. After
his death, the story follows George's pets, the horse Charlie and the dog
Governor Wise, as they return home from the war in his stead, and details
the grieving family's attachment to these animals that now serve as surrogate children. After making it clear how much George was esteemed and
how much he is missed, the author concludes with an appeal to the audience: "Boys, if you would be like George when he was a man . . . you must
try to be now what he was as a boy. No cruel or cowardly boy ever made
a noble man. Begin now. Be kind to all little, dumb, dependent creatures,
and never be afraid to do anything which it is plainly right to do."[49] Not
only compassion, but also bravery, the story suggested, made one a noble
man, like George the war hero, or a fair man, like the Judge.

Some of the men involved in anticruelty reform had, like the fictional
George, direct experience with the Civil War. John Day Smith served as a
color guard in a Maine regiment and was wounded in the Civil War before
becoming a lawyer, a judge, a longtime president of the Minneapolis Hu-

mane Society, and later a judge in the city's juvenile court. In recollecting
his war experience late in his life, Smith suggested that the war had taught
him about suffering and solicitude. Shot in the face at the battle of Jeru-
salem Plank Road in Virginia, Smith was told by army surgeons that his
case was hopeless and they left him to bleed to death in front of a hospital
tent. But when he saw wounded men being moved onto wagons he begged
an army nurse to let him on. Piled in with five other wounded men, Smith
lay on the hard floor of the wagon listening to the "crying and moaning"
of the other men, some of whom died en route, lying next to him. "I shall
never forget the agony and suffering of the night," he recalled. Smith described the painful surgery on his face—done without anesthesia—and a
painful train ride north. "The jarring of the train made my wound almost
unbearable. . . . I was suffering intense pain." Smith only managed to make
it back to Augusta, Maine, with the help of kind strangers—someone from
the Sanitary Commission who finds him lying on a bench at the Baltimore
train station, a tender nurse, a man on a bus in New York who gives him
one dollar. Smith reckoned that his wounded face was "sufficiently hid-
eous to extract sympathy" from strangers.[50] Having suffered extreme pain,
helplessness, and having learned the importance of sympathy and the
kindness of strangers, Smith went on to a career that combined concern
for suffering with legal enforcement. In his person, he combined what anticruelty reformers believed were the crucial components of their distinctive institutional identity.

Where popular fiction suggested that manly sympathy could be expressed either through the law or through military action, anticruelty organizations combined the two. While much anticruelty rhetoric sought to
masculinize sympathy by arguing that its entailments were closer to cou-
rageous and protective chivalry than to self-indulgent tears, anticruelty
organizations also believed that they differed from mere sentimentalists
because they practiced law enforcement rather than charity. As Elbridge
Gerry put it, the humane society served as "the hand of the Law, attached
to the arm of the Law, created for the enforcement of the Law."[51] Beginning with Bergh's ASPCA in New York, animal and child protection agencies were delegated police powers by the state. "The objects of this society," declared the ASPCA bylaws, are "to enforce all laws which are now,
or may hereafter be, enacted for the protection of animals; and to secure
by lawful means the arrest, conviction and punishment of all persons violating such laws."[52] As Bergh, Gerry, and other anticruelty leaders saw the
matter, police powers expressed rather than conflicted with their humanitarian ideals. Illinois Humane Society president John Shortall explained

that by performing good deeds, his organization had earned its "Christian-like name—humane society." But what Shortall found especially gratifying was that the society had a police power. "It seems a misnomer," he admitted, that an organization so clearly dedicated to Christian ideals of "mercy, charity, love" should be undertaking arrests and prosecutions. "But in this case," Shortall explained, "the dove has claws—sharp claws—and uses them, too, as it has occasion." By using its police powers, the Illinois Humane Society could arrest "the arm uplifted to strike" even as it taught lessons of kindness. This "dual nature," as Shortall called it, was, he claimed, "patterned after the highest condition taught in the Word."[53]

Incorporated as private organizations, SPCA, SPCC, and humane society agents nonetheless roamed the streets wearing badges that entitled them to arrest violators of state anticruelty statutes and relevant municipal ordinances (see fig. 10). As one SPCA president put the matter, "The officers of the Society are clothed with ample police powers. They wear a distinctive uniform and patrol the streets by day and by night. They have full power to arrest and prosecute offenders against laws relating to animals." The delegation of police powers varied according to an organization's charter and the statutes governing its operation. Most states, though, followed the same arrangement as New York and Illinois. In those states, men who had been chosen as agents by a duly incorporated humane organization applied to the local magistrate, police, or sheriff, who awarded the powers individually to applicants. In Colorado, for example, when humane society secretary Hugo Preyor wrote to Henry Deitz to inform him that he had been made the organization's agent for Boulder, he explained that "you will have your Mayor swear you in as Special Police officer, also the sheriff of your county as Deputy Sheriff, enabling you to make arrests anywhere in the county." While applicants could be rejected on any number of grounds (and in fact Boulder County's sheriff refused to make Deitz one of his deputies), once an agent was given police powers, they could not be taken away so long as the agent remained in the employ of the humane society.[54] And in most states with an active humane society, statutes governing cruelty required that all peace officers cooperate with the enforcement efforts of anticruelty organizations and their members. Commonly, statutory language provided that any member of a humane society "may require, and it shall be the duty of any sheriff, deputy sheriff, constable, or police officer, or the agent of any such association . . . to arrest any person found violating the laws in relation to cruelty to persons and animals." Besides having police powers and the mandatory cooperation of other law enforcement bodies, the close identification of humane societies

**Figure 10.** Private police: ASPCA officers in uniform. American Society for the Prevention of Cruelty to Animals, *Twenty-Seventh Annual Report* (New York: s.n., 1893), frontispiece.

with the law was maintained in other ways as well. In many towns and cities, humane society leaders were composed of lawyers, while agents were sometimes active or former members of the constabulary or the judiciary. Society agents often appeared before the bench to prosecute their own cases in court, while the largest humane societies employed staff attorneys.[55]

When they incorporated law enforcement as a goal, anticruelty organizations identified their activities with law, justice, and the state. It was not just their rhetoric, but also their organizational form that anticruelty leaders used to masculinize benevolence. The identification of anticruelty with law enforcement virtually guaranteed that the public face of the societies would be male. Operating in the years before women were added to municipal police forces, anticruelty leaders simply assumed that police work, whether public or private, was the province of men. Likewise, the lawyerly aspect of their operation—the trying of cases—was also coded male. They were hardly alone in thinking that women were fit neither for law enforcement nor lawyering. In 1875, a Wisconsin judge denied a woman's right to practice law in that state by arguing from the conventional wisdom that "nature has tempered women as little for the juridical conflicts of the courtroom, as for the physical conflicts of the battlefield." Widely excluded from the bar for most of the nineteenth century, even in 1910 women amounted to just over 1 percent of American lawyers. By that date, some municipalities had begun to add female officers to their police departments, but they nonetheless resisted giving them the important symbols and mechanisms of police authority: uniforms and weapons. "You might just as soon send out so many children," sniped Chicago's chief of police. Nor was the masculine character of the anticruelty movement unique. The displacement of women from their prominent antebellum role in charity organizations was a feature of Gilded Age reform in general. With the rise of "scientific charity"—a turn away from outdoor relief and toward the secularization and systematization of charity work—leaders of private relief organizations across the nation wrested organizational control from female volunteers.[56]

The assumption that only men could perform the law-enforcement functions of the anticruelty organization was so widespread that it was rarely discussed. Rather, it surfaced when challenged. Such was the case in Philadelphia, where the all-male PSPCA was often in friction with its sister organization, the Women's Branch. Though the organizational force behind the PSPCA was a woman, Caroline Earle White, when the society was formed she was not allowed to serve on the board of directors. Instead, while her husband served on the PSPCA's board, White formed the Women's Branch. More than a traditional auxiliary, its female members did a good deal of the same work as the male society, except for arrest and prosecution. Whether the Women's Branch had any police powers was the subject of some dispute between the two organizations. Though the female auxiliary was organized under the same general laws that granted police powers to the PSPCA, that organization denied that its sister society could conduct law enforcement. White went before the state legislature in 1883 to lobby for a bill that would explicitly grant police powers to her branch organization, but despite the fact that all her branch agents were male, Pennsylvania legislators could not countenance a grant of state police authority to women. White probably was not even seeking police powers for women; rather, just for a woman-run organization. For even the leaders of women's auxiliaries assumed that their agents should be male. When Mrs. E. F. Brady of the Women's Humane Society of Missouri wrote to the Illinois Humane Society about the horrible condition of mules and horses over the border in East St. Louis, she assumed that only a man could clear up the situation. "Do you happen to know of a suitable man who would be willing to act as a Spec. Agent at East St. Louis," she asked, "or could you direct us to some person in that city who would look up such a man for us?" Though Brady wanted her all-female organization to help stop cruel treatment of animals in the industries along the Mississippi River, she did not believe that she, or any of her members, should directly remonstrate or arrest the male handlers of the city's myriad working animals.[57]

Records of the Illinois Humane Society reveal that from the turn of the century forward, some humane societies did begin to employ female agents. Perhaps unsurprisingly, the practice was presented as a novel departure. Organized in 1899, the Anti-Cruelty Society (ACS) was formed as a woman's auxiliary of the Illinois Humane Society. Several years before it would employ its first female police matrons, the city of Chicago awarded the women of the ACS badges to enforce municipal ordinances. Chicago newspapers found the new arrangement startling. Similarly, in 1900, a local organizer wrote to the IHS to announce that her branch society had begun to employ a female agent. "We have with us what the little boys call a *lady police!* We have in fact a most energetic woman agent, who confounds the gentlemen police to their most utter confusion. She has the insignia of office, a policeman's star." The sight of a woman endowed with police powers continued to confound many of Illinois's boys and men for years to come. Even as late as 1912, Shelbyville, Illinois, activist Emma Hamlin wrote to complain that though she had been appointed the society's special agent for her town, she could not receive a grant of police powers from her local authorities. This, she believed, rendered her useless. "I find that a woman being special agent with no police power is just the same as running things alone," she confided. Even if she could persuade local police to make an arrest, she predicted that she could not win in court. "If I arrest them they will beat me—because I'm a woman as much as any reason."[58]

Where male anticruelty officers could present themselves as the "strong arm of the law," female officers ran the risk of stirring up scorn and resentment; a woman could appear meddlesome rather than just. In 1913, Mrs. Merle F. Eshbaugh, the president of the Evanston (IL) Humane Society brought ten cases of cruelty to horses before her local judge, Justice Harrison. He promptly dismissed all ten cases. Accusing Eshbaugh of overzealousness, Harrison remarked that she "wouldn't know a horse from a hornless cow." Besides heaping scorn on her for acting out of emotion rather than expertise, Harrison infantilized her, claiming that "since Mrs. Eshbuagh was elected president of this society she has been like a small boy with his first little red wagon." Chicagoan Mrs. Fred Packard also found herself to be the object of disdain when she started a splinter organization specializing in horse protection. In the beginning, Packard recalled in 1911, she "met with some unpleasantness." When she approached teamsters and reprimanded them for overloading, beating, or working sore horses, "they insisted my place was home 'washing the dishes.'" Undeterred by the suggestion that her interference with men's business was unwomanly, Packard assured the teamsters that they need not worry about her—her dishes were clean. Teamsters were used to dealing with male police and Packard found that "for a woman to interfere did not meet their approval."[59] And though it is likely that the teamsters' dislike of Packard rested as much on class resentment as sexism, the discord between law enforcement and womanhood gave shape to gendered expressions of scorn.

The degree of ire aroused by women endowed with police power may have been inflected by which anticruelty activities, in particular, women were engaged in. The examples above suggest that women were not welcome when they tried to enforce animal protection statutes. But the records of the Minneapolis Humane Society, which also employed female agents beginning in the early twentieth century, do not record the same opposition. Its female agents, however, only worked on cases involving domestic affairs. In 1911, the MHS had two female agents: Mrs. E. C. Bascomb and Emilie Glorieux. While the society's male agents worked on both animal and child cases, Bascomb and Glorieux attended solely to cases of girls and women, and only Glorieux, who was a municipal policewoman detailed to the humane society, appears to have had police powers. Among the first generation of policewomen, Glorieux's limited duties would have been typical. Similar to other early-twentieth-century maternalist rhetoric in reform and suffrage circles, the creation of female police was justified in terms of gender difference. Female police were not designed to perform the same activities as male police; rather, they would bring their nurturance and empathy to assist the women and children who wended their way through the legal system.[60]

While women infrequently served as anticruelty agents even in the twentieth century, they nonetheless performed a number of critical functions. In Philadelphia, for example, the Women's Branch concentrated its considerable energy on running the nation's first animal shelter and developing boy's branches of the PSPCA. In its focus on direct relief and humane education, the activities of Pennsylvania's Women's Branch reflect the gendered division of labor that characterized many SPCAs, SPCCs, and dual humane organizations. Though female membership hovered around a third of its total, the New York SPCC, for example, did not create a women's auxiliary until 1912. Once formed, the auxiliary was charged with overseeing the work of sheltering, feeding, and clothing the children who required temporary shelter in the society's rooms.[61] When, in 1910, the women's auxiliary of the ASPCA officially incorporated as the New York Women's League for Animals, its members busied themselves running a dispensary for animals, putting on an annual workhorse parade, and promoting humane education.[62] Likewise, the participation of the Woman's Christian Temperance Union in animal and child protection mirrored the split within existing organizations. Though the WCTU adopted the anticruelty cause in 1888 under the auspices of its Department of Mercy, this all-female organization never sought police powers as a part of its work but instead focused on humane education efforts, ending the use of birds in millinery, and antivivisection legislation. As Christians, they felt the duty of mercy called them; as mothers, they felt it their duty to mold children properly; as women, they aided the formal incorporation of humane education into the duties of the largely feminized teaching profession. Reflecting the drift of their work, in 1914 the WCTU changed the name of the Department of Mercy to the Humane Education Department.[63]

Well into the twentieth century, the female face of the anticruelty movement was associated with humane education, direct relief to sick animals and children in temporary custody, and the creation of "homes" for animals—animal shelters. By contrast, the male leadership associated itself with decisive action born of tender feelings. The man of feeling was now a private policeman; he brought not only his personal feelings, but also the force of the law, to protect those he deemed helpless.

Harnessing sympathy to police power changed more than just the popular image of the humanitarian or the gendered terms of reform. Commenting on anticruelty legislation, one contemporary legal scholar noted that their "peculiar feature" was the "partial reliance upon voluntary associations for the enforcement of the law."[64] The arrangement was "peculiar" because it blurred the boundary between public and private, between state responsibility and voluntarism. In other ways, however, the arrangement was typical of the relationship between urban police and urban reform in the second half of the nineteenth century. Indeed, the line between public and private responsibility for crime, public order, and social welfare was often in flux. Anticruelty organizations not only contributed to this flux, but by using the law to effect reform, they helped create a new role for law as a preventative, even therapeutic tool for shaping the social order.

The unsteady division of responsibility for governing the nineteenth-century polity was due in part to the fact that, for much of the century, police were not identified chiefly as specialists in fighting crime. Rather, as a formalized and professional police force grew out of the ancient constable and watch system, police were charged with the broad mandate to maintain peace and order. This involved police in cities from New York and Boston to New Orleans and San Francisco in a wide array of duties, including tending to social welfare and public health. As one historian has argued, "the political ideal in police work was routine municipal housekeeping." Besides prosecuting crime, urban police tended streetlamps, maintained sewers, removed obstructions from the roadways, fed and lodged the homeless, returned lost children to parents, inspected docks, carriages, and omnibuses, issued licenses for serving liquor, controlled building permits, and rang fire alarm bells. Many of these duties had been incorporated into police work during the antebellum years, and both the development of professional police forces and the broad set of duties assigned them reflect the changing character of municipal government. In response to rapid urban growth, cities began taking over, and attempting to rationalize, services—everything from sewage, police, fire, and road construction—that were formerly provided on a private, for-profit basis. Thus the initial formalization of police forces and myriad police duties represented an expansion of the public sector. But by the century's end, as police increasingly specialized in crime control, municipalities redistributed the responsibilities of police. Some of these they gave to newly created departments of city administration such as health, and streets and sanitation. Other functions were in essence reprivatized as, for example, proponents of scientific charity in cities like New York and Chicago lobbied to prevent police from distributing soup and housing the homeless in an effort to monopolize, and hence to control the terms of, poverty policy.[65]

The drawing of firmer lines between police and charity functions, and between public and private forms of charity, was one dimension of policing's late-nineteenth-century flux; the privatization of specific law enforcement duties was another. Even though the narrowing of police responsibilities was designed in part to make urban police more effective at controlling crime, many elite reformers were dismayed at what they saw as police inability, or unwillingness, to control the dens of vice and sin that bred the intemperance, prostitution, and poverty that threatened to destabilize the fragile social order. Beyond being ineffective, elites suspected that the police were in outright collusion with the purveyors of vice. As one midcentury New Yorker described his city's police, they were "partly awed by the blackguards of the local brothel and groggery, partly intimate with them." This assessment was not without merit. By the end of the century, investigative commissions in Atlanta, New York, Philadelphia, Baltimore, Chicago, Los Angeles, San Francisco, and Kansas City had all concluded that most police in large cities operated as cogs in the powerful political machines controlled by Democrats. Beholden to ward bosses whose political power rested, in turn, with the very populations whom elites, mostly Republicans, wanted to reform—the immigrant poor—most police had little incentive to enforce existing morals legislation.[66]

In response, frustrated elites in several cities formed quasi-vigilante organizations designed to enforce the vice laws that the regular police steadfastly ignored. During the 1860s, the New England Society for the Suppression of Counterfeiting received state funds to combat graft. In the next decade, Anthony Comstock founded the Society for the Suppression of Vice (SSV) in New York City, Presbyterian minister Howard Crosby founded the Society for the Prevention of Crime (SPC) in the same city, and Boston reformers formed a New England branch of the SSV and a Citizens Law and Order League. Though SPCs and SSVs differed from anticruelty organizations in terms of specific goals, they also, as historian Timothy Gilfoyle has argued, shared a similar orientation to reform. Like anticruelty organizations, other self-styled preventative organizations adopted a masculine rhetoric of aggressive protection and comprised male reformers who believed that law enforcement was critical to social reform; they also were granted—or simply exercised—police powers to enforce select laws. And, as we have seen, animal and child protectionists defined cruelty in ways that overlapped with the concept of "vice." Not only were specific antisocial activities—such as prostitution, intemperance, "immoral" entertainments, and animal fighting (associated with gambling)—deemed exemplary of both cruelty and vice, but also both anticruelty and antivice reformers shared a fundamental revulsion at behavior that indulged base passions at the expense of self-control. In San Francisco, the institutional and conceptual similarities between anticruelty and antivice reform were made manifest in the union of the Pacific Society for the Suppression of Vice with the Society for the Prevention of Cruelty to Children and Animals. In addition to working to "prevent cruel and inhuman treatment of children, animals and human beings," the combined organization sought "the promotion of the public morals and the removal, as far as possible, of all corrupting influences."[67]

At the same time that urban elites sought to purify police work—and the social body—by privatizing select law enforcement functions, a host of other private police functioned to blur the lines between municipal police and the private sector. Private detectives, of which the Pinkerton National Detective Agency is but the most famous, prowled streets and workplaces, often indistinguishable in appearance, manner, and authority from municipal police detectives. Not until the Pinkertons' bloody intervention in the 1892 Homestead Strike did public officials begin to worry that, in the words of a congressional committee, "such use of private armed men is an assumption of the State's authority by private citizens." Though it was the Pinkertons that became famous for their role in strikebreaking and labor discipline, they were not alone in patrolling the private interests of capital while cloaked in public, or quasi-public, powers. In Massachusetts, as in other states, the legislature could create "special police," a grant it often used to license men to guard businesses, monitoring customers and employees alike. Since 1865, the state of Pennsylvania had granted its police powers to designated employees of railroad, coal, and iron companies. As one analyst of the state's private police noted, "this gives rise to a legal anomaly—a public police officer who is at once a private police officer."[68]

Certainly the grant of public powers to private interests had inherent dangers. Some observers worried that the existence of private police forces like the Pinkertons would undermine the credibility of regular police. While that fear was grounded in a sense that private police might be more effective than their uniformed brethren, it was just as likely that private police might use their powers in highly selective and destructive ways.

The participation by Pinkertons and other private police in battles between capital and labor certainly illustrates this, but the problem plagued even humane societies. Some anticruelty organizations in California and Illinois, for example, had to fend off pretenders, organizations that falsely incorporated under the anticruelty laws in an attempt to gain their powers for vigilante or political ends. In San Francisco, the Pacific Humane Society was organized by a group of strikebreakers. Unable to find any other way to secure weapons permits, the men incorporated as a humane society.[69] Thus, even as municipal police forces sought to more clearly distinguish themselves as a set of distinct professionals (all city forces adopted the trademark blue uniform during the nineteenth century in order to signal the separation of police from civilians), a range of factors—from the shifting array of police responsibilities to the growth of private policing practices—acted to blur public and private, state and society. In some respects, the privatization of law enforcement contracted state responsibility; in other ways, however, more individuals, in more places, and at more times, carried the state with them not as an abstraction, but as a force they embodied in their person.

Embodying police power in their persons was, in the minds of many anticruelty reformers, an essential tool. Certainly anticruelty leaders believed that state authority was a crucial component of reform. One reason Henry Bergh wanted his ASPCA vested with police power was because he had discovered the efficacy of official power while serving as a diplomat in St. Petersburg, Russia. Appalled by the treatment of draught horses, Bergh found that, dressed in his civilian clothes, his personal efforts to end the beating and overloading of carthorses were useless. Drivers simply ignored his requests for gentler treatment. But when he remonstrated with drivers while dressed in his diplomat's uniform, their response was different. Apparently awed by his official insignia, they bowed to his requests.[70] Local humane society officers similarly prized their badges as symbols of legal power without which they could not function effectively. President of the Chicago Heights branch of the Illinois Humane Society, C. S. Tisdale, for example, wrote to the parent organization requesting more badges for the branch's members. "This to show that these people have some backing in their work," he explained in his appeal.[71] Like Bergh, Tisdale and his branch members believed that their ability to stop cruelty lay in their power to appear before offending cruelists not as individuals but as representatives of the law; it lay, in other words, in their power to prosecute.

Though Bergh and other anticruelty agents prized their legal powers and the aura of authority associated with uniforms and badges, their relationship to municipal police was both ambiguous and ambivalent. Not only did organizations privately incorporated to enforce public laws with public powers strain the distinction between state and personal authority, but also individuals shuttled back and forth across the line. In some cities, for example, municipal police appointed officers to detail work in the service of anticruelty organizations. Police officer Stuart Dean served twenty-three of his twenty-seven years in the Chicago Police Department on assignment to the Illinois Humane Society. In smaller towns across Illinois, the state humane society appointed local policemen as its special agents. In Minneapolis, the humane society also had police assigned to serve fulltime as its agents.[72]

Besides being confusing, relations with police could be either cooperative or strained. From its beginning, the Massachusetts SPCA found Boston's police quite helpful. At the behest of their chief, the force distributed thousands of copies of the state's new animal protection laws and of George Angell's brainchild, *Our Dumb Animals*. Where antivice organizations tended to openly criticize local police as inept and corrupt, anticruelty spokesmen generally put the matter in softer terms, explaining that private enforcement of humane laws was necessary not because the ordinary police were immoral, but because, as Wyoming's Humane Society said of the police, "these men have their hands full with the ordinary affairs of life and they are not experts in every line." Though anticruelty organizations were happy to assume responsibility for enforcing the very same laws that were their raison d'être, they still wanted to cultivate good relations with police. Some societies took the time each year to pass resolutions thanking the police for their assistance and cooperation; others made all local police officers honorary members.[73]

Nevertheless, audible rumblings of discontent could be heard. Perhaps unsurprisingly, San Francisco's combined SSV, SPCA, and SPCC used its annual reports as a platform to lambaste the police and the judges in police courts for putting political favors above public-spirited law enforcement. And in a synopsis of its 1877 annual meeting, the Illinois Humane Society reported that while many Chicago policemen had been helpful to the society, "we feel constrained to say that our city police do not seem to comprehend that the enactments for the protection of animals are as much the laws of the state as any upon the statute book, and equally entitled to enforcement." The problem was not unique to large cities like Chicago and San Francisco. Small-town police could be equally reluctant. When Mrs. McOwin of Aurora, Illinois, wrote to the Illinois Humane Society, she complained that "this city like all other citys is run Politically, and when a city is run by politics you may never expect people so connected will do much Humane work." Juxtaposing politics with true humanity, Mrs. McOwin explained that the local police "will not do this work for fear of enemies and they will loose their job." With no police support, the woman recommended that the state humane society appoint a special officer. She suggested Aurora resident Ervin Davis because he was "a man that is out of politics." Unlike the police, Davis "stands alone on principles" and is "independent of the support of the public."[74]

The dangers of police collusion with the "public" rather than with "principles" was made all too clear in the case of Colorado Humane Society agents Mr. and Mrs. S. A. Bella, a rare husband-and-wife team. In January of 1902, the Bellas attempted to arrest a man who had left his team of horses standing out "on one of the coldest nights" while he went inside a tavern to drink. The notion that men all too readily abandoned their horses to the elements in favor of drink was, by the turn of the century, a recurrent trope in anticruelty literature. Clearly, the Bellas believed it was coming to life before their very eyes. And though both Bellas had been involved in the attempted arrest, it was Mrs. Bella who bore the brunt of popular anger. According to the local newspaper, a crowd of "Durango toughs" not only had Mrs. Bella arrested for *making an arrest*, but also they subjected her to an encyclopedic variety of vigilante methods. An angry crowd captured and tortured her pet dog, dumped garbage on her doorstep, and nailed a sign to her door "warning that she will be tarred and feathered and ridden on a rail if she does not cease prosecutions for cruelty to animals." While being led to jail by the town marshal, Mrs. Bella was followed and jeered by "a mob of a hundred or more." Acting in collusion with the marshal and the mob, the local district attorney asserted that "the state agents have no right to interfere in cruelty cases in the town." Upon hearing the news, secretary of the state humane society retorted that "state laws always take precedence over district attorneys and town marshals who are not in sympathy with them."[75] Partially a contest over prevailing standards of morality, partly a misogynist attack on Mrs. Bella's attempt to exercise police authority, and partly a battle for sovereignty between the forces of localism and state centralization, the Durango case was but an extreme example of the tensions created by the transfer of state power to private citizens.

In turning to law enforcement to enact change, anticruelty organizations remade the ideal humanitarian into a man not simply of feeling, but also of action. By deploying police powers, they also participated in shaping the confusing landscape of nineteenth-century policing, helping both to expand and to contract the powers, presence, and responsibilities of municipal and state governments. At the same time as they competed, cooperated, and intersected with municipal police forces, anticruelty organizations had a close relationship to another, more abstract notion of police. The laws enforced by anticruelty organizations fell under the purview of the notoriously vague police powers afforded to state and municipal governments. According to Blackstone's 1769 *Commentaries*, police was the power to make "individuals of the state, like members of a well-governed family, conform their general behavior to the rules of propriety, good neighborhood, and good manners." Before the development of formal police forces, "police" referred as much to a state of affairs (the achievement of social harmony, security, and collective wellbeing) as it did to the mechanisms (constabulary, regulations, government administration) by which that state might be achieved.[76]

By the time that anticruelty organizations were founded following the Civil War, American states and municipalities had already used their police powers to develop an extensive body of laws regulating private property and personal conduct; there was, moreover, a well-developed jurisprudence upholding state regulation on the grounds of state police power. In his influential 1904 treatise on police power, legal scholar Ernst Freund surveyed the explosion of regulations enacted during the nineteenth century and surmised that police power could be differentiated from other powers of the state by its unique combination of goals and methods. Its goals were "to secure and promote the public welfare," and its methods were "restraint and compulsion." According to Freund, police encompassed legislation protecting safety, order, morals, and legislation regulating both labor and capital. Laws protecting animals from cruelty also fell under police regulation. Freund placed such laws under the heading of "public morals" protection. Fellow treatise writer Christopher Tiedeman, however, considered such laws under "state regulation of personal property." Both, however, agreed that state regulation of the family—and hence of children—was properly undertaken, as Tiedeman put it, "for the promotion of the general welfare."[77] At least some anticruelty reformers were aware that, in addition to being delegated police powers, their very ability to control peoples' treatment of animals and children was a function of a more abstract notion of police. According to one, "the rights of property and their invasion under the police power . . . [are the] most important and least understood point in humane work."[78] Acting as proponents for an enlarged police power, humane societies supported regulation of property and the redefinition of property interests in terms that linked private behavior with the public good.

Though police powers were well established under America's federalist system, and though a substantial body of police legislation existed by the time that most anticruelty legislation was enacted, it was also embroiled in controversy. Indeed, the postbellum years saw not only the flourishing of police legislation, but also significant challenges to state regulation. Because the Fourteenth Amendment made the Bill of Rights applicable to the states, challenges to police regulations could now be brought on the grounds that they violated equal protection or due-process rights. Thus in a host of cases, plaintiffs during the last third of the nineteenth century mounted challenges to local and state rules governing slaughterhouses, the sale of liquor and cigarettes, the location of particular types of businesses, the hours and conditions of labor, the terms of carrying railroad freight, and more. This is not surprising given that, as Christopher Tomlins has argued, "police," rooted in notions of the commonweal, was conceptually at odds with "law," rooted in individuals and a vision of their antagonistic relations with both state and society. In the late nineteenth century, these tensions came to a head as courts were asked to weigh the inalienable rights of private property against the claims of the public welfare. In response, courts began to apply a more careful scrutiny to regulations to determine whether they actually, or merely purported to, serve the public order, morals, or wellbeing.[79]

Humane societies were not immune to these challenges. Particularly because their animal protection duties gave them the right to seize, and even kill, maltreated animals, they frequently encroached on private property rights and were challenged on due-process grounds. Likewise, when some locales established dog licensing laws, and made anticruelty organizations into the administrators of such laws, aggrieved dog owners charged that the state had given humane societies an illegal monopoly.[80] Because parents and guardians could not claim that external regulation of their children was an invasion of property rights, police-based challenges to child protection laws were less frequent. But they did happen. In *People v. Ewer* (1894), Charlotte Ewer was convicted of violating a New York law prohibiting the "employment or exhibition" of girls under 16 in a theater. Citing the *Slaughterhouse* cases, Ewer appealed her conviction on the grounds that the law under which she was convicted was an unconstitutional violation of "natural and inalienable rights" and an invalid "exercise of the police power of the state." The New York Court of Appeals upheld

Ewer's conviction, declaring that the because children's development was of "paramount interest" to the state, legislation like that in question, designed to ensure that "the child shall become a healthful and useful member of the community," was a legitimate function of police power. Elbridge Gerry, who had argued the case for the New York SPCC, explained the grounds of the decision before a gathering of his organization's members. It "cannot be disputed," he claimed, "that the interest which the State has in the physical, moral and intellectual well-being of its members, warrants the implication and the exercise of every just power which will result in preparing the child in future life to support itself, to serve the State, and in all the relations and duties of adult life to perform well and capably its part."[81]

Though, as we have seen, anticruelty organizations often spoke of their protections in terms of "rights," here they offered justifications for protecting animals and children that had more to do with the public welfare than with individual rights.[82] And though these justifications might seem contradictory, humane societies' confusion was in some respects typical of the postbellum period. For as legal historian William Novak has suggested, in the years after the war states greatly expanded police legislation and, with notable exceptions, courts gave it great latitude; but at the same time, individuals, and individual rights, became more important jurisprudential units.[83]

Whether they conceived of the legislation they enforced as protecting the rights of animals and children, or as protecting the public welfare, humane societies had no doubt that the law—as an idea and as a set of institutions—was critical to their mission. In turning to the law to achieve social change, humane societies in many ways typified the transformation of reform strategies in the wake of the Civil War. Before the war many reformers had eschewed politics and legislative action in favor of "moral suasion," or moral reform. Like the evangelical ministers who traversed the county during the same period, reformers endeavored to create social change by transforming individual hearts. Rather than dispensing material assistance to the poor, for example, antebellum benevolence organizations defined poverty as a spiritual and moral problem, and sought to evangelize the poor, convinced that conversion would bring solvency if not prosperity. Rather than trying to ban the sale of liquor, antebellum temperance societies asked men and women to take a pledge not to drink. Likewise, many abolitionists initially rejected politics in favor of persuasion. As one author put the matter in 1832, he and his compatriots would seek to end slavery not by the "exercise of political supremacy," but "by pricking the conscience of the planters . . . by moral suasion—by concentrating public sentiment against slavery . . . and by the use of those spiritual weapons which are mighty, through God, to the pulling down of the strongholds of Satan."[84] In this vision, social change would result from moral change, and it would not be foisted upon unwilling and unregenerate sinners, but would come from the inside out. To turn to the law to end drinking, slavery, or other social vices was to admit defeat.

But in the years following the war, many reformers crystallized a trend that had begun even before the war: they abandoned a voluntaristic approach to change; they replaced the moral reform of the individual conscience with the coercive power of the law. After the war, reformers increasingly sought to create new rules and to harness the power of the state rather than to reawaken the dormant moral sense. Where the story of the kindly Judge and his brave son George suggested that sympathy was consistent with military action, to some reformers, the Civil War seemed to prove that people would not change unless forced to. Not appeals to sympathy, universal humanity, and conscience, but a violent and bloody war had ultimately ended slavery—swift action had trumped sentimental appeal. This taught reformers a lesson not only about what worked best, but also it dampened their optimistic view of human nature; some people, apparently, did not wish to be good.[85] As many reformers abandoned the bundle of assumptions associated with sentimentalism, they adopted a new language to guide their approach to change. Many who participated in the Sanitary Commission during the Civil War, for instance, went on to become leaders in postbellum reform. From the war, these men and women learned lessons in efficiency and centralized authority, in the value of institutions; reformers and intellectuals likewise insisted that science and not sentimental morality would henceforth dictate their actions. Orienting themselves away from voluntarism and toward institutions, many more reformers after the war were willing to use the law as a tool of reform and to regard the state as a venue for their efforts.[86]

Founded on the heels of the Civil War, American anticruelty societies seem in many respects to conform to this narrative of postbellum reform. Anticruelty society leaders believed in using a law enforcement model to achieve their goals, were not afraid to associate themselves with the power of the state, tried to increase the reach of state power through new legislation, and favored decisive action over mere sentiment, power over persuasion. As the letterhead of the Mohawk and Hudson River Humane Society trumpeted, the goal of anticruelty organizations was the "protection of child and beast by authority of the law." Their propensity to cloak them-

selves in quasi-police uniforms and arrest offenders suggests a willingness
to succeed through intimidation, a declining faith in the innate goodness
of man, and a pessimistic view of the human capacity for change. Indeed,
announced one reformer, the work of the humane society does not "alone
depend on appeals to the better nature of men."[87]

Though their law enforcement powers endowed anticruelty organizations with a set of tools that would have been both repugnant and un-
imaginable to many antebellum activists, they nonetheless retained many
of the assumptions and much of the language of earlier reformers. Like
many of their predecessors, some among them were inclined toward "universal" reform, and saw cruelty as the underlying element in a number of
social problems from alcoholism and crime to white slavery, all of which
would be eliminated under the reign of a Christian-inspired kindness toward man and beast alike.[88] Likewise, the movement relied heavily on
moral suasion and faith in the ameliorative effects of education and exposure to suffering. The lesson humane activists took from the Civil War
was not, moreover, that sentimentalism was dead, but rather that sympathy itself was not enough. The desire to uphold the "rights of the defenseless" entailed action, a willingness to mimic Minerva and the Angel
of Mercy on the humane society seal: arm upraised to stay the hand of
the violent and sword at the ready. In their public rhetoric, anticruelty reformers allied themselves with abolitionists rather than repudiating them
as ineffectual—abolition was the cause of the Civil War, they believed,
and the prosecution of cruelty carried that mission forward, extending its
reach and amplifying its power.

Moreover, as they approached the law, humane societies regarded it as
a transformative, and not just a punitive, force. Before they began dubbing
themselves "humane societies," anticruelty organizations eponymously
styled themselves as *preventative* bodies. According to many officials and
agents of anticruelty organizations, the ability to arrest enabled them,
ironically, to forgo prosecution in most of the cases that came before them.
Legislation, they hoped, had an educative function; hence, humane organizations routinely distributed copies of the anticruelty laws that they
had it in their power to enforce. An agent of the Alton, Illinois, Humane
Society wrote that his organization had been busy distributing "warning
notices containing extracts from the State laws concerning the prevention of cruelty to children, and animals." These took the form of posters
and handbills. The results, the agent believed, "exemplified the adage that,
'an ounce of prevention is worth a pound of cure.'" Likewise, an official
from the Pennsylvania SPCA praised the power of publicity to educate

the public and prevent cruelty. His organization, like the Illinois branch, distributed admonitory handbills and posters. This, combined with press coverage of their prosecutorial activities, had led to a situation in which "shame, or fear, prompts the concealment of practices which were once so common as to be thought beyond remedy . . . [and] the display of our badge, or a simple indication of an intention to report an offender to our office, usually suffices to calm the most turbulent and abusive."[89]

Anticruelty activists hoped that the existence of legislation—and public knowledge of their enforcement powers—would be enough to stop cruelty before it happened. But in the event that prosecution became necessary, they hoped that it too would serve an educative function. In choosing which cases to prosecute, one agent advised his fellows, "select those whose example will intimidate the greatest number of others and do the most towards preventing similar cruelties thereafter." An 1880 letter from branch agent W. L. Goldberg to E. W. Chase, secretary of the Minnesota Society for the Prevention of Cruelty, exemplifies this attitude. Goldberg wrote that he was moving ahead with a prosecution of a local man for "unlawfully starving and neglecting" his colts in the hopes that "it will likely *teach him* as well as *others* a *lesson*." A pamphlet prepared by the Minnesota SPCA in the 1870s made a similar point. "It is to be remembered that this Society is designed to PREVENT abuses, and we confidently expect that aggravated cases of cruelty will be of less frequent occurrence, when a few arrests and convictions will show to those not reached by other means, our intention to prosecute every case of extreme brutality." [90] Like many other fellow workers, these Minnesota anticruelty reformers saw their remediation as educative and thus as preventative. They believed that prosecution would not only create a new standard of behavior and hence of morality, but also that it would create public examples according to which the general population could learn about the new standards, imbibing and applying them before they themselves would face prosecution.

Though humane societies sought to link prosecution with prevention—and with the sort of personal transformation that would eventually produce widespread social change—this approach was largely consistent with a traditional view of the law's function. In choosing prosecution as a method of producing change, they assumed that social problems were largely individual in nature. And the notion that arrest and prosecution might be linked to prevention did not originate with humane societies. Rather, it was part of the original rationale for the development of police forces in early-nineteenth-century England and in the midcentury United States. Borrowing the theories of eighteenth-century Italian criminologist

Cesare Beccaria, proponents of police argued that a coherent, uniformed force and regular police patrolling would result in greater detection of crime and more frequent punishment. For the rational criminal, these would serve as deterrents.[91]

In spite of their reliance on a traditional argument about the relationship between law, police, punishment, and deterrence, humane societies used their legal power to initiate a range of interventions that fell short of prosecution. In so doing, they began to reshape the law from a tool of punishment into a tool of reform. In the majority of cases, anticruelty agents tried to use the weight of their legal authority to reform individuals rather than to legally punish them. Internal case files of humane societies provide the opportunity to view this more therapeutic approach to law in action. In many ways, the children's case files read like those of an organization dedicated to social work. They are filled less with stories of cruelty—as in physical abuse—and much more with social problems such as truancy, teen pregnancy, juvenile delinquency, family dissolution, desertion, and nonsupport.[92] Most cases did not end in court. While rates of prosecution ranged across humane societies and over time, the New York SPCC had the highest rate of cases in court—around 25 percent of the total cases it would investigate in a given year. Humane societies attempted to make the law into a flexible tool, one capable of responding to particular persons and their circumstances.

In the spirit of educative prevention rather than punitive court action, one option frequently used by humane society agents was to warn or threaten alleged perpetrators rather than prosecuting them. Pennsylvania SPCA secretary Pliny Chase chose this route when he wrote to fellow Philadelphian Joseph Eskinrod in 1872. Chase informed him that the SPCA had received a complaint that "you frequently treat a cow somewhat cruelly, and kill chickens and birds in a cruel manner." Chase took the opportunity to make Eskinrod aware of the Pennsylvania laws against cruelty, then less than four years old. "As you may not be aware of the law on the subject," he wrote, "I hereby notify you that cruelty towards any animal subjects you to a penalty." Less than a month later, Chase wrote a similar letter to Elijah Pennington, warning that if he did not provide proper ventilation and bedding for the horses in his stables, "we shall be obliged to take legal action against you."[93] Unlike an antebellum reformer, Chase did not try to convince Eskinrod or Pennington that their actions were morally wrong; instead, he simply informed them that they could face legal consequences. Though Chase aimed to change these men, he targeted their actions—and their self-interest—rather than their hearts.

As they did with animals, humane society agents issued similar threatening letters of warning in cases involving children. In an 1884 case, for example, the Illinois Humane Society received a complaint that Mr. and Mrs. Howard of Chicago were keeping their seventeen-year-old mentally handicapped son "shut up & half clothed & half starved." After investigating the case, Agent Dudley asked IHS secretary Henry Clark to write a letter to the boy's father, Mr. Howard. In the letter, Clark informed Howard that he wrote "in the interest of humanity & kindness." Arguing that "parental love & sympathy" should make the couple inclined to help their disadvantaged son to have "every possible comfort & happiness," Clark chided Mr. Howard's neglect. "This is the humane view to take of it," he wrote. And though Clark hoped that his appeals to the man's parental feelings would right the wrongs Dudley had found upon investigation, he did not rest there. "You are asked to remedy this case," Clark concluded, "without compelling this Society to take further action & thus avoid public notoriety, which would necessarily ensue in case of prosecution."[94] Clark, unlike the PSPCA's Chase, added a dose of moral suasion to his warning; he peppered his letter with appeals to principles—humanity—and to the affections that his organization believed should reign supreme—love, sympathy, and kindness. But, like Chase, he ended by reminding Howard that, ultimately, should he fail to reform himself, the IHS held the power to bring the force of law—and with it shame and public humiliation—down upon him and his family. Though the IHS did not ultimately use its legal powers against Howard, their ability to do so was precisely what made nonprosecutorial interventions successful.

Minnesota's agents were similarly inclined. In 1905, an anonymous report brought a south Minneapolis man to the attention of the humane society's Agent Bean. According to Bean's report, the man "drinks and does not support his family." Bean tried to visit the man at home to give him "a good talking and ask him about taking the cure," but not finding the man at home, he wrote a letter instead. Bean approached the man with friendly advice, writing that "If it is drink that causes all this trouble, why not try one of the cures that has been found effective." He even offered the nonjudgmental observation that "the drink habit is just like any other disease and ought to have proper medical treatment." On the other hand, Bean underlined his "suggestion" that the man seek help with the reminder that "there is a law that could make you support your wife and children properly if the matter were brought into court," and he ended his letter with an admonition: "you must arrange to provide properly for your family in the future or more radical measures will have to be taken."[95]

In other letters, agents were more forward about their legal power. "We trust within the next week you will make some arrangements for the support of your wife and children, and if you do not, we will do all that we can to see that you are punished," wrote one agent to a deserting husband.[96] When a boy was reported by his school for being "disorderly," Agent Strelow had the boy visit the society office and told him that he had two months to shape up or "he would be brought into Juvenile Court."[97] The frequency with which Minneapolis Humane Society agents used the threat of legal action suggests that they viewed having—but not using—the power of arrest as critical to reforming individual behavior. Criminalizing behavior like nonsupport and desertion did not necessarily mean that reformers wished to arrest and jail every offender; rather, they wished to use criminalization as an entering wedge, a tool to gain access to disordered lives and to make a series of interventions short of arrest.

Besides writing letters to alleged offenders, humane society agents also relied on personal visits to produce change. Officers recorded these visits in more or less detail, sometimes simply noting that they went out and "reprimanded" the alleged cruelist. But often the relationship between agent and respondent was more involved. When the IHS's agent Little received a complaint that Jane Monroe "gets drunk every day and beats & abuses her two children," he went to Monroe's home to investigate. In his report book, Little recorded that "this charge is true so far as getting drunk is concerned." He found that while Monroe did neglect her children when she drank, she did not abuse them. Little felt Monroe was not beyond hope or help, so he extracted promises of reformation from her. "I have agreed with her," he reported, "that if she will get out of the house that she is living in and away from the society that surrounds her and stop drinking and take care of the children as she should I will give her a trial, which she promises to do." Monroe also promised to let Little know her new address "so that I can watch and see if she does it." Humane society case files are filled with similar examples. In another case, IHS Agent Dudley investigated an anonymous tip that a Mrs. Lowrey would go out to work and leave her children in the care of a drunken woman who neglected and abused them. After visiting Mrs. Lowrey and observing that "the children are well clothed and I think [Mrs. Lowrey] is trying to take good care of them," Dudley settled the case with a reprimand and a promise from Lowrey that she would find a more suitable, sober babysitter for her children.[98]

Even when agents did use their powers of arrest and dragged offending men, women, and children into court, cases were often extended and carried over, suggesting that agents and judges viewed the law less as a means of balancing the scales of justice and more as a means of convincing individuals to change their behavior in the present. In a Minnesota case, for example, neighbors reported a man for drinking and neglecting his family. Humane society Agent Van Etten issued a warrant for the man's arrest on a charge of drunkenness. The man pled guilty to the charge and was sentenced to the workhouse for ten days, but the humane society requested that he be granted a stay because he had promised to quit drinking.[99] In another case of nonsupport, a woman came to the Minneapolis Humane Society complaining that her husband failed to provide for her and their one-year-old girl. After Agent Graves's "severe warning" failed to remedy the man's behavior, Graves issued a warrant for his arrest. Rather than trying the man, the court ordered the man to pay child support through the humane society, and continued his case for two weeks. At the end of that time, the court continued the case again for another month with the same arrangement: the man would pay child support through the humane society. The case file lists no trial and prosecution, only these continuations. The file concludes on a note that suggests these interventions worked: "he formerly hung around poolrooms, but now seems to be trying to work and do right."[100] As far as the humane society was concerned, the point was less to exact revenge on these men and more to restore them to their proper role: husband, father, provider. Courts, in their willingness to go along with the humane society's requests for, and even to initiate, continuations, seem to have agreed.

In dealing with instances of family dissolution and instability, humane society agents and court justices viewed the law, and the institution of the court, as one node in a network of institutions intervening to try to restore what they viewed as order. In certain respects, anticruelty organizations functioned as a new instrument in an old practice: community self-regulation. Before the development of formal police, responsibility for regulation was vested in all citizens. Constables, themselves community members appointed on a part-time basis to field complaints, had no greater powers of arrest than anyone else. They simply agreed to serve as conduits connecting their neighbors with the local magistrates. Magistrates, who had the power to swear out arrest warrants, were also laypersons, not formally trained professionals. And just as often as they went to constables, men and women came directly to magistrates to register complaints.[101] Constables and courts were porous with communities, not rigidly separated from ordinary citizens; they were men and institutions to which ordinary citizens regularly went to untangle relationships that had become knotted beyond community control.

In the late nineteenth century, communities used humane societies in similar ways. As other studies of SPCCs in Boston and Philadelphia have recently noted, anticruelty organizations did not simply exercise a form of top-down power over their clients. Most investigations conducted by humane society agents were the result not of agents' own discoveries, but of complaints received by the central office. And though some reports were anonymous, arriving on postcards or in unsigned letters, complaints also poured in from friends, neighbors, family members, and the aggrieved themselves. When neighbors reported each other, they often brought humane society agents into the middle of longstanding disputes. In May of 1885, Mrs. Johnson wrote to the Illinois Humane Society to complain that her neighbor, Mrs. Messer, was poisoning her chickens. When IHS agent William Mitchell went out to investigate, he found himself enmeshed in "a very old quarrel" between the two women. While Mrs. Messer used a pesticide on her plants, Mrs. Johnson allowed her chickens to wander into her neighbor's yard. Mitchell told Johnson to keep her chickens from Messer's plants, and left the two women to their rancorous relationship. In Minneapolis, the humane society received a petition signed by twelve men living near the northside home of the Kramer family. Carefully mimicking the language of a citizens' pleading, the petition began "We the undersigned residents and citizens . . . respectfully request that some steps and action be taken to abate the nuisance caused and engendered by [the Kramer family]." The petition went on to claim that the family was "a public nuisance . . . constantly committing breaches of the peace and provoking breaches of the peace." Because neighbors alleged that the Kramers involved their children in this disorder, they contacted the humane society. Upon investigation, the MHS discovered that the Kramer's neighbors, Orthodox Jews, resented the fact that Kramer, also Jewish, did not observe the Sabbath: he worked on Saturdays. Kramer's friends, Reform rather than Orthodox, vouched for his good character.[102] While some neighbors clearly used humane societies to try to remedy instances of cruelty and neglect that they found troubling, others realized that the anticruelty organization's powers could be brought to bear on a wider range of disputes. All that was needed was to translate complaints into the anticruelty idiom.

Families also brought humane society agents to their doorstep. Aggrieved wives were the most likely to make complaints, followed by husbands and, much less frequently, children. Wives complained that their husbands drank too much, refused to work, failed to support the family, deserted, and were adulterous and abusive. In 1895, for example, Mrs. Jones mailed a postcard to the IHS. She asked a society agent to come see her at home. "I have a sick baby and three other children, my husband won't work and drinks all the money he can get." Some women even came asking anticruelty agents to help them obtain a divorce. In addition to wives and mothers, children also made complaints to humane societies. In 1884, an eleven-year-old girl came to the IHS. With two witnesses for support, she accused her adoptive parents of abusing and neglecting her. The same year another girl of the same age came into IHS headquarters to complain that her father abused her and had threatened to kill her. Understandably, she was afraid to go home. Thus, although some families and family members undoubtedly resented the intrusion of anticruelty agents into what they regarded as their private affairs, for others the humane society was a resource they used to curb undesirable and destructive behavior.[103]

With such complaints, humane societies found themselves acting as intermediaries in a complex dynamic that spun out beyond the boundaries of the nuclear family. In one such case, Minneapolis Humane Society Agent Farmer found herself shuttling among several family members and between the family and other local institutions. The case was initiated by the principal of a local school who contacted the humane society because four of the Keeler children were delinquent in school attendance. Farmer's notes indicate that the principal described the children's mother as "shiftless," and the father as a "worthless" man who had lately left town for St. Louis, leaving his family near destitution. The city's truant officer had already been to the Keelers, but the children's school attendance had not improved. When Farmer paid her visit to the family, she found Mrs. Keeler trying to support her six children on a small inheritance and the meager supplement she could earn by taking in laundry. Because of her poverty, Mrs. Keeler had taken some of her children out of school to work. Farmer contacted both family members and charities. From the latter, she tried to get Mrs. Keeler a supply of firewood for the winter. And she located Mrs. Keeler's well-to-do brother-in-law. He administered the monthly payment of Keeler's inheritance through his business, the Minneapolis & Northern Elevator Company. In a letter to Keeler, Farmer explained that she had told him that she "did not see how a woman and six children could live on ten dollars every three weeks." He promised "he would give you more money if you needed it and they would look after your wants." Given more money, Farmer believed Keeler would not need to take her children out of school. She ended her letter by urging Keeler to keep in touch. "If the money is not forthcoming you would better notify us, and we will see to it again." She also offered to help Keeler find her husband, even though the brother-in-law thought the idea, and his brother, "useless."[104] Originally brought in to mediate between the local school and Mrs. Keeler, Farmer ended acting as a liaison between Keeler, local charities, and members of her extended family. In this and other cases of nonsupport and destitution, the humane society wanted first and foremost to bolster family members' obligations to one another. But the presence of the principal, the truant officer, the humane society, and the extended family in Keeler's case revealed that the family was situated in a web of institutions both supporting and regulating it.

As the Keeler case also suggests, humane society agents received cases not only from anonymous tips, neighbors, and family members, but also on referral from other local institutions. Just as frequently, they referred cases out to other benevolent organizations. Illinois Humane Society agents, for example, frequently noted in their case reports that they referred cases of destitution out to other agencies. "I found this a case of charity and referred them to the County Agent," noted Agent Williams in one such instance. Similarly, in cases where charges of neglect turned out to be the result of simple destitution, Minneapolis Humane Society agents were likely to refer respondents to the city's Associated Charities bureau.[105] Officially, humane societies tried to maintain a firm line between law enforcement and charity work, emphasizing that the latter was not their duty. Though they saw themselves as relieving suffering, humane societies were not organized to offer material relief. Disavowing charity not only helped anticruelty organizations distinguish themselves from others in the field of private philanthropy, but also it emphasized their unique approach to rights protection through law enforcement.[106]

But on the ground, the lines between charity and law enforcement were often not as firm. Humane societies sometimes did provide material relief or help men to find jobs. Sometimes the lines blurred in a single person. George Ellman, employed as the branch agent for the IHS in the Quad Cities, for example, was also the agent for the local Jewish charity. When Ellman resigned, town authorities considered combining the duties of the humane society agent with that of the agent for the Associated Charities. Similarly, in Minneapolis, when one agent switched jobs from the Associated Charities to the humane society, she brought some of her cases with her. In the early twentieth century, when laws criminalizing nonsupport began to be administered through juvenile courts, Minneapolis's Humane Society acted as the collector and distributor of judicially mandated family support payments. And though such material support did not come from the coffers of the humane society, and was the result of prosecutorial action, it nonetheless blurred the lines between law enforcement, charity, and social work.[107]

The multiple ways in which late-nineteenth- and early-twentieth-century humane societies functioned—as charities, as law enforcement agencies, and as informal social work organizations—is another instance of their hybridity. Not only did these reformers blend animal with child protection, status-based with individualist conceptions of rights, sentimentalism with liberalism, and humanitarianism with law enforcement, but also they stood at the cusp between old and new approaches to law and governance in the United States. As legal and political historians have noted, law was the dominant instrument of governance through the end of the nineteenth century. Though the federal government was weak compared to its Western European counterparts, America was hardly a stateless society. Rather, most governance was conducted on the local level through what Stephen Skowronek has called "the state of courts and parties." As the French observer Alexis de Tocqueville noted during the 1830s, "there is hardly a political question in the United States which does not at some point, sooner or later, turn into a judicial one." While political parties greased the wheels of democratic political participation, nineteenth-century courts made most substantive policy decisions. This was true not only for the rules governing property, but also for the reshaping of domestic relations. Though some important changes in the status of dependents—such as married women's property acts—were the result of legislative action, many others were "judge-made law." The development of the "best interests of the child" doctrine is perhaps the primary example of how judges, rather than legislatures, acted to shape social norms and practices for much of the nineteenth century.[108]

And as we have seen, local and state-level governance through police-based regulation was quite robust. But without much administrative machinery, municipalities relied on courts to make their police powers functional. The local patrol systems that did operate in the antebellum period, the constables and sheriffs, acted as agents not of municipal governments, but of the courts. Ordinary citizens also depended on courts to regulate behavior, dragging friends, neighbors, family members, and business associates into court with a frequency and a vigor that earned Americans a reputation as a highly litigious people. In their reliance on courts to make policy and regulate behavior, antebellum Americans not only relied on law as what Christopher Tomlins has called the "modality of rule," but also they located its function—social control—on a local level.[109]

While anticruelty organizations' willingness to use legislation and law enforcement to produce change represented a departure from antebellum reform tactics, their reliance on law as a mode of governance and their largely local organization shows them operating within the bounds of the existing state. They assumed that law was the primary mechanism for regulating social order and they relied on courts, or the possibility of legal action, to make that order function. But rather than relying on judges to make new law, anticruelty organizations also lobbied for new legislation, transferring governance to the legislature and making courts into the interpreters of statutes rather than the creators of policy. This changed role for the courts was particularly pronounced where animal protection was involved since, unlike with domestic relations, there was virtually no common-law precedent for such laws. In other ways, too, anticruelty organizations participated in the same transformation in modes of governance represented by the development of municipal police forces. In making formal police, cities transferred authority from courts to municipal bureaucracies and shifted traditional responsibility for social control from community members to professionals. When local neighborhoods and families brought their complaints to humane societies, they simultaneously turned to the law in an old way—as a local institution designed to take up the task of quotidian dispute settlement—and they recognized something new—the development of specialized organizations designed to regulate specific domains of social life.

Anticruelty organizations privatized police functions by assuming law enforcement duties that would otherwise have fallen on the regular police force; but in other ways they expanded not only the domain of law, but of the state. For while the state had always, through the police power, maintained an interest in, and a power to regulate, the orderly functioning of households, businesses, and all other relationships that might affect the public welfare, anticruelty organizations gave those interests greater depth and greater specificity. Where antivice organizations viewed the law and the state in static terms, asking only that existing laws be enforced, humane society activists pursued new legislation. As George Angell remarked in response to a question about why private groups should enforce the law, without anticruelty organizations, there would be no anticruelty laws to enforce in the first place. Those outside the movement realized this as well. According to the *Breckinridge Bulletin*, Colorado's humane society had been "instrumental in having wholesome laws placed on the statute books of the state for the protection of these dependents [animals and children]."[110] Using the law to pursue their goals, anticruelty organizations developed close relationships with not only the machinery of justice, but also with a variety of other branches of burgeoning municipal and state bureaucracies. The lines between privately incorporated anticruelty organizations and local and state governments were often vague, were occasionally contested, and in some Western states, they disappeared altogether.

One such contest highlighted not only the departure of anticruelty organizations from the timeworn tactics of moral suasion and charitable relief, but also the state of public-private partnerships in late-nineteenth-century America. Anticruelty organizations' blending of public and private functions was pronounced but not singular. Policing, as we have seen, was one activity that blended the two; the administration of charity was another. Many privately chartered charitable organizations received public monies. Children who had been made wards of the state, for example, were often housed in private orphanages that received state funds in exchange for the wards' care. After the Civil War, reformers involved in the Charity Organization Society and allied with the scientific charity movement began to call for greater uniformity, efficiency, and state oversight of private, but publicly funded, charities. Beginning with Massachusetts, many states formed public advisory boards to oversee and inspect all state-supported charitable institutions, including those that were formally private but which received some state funds. By the last decade of the nineteenth century, sixteen states had followed the lead of Massachusetts.[111]

In 1894, New York created a State Board of Charities to inspect all private charitable organizations that received any state funds to carry out their programs. As part of its work, the New York board wanted oversight of the New York SPCC. The NY-SPCC seemed, on the face of it, to fall under the purview of the board because it received public funds for two of its functions. First, the organization was the clearinghouse for the support payments that the courts required parents to pay to the institutions that housed children who had been removed from their homes owing to poverty, cruelty, or delinquency. Though the organization did not keep any of the funds, it did receive and distribute them. Second, the society received compensation for the legal work it did assisting district attorneys in prosecuting cases of cruelty (SPCC agents collected necessary evidence and wrote briefs for the attorneys to use in court). And, when the society temporarily housed, fed, and clothed the children that were awaiting a ver-

dict in cases against either their parents or themselves (for juvenile delinquency), it seemed to offer the sort of direct relief that met the definition
of charity.[112]

The State Board of Charities believed that the NY-SPCC was a charity
and hence fell under its purview, giving it the right and obligation to oversee the society's administration of its cases. In a legal battle that stretched
over several years, the SPCC vigorously fought this encroachment by insisting that it was not a charity in either philosophy or method. Charity,
explained Gerry in the midst of the fracas, offers immediate relief, while
philanthropy takes a view both wider and more long-term—"it looks more
to the surroundings than it does to the individual case." The long-term
goal of the anticruelty society was, Gerry explained, preventative in nature; by sending a message, through arrest and prosecution, that cruelty is
unacceptable, it is stanched; by removing children from vicious homes, the
cycle of poverty and vice is broken. Nor, Gerry insisted, were the society's
methods charitable. Far from relief-giving, the SPCCs were "subordinate
governmental agencies" created by the state legislature for "the specific
and express purpose of protecting the helpless, who otherwise would have
no legal representative in the Courts to press their claims for protection
from cruelty, [and] for rescue from lives of misery."[113] Identifying law enforcement with the state, Gerry argued that the society was neither private nor charitable, but rather the helping hand of the state extended to the
helpless (and dependent) to offer not relief, but protection of their rights.

Though courts originally granted the Board of Charities supervisory
authority over the SPCC, the state court of appeals eventually agreed with
Gerry's arguments and revoked the board's powers. Court of appeals justices argued that the money received by the SPCC was not for the food,
clothing, or shelter of children, but was paid to the society for its police
work. Hence it was not an organization that received and disbursed state
money as a form of relief but was a law enforcement organization paid by
the state to perform police duties. It was, in this sense, no more a charity
than are the regular police. "All the things that it does or can do would
naturally and primarily devolve upon the police department," wrote the
court, "and the society exists only because it can do the work of the police
more efficiently than they can." The society is, finally, "a quasi public corporation, authorized for the greater convenience and certainty of accom-
plishing that governmental work."[114]

When the ASPCA encountered challenges to the constitutionality of
its enforcement of New York City's dog-registration law, the court's findings similarly supported the organization and emphasized its "quasi pub-

lic" nature. Part of the grounds of the case questioned whether the legislature could vest its regulatory powers in a private organization such as
the ASPCA. In language nearly identical to that of the SPCC's case, the
presiding judge declared that while the organization was technically private, it was created by the legislature "for public purposes. It subserves no
private interest. Its duties and power relate exclusively to matters which
have always been deemed suitable for public regulation." Here the court
acknowledged the fact that animal control had long been the subject of
police-based regulation. The propriety of the regulation of animals was beyond question. Moreover, if it was proper for the legislature to regulate, it
was proper for the legislature to vest regulatory power in some body. The
court saw no reason that the ASPCA could not, constitutionally speaking,
be so invested. It was not, after all, the court reasoned, a typical private
entity. "The Society is a subordinate public agency," asked simply "to perform a service which the Legislature might delegate to a citizen or public
body."[115]

Though the officials of the New York anticruelty organizations went
to court in the interest of preserving their organizational autonomy rather
than to prove that they were engaged in governmental work, these cases
nonetheless revealed the patchwork of assumptions that had come to sur-
round the place of anticruelty organizations in the wider network of late-
nineteenth-century reform. Without developing a theory, as some later
progressive reformers would, about state responsibility for animal and
child protection, anticruelty activists had nonetheless succeeded in insinuating their priorities into the machinery and the identity of the states in
which they operated. When state courts wrote that anticruelty organizations performed work that would otherwise fall to the police, they failed to
realize, as Angell and other reformers did, that the relationship was more
circular than linear. Anticruelty organizations lobbied for new legislation
to protect animals and children, and were then given the power to enforce
it. They did not, in large part, assume functions that were a predefined
portion of local and state governments. Even though they were privately
incorporated, they enlarged government by securing legislation that specified, in ever more detail, how animals and children were to be governed.
Once on the books, and being enforced by the private anticruelty organizations, state officials believed that these organizations performed duties
that would otherwise fall to public officials. Technically, this was true;
but many of the duties would not have existed at all except at the behest
of the private organizations. And sometimes, as we have seen in the case
of municipal police who were detailed to the humane society beat in cities

such as Minneapolis and Chicago, the mingling of private and government priorities could be quite explicit.

For much of the late nineteenth century, the close relationship between the state and the anticruelty organization remained implicit, except when openly challenged. But in the early twentieth century some states carried the logic of the New York courts to its final conclusion. After the turn of the century, the statewide humane societies in Colorado, Wyoming, Minnesota, and Texas became state bureaus. This happened first in Colorado. Organized in 1881, just five years after Colorado became a state, the humane society was responsible for creating all of the state's animal and child protection laws. After several failed attempts, in 1901 the state legislature approved a bill making the CHS into the State Bureau of Child and Animal Protection. This change in status affected little about the organization's internal operations. Besides making the governor, the superintendent of public instruction, and the attorney general ex officio members of the board of directors, the change in status also supplied the society with a more regular revenue stream. The situation was similar in the three other states that made the humane society into a state agency. In Minnesota, while the humane society had been originally formed as an SPCA in 1869, it did not become a state agency until 1905. Wyoming followed suit in 1907, transforming its three-year old humane society into the State Board of Child and Animal Protection. Last, the Texas State Bureau of Child and Animal Protection was formed in 1913.[116]

In 1900, a Colorado Humane Society handbook laid out the case for the transformation of the humane society into a state agency. Employing the same language as its Eastern predecessors, the handbook claimed that the CHS acted not as "a charitable or benevolent organization but [as] an arm of the law." It also relied on the same imagery of chivalric, martial protection. Emblazoned on the front of the handbook was the society's logo: a sword crossed over a shield engraved with the words: "we protect the helpless." According to the CHS, it was an "arm of the law" because it was responsible not only for procuring legislation for animals and children, but also for enforcing that legislation. Though technically, the CHS pamphlet noted, "it is as much the duty of courts, sheriffs, prosecuting attorneys, and other officers" to enforce existing animal and child protection legislation, the CHS was necessary because, in reality, public officials rarely found the time or took the initiative to look into cases of cruelty. "The attention of such officials," the CHS wrote of regular police and courts, "is sure to be monopolized by the complaints of those who are able to demand protection." Animals and children, by contrast, were "helpless classes" unable to secure the attention, and hence the protection, of established law enforcement bodies. Because they engaged in law enforcement, the society reasoned that its agents performed a duty not only on behalf of animals and children, but also on behalf of the entire state. In its own view, the CHS helped the state of Colorado to fulfill the letter of its laws, and hence the spirit of its people. As such, the CHS pamphlet argued that its activities "should be supported by general taxation, as the other official agencies of law and order are." Addressing colleagues at the American Humane Association's annual meeting, G. H. Thomson of the Colorado Humane Society concluded that his organization's good work proved that it was "an indispensable feature in the social machinery of the State." The ability of the organization's agents to accomplish their investigations was, he claimed, a result of their identification with the "resistless power of the State back of all."[117]

As humanitarians like Colorado's Thomson saw it, their organizations not only employed the power of the state, but they also played an active role in what historians would subsequently regard as a transformation in the role of the state. Initially associated with a monopoly of force in the early modern period, the legitimacy of modern liberal governments slowly came to rest instead on the ability to relieve rather than inflict suffering and to rehabilitate rather than to wound.[118] E. P. Bradstreet, an agent of the Cincinnati, Ohio, Humane Society described this process in a talk, delivered in 1890, entitled "The Power of the State to Protect against Cruelty." For centuries, he claimed, rulers had abused their powers, inflicting tyranny and abuse on their own populations. Somehow, Bradstreet said, "it never occurred [to them] that one of the prime duties of that central power we call 'the State' was to care for the needy, weak, and unprotected, to cover the head of an abused subject with the shield of governmental power." After considering thinkers from Aristotle and Plato to Montesquieu, Bradstreet asserted that all venerable theoreticians had reached the "irresistible" conclusion that government was permitted, even required, "to legislate for man's best good, and therefore against cruelty to man and beast." The task for humane activists, then, was to pursue not just moral suasion through humane education efforts, but also to secure new legislation. They had to force governments into adopting their duty, in Bradstreet's words, "to smite as with a rod of iron the arm upraised against helpless weakness."[119]

Humane organizations were, however, divided about how far their activities and their relationship with local, state, and national governments should extend. Though anticruelty reformers had made the man of feeling into a man of action by deploying state power, and though humane societies across the country repeatedly heralded their function as arms of the state, many individual reformers remained suspicious of too much entanglement with the government, which, like antivice crusaders, they associated as much with the mire of self-serving and corrupt politicians as they did with beneficent power. The question of how to relate to an increasingly powerful state was not, however, easily resolved. Perhaps surprisingly, the question also brought anticruelty reformers face to face with another long-submerged issue: the logic of joining child with animal protection.

# From Cruelty to Child Welfare

In fall 1910, the ASPCA found its nearly singular authority challenged by the formation of a new animal protection organization: the Horse Aid Society of New York. Founded by Mrs. Jacob M. Ehrlich, the organization declared that its motto was "A Square Deal for the Horse." A new organization was necessary, their annual report explained, because they objected to the methods of the ASPCA, which they believed was more interested in punishing human transgression than in preventing animal suffering. The older, established organization "seemed more concerned regarding positive punishment of the human being for injuries inflicted upon the animal than in teaching the human how to relieve the suffering of the dumb animal." In their focus on prosecution and punitive measures, the ASPCA was missing the point, which was to relieve suffering.

To that end, the new organization proposed "systematic relief" for both horses and their drivers. The first step was to establish objective criteria for cruelty, to put the "determination as to what is cruelty into competent hands." Veterinarians alone, they believed, were competent to determine a horse's fitness for work and the amount of pain it suffered. Second, recognizing that many horse drivers were either ignorant or poor, and that this situation might bear some relation to cruelty in the form of overworking horses, the Aid Society set up a free dispensary for veterinary care, a driver's club to distribute lessons in proper animal care, and a mutual aid society that would provide an employment bureau, dorms, free baths, a gym, a reading room, and sick, death, widow, and orphan benefits to drivers' families. This approach, they believed, substituted an undue focus on human depravity for a systematic method of rooting out the underlying causes of cruelty, which, the Horse Aid Society suggested, lay not in the human heart but rather in external circumstances.[1] The Horse Aid

Society was never in a strong enough financial or organizational position to make many inroads into ASPCA territory, but its critiques and alternative methods illustrate some of the ways that the reform environment had changed since the first animal and child protection organizations had been founded.[2] Its efforts to address the root causes of cruelty to working horses in a "systematic" way and its appeal to professional expertise to determine cruelty were part and parcel of a larger shift away from individual and moral explanations for social problems and away from reliance on laymen and volunteers to address such problems.

In the first decades of the twentieth century, the Horse Aid Society was not the only voice advocating a new and systematic approach to the problems that anticruelty societies tried to remedy. The same year that the Horse Aid Society was founded, Owen Lovejoy, the general secretary of the National Child Labor Committee, addressed an international conference of humane societies. "Our new industrial processes call for a new definition of cruelty," he declared, for "the powers inflicting cruelty on the working child are not personal, but institutional. It is not usually the harsh mother or the cruel father against whom we must guard the child; now is it the individual employers."[3] Lovejoy, an outsider, appealed to anticruelty activists in their own terms, but stretched them to the breaking point. Both he and men such as Elbridge Gerry and John Shortall thought child labor a disgrace, but they framed the problem differently from one another. In asking them to shift cruelty's locus from individual to institutional acts, Lovejoy transcended cruelty's conceptual limits, for anticruelty reformers seldom understood cruelty in impersonal or institutional terms. Gerry and Shortall thought child labor cruel when it was the product of parental vice and greed, and when they thought it might harm a child's moral fiber, but outside that framework and without some element of ill intention, they could not understand it as inherently cruel. Other anticruelty reformers had a similar logic. The superintendent of the Wisconsin Humane Society, for instance, reported complaints that the society was not doing more to end or regulate child labor. To this charge, he replied that he had "noticed only such cases as bear upon them the aspect of cruelty."[4] It was not that humane organizations refused to see child labor as a problem but that they understood it in moral terms rather than institutional or systemic ones.

As Lovejoy's appeal suggests, early-twentieth-century reform was moving away from the sort of model within which anticruelty societies had operated. Rather than rooting social problems in individual behavior, this new approach to reform focused on structural causes and suggested that

manipulating environmental factors according to social laws would produce an orderly and harmonious society. What Lovejoy and the Horse Aid
Society represented was the emergence of an approach to social reform
that historians identify with the Progressive Era. Typically, historians
date its emergence to the turn of the twentieth century and characterize it
as an attempt to overcome the strategies and ideologies that characterized
Gilded Age America. If the Gilded Age is seen as the era of laissez-faire
economic policy and ideology, the Progressive Era marks the emergence
of the regulatory state and the recognition that the government can and
should intervene to protect workers and consumers from the worst consequences of unfettered capitalism.[5] Legislation to limit the condition and
number of hours that women and children work, to prevent monopolies, to
regulate the production of food and medicine, and to provide compensation
for injured workmen are characteristic of this new approach. The change
was not simply tactical, but ideological. Likewise in social reform. If the
harsh and punitive tactics of scientific charity were the philanthropic dou-
ble of laissez-faire, in the Progressive Era reformers were likely to recognize that circumstances beyond individual effort and choice (such as low
wages and chronic boom-and-bust cycles) contributed to poverty, and that
the immiseration of the poor was exacerbated by poor housing, education,
and sanitation in urban America.

Recognizing the interconnection of social and economic inequality to
issues like municipal politics, sanitation, and health, Progressives viewed
society not as a series of independent individuals, but rather as an interdependent whole, a complex system. Framing social and economic problems in this more systemic way led Progressives to turn both to the use
of the state and to the strategy of prevention. In a complex and interdependent society, it no longer made sense to respond to problems in a local
or piecemeal way, but rather to try to use the largest and most powerful
mechanisms—state and federal governments—to craft solutions on the appropriate scale. But this systemic view also led many reformers to search
for environmental ways to prevent the problems they saw. If social and
economic problems were caused not simply by individuals but by larger
structures, then the prevention of those problems also required a strategy
that sought to reform not just individuals but the conditions in which individuals lived and made choices.

The focus on system and prevention also led to an explosion in child
welfare reform activity from the 1890s forward. From the establishment
of juvenile courts, campaigns against child labor, and the movement for
compulsory schooling to efforts to decrease infant mortality and provide

wholesome recreation for children, reformers targeted children as critical nodes in the social order. As one 1916 textbook on child welfare explained, "In modern social work the emphasis has been shifted from the parent to the child. . . . It is well then to begin with the child, for he presages the coming man. He is the plastic material that can be molded ill or well; he is gigantic in possibilities, but dwarfed if without opportunity."[6]

Both the changes in the ideology and strategy of reform and the expansion of child welfare organizations affected the status of anticruelty societies. Products of the Gilded Age, humane societies defined the social problem of cruelty in moral terms, they identified individual perpetrators as the object of their reform efforts, and they placed law enforcement at the center of their approach to reform. Men and women involved in Progressive Era reform were interested in preventative work, not law enforcement. Defining abuse as a product of bad circumstances, they believed that proper interventions and material supports could forestall the need for the punitive work of anticruelty societies. Just after the turn of the century, Carl Carstens, who became the head of the Massachusetts Society for the Prevention of Cruelty to Children (MSPCC) after leading the Child Welfare League, broke with the dominant anticruelty society approach, declaring that his organization would adopt the preventative, casework strategy of social work.[7] Carstens's move was controversial among anticruelty societies, and it was rejected outright by stalwarts such as Elbridge Gerry and AHA president William O. Stillman, both of whom maintained that SPCCs should stick with what they knew and continue to provide the service that no one else did—punishing cruelty through prosecution and removal of children from unfit homes. Gerry did manage to keep the NY-SPCC on this track, but Carstens's approach was the future of reform in general. Though the MSPCC kept the word "cruelty" in its moniker, in practice it and the rest of the child welfare movement abandoned the language and tactics of anticruelty reform.

Prosecution of parents and separating children from their families in particular fell out of favor as family preservation and rehabilitation became the new child welfare ideal. This was accompanied by a shift in focus from abuse to neglect as the chief problem facing troubled children and their families. Many progressive reformers believed that dependency and neglect could be prevented by assisting the entire family unit rather than simply isolating the child as the object of intervention and assistance. Though earlier reformers like those involved in SPCCs and humane societies believed that the family was the natural social unit, the birthright of every child, and the best environment in which to grow to a sound adulthood, they also believed that a bad family environment was worse than no family at all and that preserving a child's right to a fair chance in life might mean taking him or her away from a cruel, immoral, or irresponsible parent. The new generation of child welfare advocates, however, believed that much dependence, neglect, and delinquency were the result of poverty, and they viewed the dissolution of the family as a larger threat than the specter of bad parents ruining good children. They emphasized that environmental factors rather than parental immorality or irresponsibility contributed to the problems that landed children on the doorstep of social welfare agencies, and they perceived helping the child as a means to strengthen and rehabilitate the entire family. This new orientation took several forms. On one hand, this new approach was adopted by those in favor of doing social work, performing casework with individual families to improve their ability to function in their children's interests. On the other hand, reformers who favored family preservation rather than the removal and institutionalization of dependent and neglected children also tried to enact legislation—such as workers' compensation, mothers' pensions, and tenement housing reform—that they hoped would help prevent some of the problems facing poor families.[8]

As the child welfare field grew more crowded, SPCCs and humane societies struggled to maintain their organizational identity and to defend their approach to child protection. Part of the problem was that as the number of organizations dedicated to improving children's lives proliferated, the role of the traditional SPCC grew less distinct. In some areas, the existence of humane societies was threatened by encroachment. In 1915, AHA president William O. Stillman acknowledged that "complaints have reached us from time to time that charity organizations were seeking to capture the work of our societies or drive them out of business." Officials from the Ohio Humane Society made similar charges. According to the OHS's attorney, Eugene Morgan, a bill before the state legislature would require that "all non-support, abandonment of, and cruelty to children cases must be prosecuted before the Juvenile Court." Morgan charged that the bill would give the juvenile court exclusive jurisdiction over cases that the OHS had formerly handled and was designed to "destroy the efficiency of the Humane Societies rather than to add to the efficiency of the Juvenile Courts." The major task that the legislation proposed taking away from the OHS was the collection and distribution of child support in cases of nonsupport. Formerly done by the OHS, under the new law it would be done exclusively by the juvenile court. Stillman opined on the OHS's plight, complaining that "this is not the first time that social and charitable agencies have sought to oust anti-cruelty societies from their special field of work for children, although it seems very ill-advised for them to attempt to do so. There is ample room for each kind of work along its own lines, and all of these reformative agencies should work together in perfect harmony."[9]

Though the OHS faced an external threat—the encroachment of the juvenile court on its territory—the problem of preserving a distinct identity was compounded by both external and internal pressures. If, as leaders like the MSPCC's Carl Carstens advocated, humane societies began doing casework and child placement, what was to distinguish an SPCC from another agency that did such work? To combat this internally driven threat, stalwarts argued that SPCCs should stick to law enforcement since this was what they, and no one else, did best. On the other hand, critics outside of humane organizations criticized law enforcement as anathema to child welfare work. To combat this externally driven threat, stalwarts defended the necessity of prosecution and legal protection of children. Seizing on the main trends in social work, many early-twentieth-century anticruelty reformers melded these strands of their argument into a claim on behalf of professional specialization. SPCCs and humane societies, they sought to prove, had a specific role to play among the panoply of child welfare services, one they should neither abdicate in order to perform other functions nor allow others to encroach upon.

Stalwarts laid out the case for preserving the traditional specialization in law enforcement at regional and national meetings and in the pages of the *National Humane Review*, the American Humane Association's monthly journal. Stillman and others discouraged existing SPCCs and humane societies from branching out beyond their traditional law-enforcing function and defended the continued necessity of law enforcement. Writing in 1913, Stillman asserted that "there should be no overlapping in the different departments of philanthropic and charitable work." Traditional charities that do relief work should not, he went on, "invade the field of the anti-cruelty societies for children." Likewise, no SPCC should "undertake to do relief work" unless no other agency in the community existed to do so. "Concentration and specialization," Stillman concluded, "are necessary for the greatest efficiency." In other columns Stillman repeated this same basic message: that SPCCs should stay out of the business of relief or "general social reform work" so as not to engage in "inefficient" duplication of services.[10]

Stalwarts argued that SPCCs should stick to their traditional functions not simply to avoid redundant duplication of social services, but also because law enforcement was a legitimate and necessary tool of child protection that, if abandoned by SPCCs and humane societies, would be performed by no one, leaving vulnerable children at the mercy of vicious adults. Robert J. Wilkin, the president of the New York State Convention of Societies for the Prevention of Cruelty, laid out this case in an essay entitled "The True Mission of the S.P.C.C." Wilkin began by recounting why and how the first SPCC had been formed, rehashing the tale of Mary Ellen Wilson and her abuse, and reminding readers that there had been "no special instrument" for protecting children from abuse at that time. The first SPCC was designed, then, to be that "special instrument" to enforce laws protecting children from abuse and neglect and it should not now abandon that mission, which remained as critical as ever for the same reasons it had some forty years earlier: the police were too busy to take it upon themselves to enforce such laws and no other organization existed to pick up the slack. "In brief, then," Wilkin concluded, "let my appeal be that we will not forget the cause of the origin of our societies and permit ourselves to be led off . . . and have us neglect what no one else can do."[11] Wilkins's plea—combining an appeal to the founding myth of Mary Ellen with an argument for the continued necessity of the SPCC's specialization in law enforcement—was typical of the defense mounted by traditionalists against both the internal and external threats faced by child protectionists.

The same forces that were driving a wedge between traditional child protectionists and newer child welfare advocates also began to strain the link between animal and child protection. In 1917, George Scott of the Illinois Humane Society stepped behind the lectern at the annual meeting of the AHA to consider the question, "Should anticruelty work for children and animals be handled by separate societies?" Some of the association's members must have been contemplating just such a division of labor. Scott's answer to this question was not documented, but the query itself records the strains that threatened the humane movement's linkage of animal with child protection. Among the factors threatening this combination, William Schultz, in his 1922 survey of the current state of animal and child protection, identified one of the most salient: changes in the philosophy and practice of child welfare reform. Though most anticruelty organizations were still dual in focus—307 out of 539 active humane societies—there was, Schultz contended, a "fundamentally wide divergence between the two types of activity." The gap between the two functions was not, Schultz believed, initially very significant, for when the aim of all anticruelty work had been to attend to the immediate relief of suffering and the prosecution of perpetrators, the methods and goals of both animal and child protection converged. By 1922, however, Schultz continued, most child protectionists regarded a law enforcement model as too simplistic and outmoded to deal with the complex factors shaping the lives of children and their families. The goal now was to regard the child in the context of his or her family, and the family in the context of the social structure. "The new tendency," he wrote, "is to deal with the environment" and to aim at "family rehabilitation" through casework rather than to isolate the child as an individual in need of protection. Summarizing this new approach, Schultz wrote that "we are asked to consider the injured child not only as an individual who suffers, but as an integral part of our social system," one whose success or failure will impact "the state a generation hence."[12] Viewed as a critical node in the social system, the child claimed a greater share of public interest than the animal, a being whose abuse and ill treatment seemed to threaten the moral standing of individual perpetrators more than it did the strength of the social fabric. Children formed the basis of the structure of society, while animals were a commodity within it.

New approaches to child welfare not only displaced the law enforcement methods that had made the link between animal and child protection organizationally possible, but also provided a new discourse—competitive and biological in nature—for describing the relationship between the two sorts of beings. Across progressive child welfare circles, reformers compared the government's treatment of animals with its investment in children. Officers and agents of the National Child Labor Committee, for example, frequently invoked the state's protection of its animal resources in order to highlight the shameful neglect of children. Writing in a 1913 issue of the *Child Labor Bulletin*, NCLC special agent Edward F. Brown set out to "show the comparative esteem in which the gulf states hold children and shellfish." Brown went on to point out that Louisiana had passed laws for the protection of game as early as 1857 but had not passed a law regulating child labor until nearly a half century later. Even then, the state continued to allocate many more resources for game management than for the administration and enforcement of child labor laws. In Mississippi, he claimed, the state government had spent more on "paper clips for the office of the Oyster Commission than it spent on the protection of the children who toil in the state."[13]

The argument that Brown and others in the NCLC made was not so much that children, like animals, had rights that deserved protection, but rather that children, like animals, were part of the state's resources that deserved conservation and proper management. "When we plead for the little children we are not pleading alone for the little child," wrote one child labor opponent, rather "we are pleading for the nation." Child labor, NCLC reformers argued, was an unwise use of the state's human resources because it harmed future citizens and thus ultimately damaged the health of the state itself. In one article, the physician W. H. Oates described the day of a young girl working in a textile mill and asked "what kind of a mother can this child make; what kind of offspring can she bring forth?" The cost of child labor was not simply to the girl herself, but also to future generations. Here, again, comparison with the treatment of animals pointed up the folly of child labor. Is not the girl, Oates asked, "entitled to the same consideration the farmer gives his colt or his calf?" After all, working a juvenile animal in harness would seem "preposterous to the average farmer. Can we not put our children of the laboring classes in the same category as the farmer puts his beasts of burden?"[14] Child labor reformers regarded animals both as a model—arguing that children should be treated as animals are—and as unquestionably inferior to humans—arguing that children should be treated as *better* than animals.

The notion that the breeding of animals and the state's management of animal resources might serve as models for how to improve children's lives demonstrates how the comparison of animals to children was not simply competitive. Rather, the two were still culturally linked in important ways. But the link was not through the discourses of domesticity or sentimental liberalism. Rather, the language of science, health, and the body made the relationship of animals to children resonate for early-twentieth-century child welfare advocates. We have already seen how the developmental view of childhood embraced by mid- and late-nineteenth-century middle-class parents had allowed them to accept the notion that their young children were consumed by "bodily exuberance" without causing them to fear, as their colonial forbearers might have, that their offspring were thus fallen or consigned to permanently live a life among beasts. The idea that young children might naturally be more animalistic gained more prominence and sharper definition at the turn of the century. Though educational theorists had long established that children developed through distinct phases of physical and mental growth, in the aftermath of Darwinian theory, it became de rigueur among many scientists and child specialists to claim that these phases recapitulated the evolution of mankind itself; children's growth demonstrated the species trajectory from animal to primitive to civilized man right before their parents' adoring eyes.

Such ideas were promoted most famously by the father of child psychology, G. Stanley Hall, who formulated a full-blown theory of recapitulation during the 1890s. Hall's work both depended upon and reinforced the notion that children were distinct from adults and it founded that difference on children's greater animality. "Hardly less than animal instinct," Hall explained, "child psychology, as Darwin [noted] in his famous observations on infancy . . . can only be explained on an evolutionary basis." Retaining a romantic conception of the child as both "fresh from the hand of God" and closer to nature than the civilized adult, Hall conceived of childhood as a period driven by biological impulses and instincts, and relied, like his predecessors, on the assumptions of comparative psychology as he freely borrowed from, first, the anthropological record to compare children to primitives and, second, from ethological data to compare children to animals. The behaviors of children, such as their tribalism and their plays, clearly demonstrated to Hall "that the child is vastly more ancient than the man, and that adulthood is comparatively a novel structure built upon very antique foundations." The child, he continued, is less the proverbial father of the man than his "half-anthropoid ancestor." Hall believed that children inhabited the animistic world of primitives, feeling an intense bond with nature and not yet experiencing themselves as separate from flora and fauna. Crucially, Hall's work rendered the suspicion that children were animalistic safer, guaranteed by evolution to be simply a stage and cast by romanticism as a valuable and vital period from which children—and even adults—might fruitfully learn.[15]

Progressive reformers took ideas like Hall's to heart as they sought the causes and cures for a range of problems plaguing urban America. Most demonstrably, reformers adopted what Dominick Cavallo calls the "physicalism" of Hall's approach—the notion that mind and body were developmentally inseparable—and argued that playgrounds and proper physical recreation for city children could help prevent the moral dissolution manifest in juvenile delinquency.[16] More generally, the physicalism inherent in ideas such as Hall's contributed to the biologicization of social problems—the attribution of social problems to ill health, bodily malfunction, or physical degeneracy. As one child welfare reformer put the matter, "defective health is the foundation of crime, pauperism, and degeneracy as well as that widespread inefficiency due to obvious disease." In making humans more and more the products of their bodies, such theories also made animals increasingly apt models. The most extreme form of this thinking was, of course, the theory of eugenics. Eugenicists believed that a host of social problems from alcoholism to criminality were heritable, passed down genetically from one generation to the next. Strict eugenicists called for sterilization of the "unfit," those likely to pass such bad genes, and their attendant social problems, on to the next generation, but much milder forms of such biological thinking also existed throughout early-twentieth-century culture and reform, not least among children's advocates.[17]

Besides building playgrounds for the expression of children's animal energies, better baby contests were one example of how the biological equation of humans and animals was manifest in child welfare reform. Begun in 1908 at a state fair in Louisiana, better baby contests measured, weighed, and tested children to find the most physically fit among the contestants. Introducing the new form of child health contest to the readers of *Woman's Home Companion* in 1913, John Biddison explained that the contest was held in "in the State of Iowa, where the finest, sleekest live-stock pasture and the bumper corn crops are raised." Applying "the same scientific methods" as those used for crops and livestock, the women of the baby health contests were "after a new crop record—better babies."[18] As pronouncements like Biddison's suggest, the valences of the animal-child comparison had shifted considerably since the previous century. Such analogizing of children and farm products allied them with animals—as, like livestock, subject to improvement through scientifically derived and biologically based rearing methods—but not as affective companions in the family circle. Where earlier reformers compared animals to children through the image of the pet, now reformers compared children to animals through the lens of livestock.

Part of the reason that early-twentieth-century reformers seized on the comparison between children and livestock had to do not simply with the Darwin-inspired biological linkage, but with the state's investment in protecting and promoting commodity animals. Even those in established humane societies seized on the competitive comparison of children to animals. At the 1917 annual meeting of the American Humane Association, E. W. Burke, the chief agent of the Wyoming Humane Society and the State Board of Child and Animal Protection, stood before those gathered to argue that the federal government was shirking its duties toward the nation's children. To illustrate this massive neglect, Burke cited the fact that the government spent twenty million dollars each year on hogs, cattle, sheep, and horses, while it spent scarcely "one-twentieth of that amount for the care and protection of children, who are the real foundation of our social fabric."[19]

Many hoped that the type of state responsibility—and financial investment—the government lavished on livestock would become a model for the care of children. Established by Congress in 1862 at the behest of President Lincoln, the United States Department of Agriculture (USDA) was an extension of the Republican Party's commitment to the federal government's role in stimulating and strengthening the nation's economy. The department was charged with assisting American farmers to improve their practices according to the dictates of both modern science and political economy. Between 1880 and 1930, the USDA not only rose to a cabinet-level bureau, but also was the fastest-growing government agency. It expanded both in terms of its size, budget, and number of functions and in terms of its regulatory capacity. Operating on the premise that the nation's economic health rested on the productivity of its farms, the USDA helped farmers to increase their yield, find the best price for their products, and protect their livestock and crops from disease. In many respects, the USDA was the model of the modern bureaucratic agency: designed to overcome the limitations of localism in an increasingly integrated economy, the department was nationally funded and staffed by scientifically trained professionals; it not only performed a regulatory function, but reached out into local communities through a network of public-private partnerships from university-based research stations to local farm bureaus. Where a patchwork of private agricultural societies and state-level assistance to farmers had once stood, there was now a coordinated, centralized, federal presence.[20]

Just as the USDA recognized the importance of farmers' (and their livestock's) welfare to the nation through concrete support and regulation, many Progressive Era reformers hoped that government at all levels would begin to assume more responsibility for managing a number of the complex, pressing problems facing the nation, including child welfare. Inclined to view government less as a threatening power and more as an instrument for efficiently coordinating a standardized and systematic set of social services, early-twentieth-century social workers and other professional reformers met with some notable success in urging local, state, and national government to assume a greater role in shaping family life. In the years straddling the turn of the century, children came under the purview of the state at a variety of levels: county boards of welfare were formed, mother's pensions were adopted in many states, juvenile courts opened, illegitimacy laws were rewritten, and uniform children's codes were crafted by some states. Reformers also aimed their sights at the federal level, lobbying for federal regulation of child labor and for the creation of an agency to coordinate the collection and dissemination of information about child welfare. Though efforts to federally regulate child labor were struck down by the Supreme Court, in 1912 Congress created the United States Children's Bureau as a federal agency housed within the Department of Labor.

Indeed, Progressives' habit of comparing the United States government's appropriations for plant and animal husbandry to its neglect of the nation's children had its origins in the battle to establish the Children's Bureau. Child welfare advocates began pressing for a federal bureau at the beginning of the twentieth century and seized on the government's assistance to farmers both as a model and as an example of the nation's misplaced priorities. When in 1909 a bill to establish the federal bureau had congressional hearings, testimonials from child welfare reformers continued to use the USDA as a foil. In her speech before a House committee, Lillian Wald, a leader in the settlement house movement, described the morning she learned of the government's boll weevil campaign. "That brought home, with a very strong emphasis to the appeal, the fact nothing which could have happened to the children, would have called forth such official action on the part of the Government." Testifying before a Senate committee, Owen Lovejoy of the NCLC defended the requested appropriation for a Children's Bureau by reminding senators that the amount requested was less than that currently being given to the Bureau of Animal Husbandry and other divisions of the USDA. Other speakers continued to use the analogy.[21]

It was not just through the USDA that the federal government invested in the nation's animals. Though no one speaking in favor of the Children's Bureau brought up the example, the national government was responsible for enforcing the sole federal animal protection statute enacted during the nineteenth century. Passed in 1877 at the behest of animal protectionists, the twenty-eight-hour law required that animals transported by "rail carrier, express carrier or common carrier" be given five hours' rest, water, and food after every twenty-eight hours of travel. In the era when the centralization of slaughterhouses in urban locations like Chicago and points further east meant that Western range cattle were transported for days on end, the legislation was crafted to overcome the inadequacies of state-level regulation of a complex interstate trade. Indeed the American Humane Association itself had been founded in 1877 to coordinate interstate efforts among animal protection organizations to attempt to better regulate rail transportation of livestock. Once in effect, infractions to the twenty-eight-hour law were monitored by agents of animal protection organizations but enforced by the federal government. And though the constitutionality of the law was challenged by litigants in an 1883 case, the measure was upheld as a valid exercise of federal power under the interstate commerce clause.[22]

Ironically, when the bill establishing the Children's Bureau was being debated by Congress, Elbridge Gerry, president of the NY-SPCC John Lindsay, and AHA president William O. Stillman all spoke out against the bureau. Their arguments centered on two claims: that child welfare work was best left to the states, and that the politicization of such work would be counterproductive. Gerry seemed to fear that the new bureau would try to standardize legislation affecting children across the states and he remonstrated that the Constitution, by design, left police powers in the hands of the states to determine what legislation best fitted the needs and problems of its population. Though Children's Bureau advocates officially disavowed a desire for such standardization at congressional hearings, elsewhere some had written of the necessity of "uniformity among the states" on legislation relating to children. Worse still, Gerry believed this attempted standardization would not only emanate on high from Washington, D.C., rather than bubbling up from the states, but the bureau would be under the direction of a political appointee, someone who might not understand child welfare much less myriad local conditions.[23]

Though the opposition of Gerry, Lindsay, and Shortall was voiced in principled terms, it may have been little more than jealous guarding of SPCCs' authority, which, as we have seen, stalwarts felt was already being encroached. Though we cannot know for certain whether principles or parochialism motivated the opposition of Gerry and his ilk, their refusal to support the Children's Bureau seems to mark them as conservative, even retrograde, blindly clinging to the past by refusing to acknowledge the drift of reform in the new century. Nevertheless, seen in context, their concerns make some sense. Heretofore, most reform had taken place at the state and local levels. For Gerry, Lindsay, and Stillman—all from New York state—this had been a hospitable forum for their ambitions. The New York SPCC enjoyed unrivaled authority in its field, a cozy relationship with the state legislature, state and municipal judges, city police forces, and an extensive police power. They had carved out this territory, moreover, at a time when municipal and state government was rife with cronyism and corruption. To them, their success owed to its apolitical, nonpartisan nature. The fact that they wielded state power without actually being part of government patronage was critical. As they and countless other Gilded Age reformers knew, political appointees not only had an unstable tenure, but many had a habit of laxly enforcing the laws.

As a student of the law, Gerry also had to know that the federal government did not have police powers and that the new bureau would therefore be toothless no matter who became its head. Indeed, at congressional hearings to establish the bureau, its *supporters* continually emphasized how little oversight the bureau would actually have. To well-established local reformers it might have seemed that the new bureau potentially drained resources, energy, and authority away from local, private organizations without offering any enhanced power to aid the nation's children. Elsewhere, Stillman expressed such a fear about even those humane societies, like Colorado's, that had become state bureaus. Stillman noted that states tended to provide less funding than the private sector and that state humane bureaus tended to enjoy less, not more power, since they were subject to politicians who "can always find means to clip its wings." Indeed, in states with well-established bureaus in fields such as public health and labor, laws under the bureaus' jurisdiction often went unenforced as states failed to provide adequate funding or enforcement bodies.[24] This was precisely the situation that the delegation of enforcement responsibility for animal and child protection to humane organizations had been designed to overcome.

The reaction of men like Gerry and Stillman was not, moreover, without parallel or precedent. The movement to create a federal version of what had begun, during the Gilded Age, as a state-level bureau occurred across a number of fields in the early twentieth century. Though the men and women who staffed state bureaus of health, charities, and labor often began their careers as reformers advocating for the assumption of state responsibility for these domains, when the federal government looked to become involved, many resisted. And officials in states with the most well-developed bureaus, the most stringent laws, the greatest budgets and enforcement powers, resisted the most. In the matter of pure food and drug legislation, for example, commissioners from Illinois and New York feared that federal legislation—and a federal enforcement agency—would actually weaken not strengthen state standards.[25] Though SPCCs and humane societies were not ordinarily state bureaus, as law-enforcing bodies they were in many respects similar and might too have feared that centralization and uniformity at the federal level would weaken the vigorous body of law and powers that they had built over decades. Such attitudes reveal less an embrace of laissez-faire than they do the extent to which reformers had been successful at the state level during the Gilded Age. While state regulation was proven and had (with important exceptions) withstood constitutional scrutiny, in many arenas, federal regulation was untried.

To Gerry and Stillman's contemporaries—and, for the most part, to subsequent historians—federal responsibility and intervention seemed the

way of the future. Because humane society stalwarts clung to law enforcement and rejected a new generation's approach to child welfare, the story
of nineteenth-century anticruelty efforts can seem little more than a historical byway. The conjunction of animal with child protection appears
as quaint or ill informed, superseded as it was by the realization that the
complex problems of human families warranted different methods than
those required for addressing the misfortunes of livestock, working animals, and pets. But that union betrayed the fact that changes in philoso-
phies of discipline, toleration of pain and suffering, and a slippery slope
theory of violence all underlay the logic of joining animal to child protection. Anticruelty organizations, moreover, not only contributed to the
postbellum transformation of moral sensibility, but also helped to transform the nature of the state, exemplifying the proliferation of regulatory
legislation in the Gilded Age. Blending animals with children, sentimentalism with liberalism, rights with dependence, and private with public
authority, anticruelty organizations straddled the past and the future.
Long after the union of animal and child protection would be forgotten,
the style of rights talk and the sort of specialized law enforcement they
pioneered would become a staple of reform rhetoric, on the one hand, and
state activity, on the other.

And though the physical abuse of children and the sufferings of animals would largely be forgotten between the World Wars, in the post–World
War II era a dramatic "discovery" of child abuse coincided with renewed
attention to modern forms of animal suffering in laboratories and industrialized meat production. Alongside the growing attention to animal and
child protection, criminologists and other researchers demonstrated a link
between violence toward animals and domestic abuse. Reviving the old
notion that "he who is cruel to his beast will abuse even his own child,"
modern protectionists have linked cruelty to crime, social disorder, and
individual suffering.[26] These recent developments might please Jacob Riis,
who wrote in 1892 that "the old link that bound the dumb brute with the
helpless child in a common bond of humane sympathy has never been broken."[27] Of course the link was broken—by developments in child welfare,
by a competitive language positioning animals-as-commodities against
children-as-investments, and by debates about the role of the federal government in protecting the weak—but its legacy remains.

# NOTES

## INTRODUCTION

1. Etta Wheeler, *The Story of Mary Ellen Which Started the Child Saving Crusade Throughout the World* (1913; repr., Englewood, CO: American Humane Association, n.d.), 1.

2. Wheeler, *Story of Mary Ellen*, 2.

3. Jacob Riis, *The Children of the Poor* (New York: Scribner and Sons, 1892), 142–43.

4. Wheeler, *Story of Mary Ellen*, 3.

5. Untitled, *New York Times*, 10 April 1874; "A Cruel Guardian Punished," *New York Daily Tribune*, 18 April 1874.

6. "Society for the Prevention of Cruelty to Children," *New York Times*, 27 December 1874; "Prevention of Cruelty to Children," *New York Times*, 29 December 1874. For a complete rendering of Mary Ellen's story, see: Eric A. Shelman and Stephen Lazoritz, *Out of the Darkness: the Story of Mary Ellen Wilson* (Cape Coral, FL: Dolphin Moon Publishing, 1998); Shelman and Lazoritz, *The Mary Ellen Wilson Child Abuse Case and the Beginning of Children's Rights in Nineteenth Century America* (Jefferson, NC: McFarland & Company, Inc., 2005).

7. Roswell C. McCrea, *The Humane Movement: A Descriptive Survey* (New York: Columbia University Press, 1910), 15.

8. Riis, *Children of the Poor*, 150.

9. For general histories of animal and child protection in the United States, see: Diane Beers, *For the Prevention of Cruelty: The History and Legacy of Animal Rights Activism in the United States* (Athens, OH: Swallow Press, 2006); Bernard Oreste Unti, "The Quality of Mercy: Organized Animal Protection in the United States, 1866–1930" (Ph.D. diss., American University, 2002); Roswell C. McCrea, *The Humane Movement: A Descriptive Survey* (New York: Columbia University Press, 1910); James Turner, *Reckoning with the Beast: Animals, Pain, and Humanity in the Victorian Mind* (Baltimore: Johns Hopkins University Press, 1980); Raelene Freitag, "Thse Peril and Promise of Nineteenth Century Child Protection: The Wisconsin Humane Society, 1879–1920" (Ph.D. diss., University of Wisconsin–Milwaukee, 1997); Louis John Covotsos et al.,

*The Illinois Humane Society, 1869 to 1979* (River Forest, IL: Rosary College, Graduate School of Library Science, 1981); Sherri Broder, *Tramps, Unfit Mothers, and Neglected Children: Negotiating Family in Late Nineteenth-Century Philadelphia* (Philadelphia: University of Pennsylvania Press, 2002); Stephen Murray Robertson, *Crimes against Children: Sexual Violence and Legal Culture in New York City, 1880–1960* (Chapel Hill: University of North Carolina Press, 2006); Linda Gordon, *Heroes of Their Own Lives: The Politics and History of Family Violence, Boston, 1880–1960* (Urbana: University of Illinois Press, 2002; orig. pub. 1988); Elizabeth Pleck, *Domestic Tyranny: The Making of American Social Policy against Family Violence from Colonial Times to the Present* (Urbana: University of Illinois Press, 2004; orig. pub. 1987).

10. Michael Katz, *In the Shadow of the Poorhouse*, 10th ed. (New York: Basic Books, 1996), 112–13.

11. "Prevention of Cruelty to Children." This language is identical to that of Jacob Riis. See Riis, *Children of the Poor*, 142.

12. "How the S.P.C.C. Originated," *Humane Journal* 21 (May 1893): 73.

13. NY-SPCC, *Fortieth Annual Report, December 31, 1914* (New York: s.n., 1915), 14.

14. Robert M. Mulford, "Historical Perspective," in *Child Abuse and Neglect: A Guide with Case Studies for Treating the Child and Family*, ed. Nancy B. Hill and Deborah A. Ebeling (Boston: John Wright, 1983), 3. See also: George Henry Payne, *The Child in Human Progress* (New York: G. P. Putnam's Sons, 1916), 333–38; Anne Allen and Arthur Morton, *This Is Your Child: The Story of the National Society for the Prevention of Cruelty to Children* (London: Routledge & Kegan Paul, 1961), 15–16; C. Henry Kempe and Ray E. Helfer, "Introduction," in *Helping the Battered Child and His Family*, ed. C. Henry Kempe and Ray E. Helfer (Philadelphia: J. B. Lippincott Company, 1972), ix; Deborah A. Ebling, "Thoughts on Intervention," in *Child Abuse: Intervention and Treatment*, ed. Nancy B. Hill and Deborah A. Ebeling (Acton, MA: Publishing Sciences Group, Inc., 1975), 7; Alfred Kadushin and Judith A. Martin, *Child Welfare Services*, 4th ed. (New York: Garland Publishing Inc., 1990), 4–5; Vincent J. Fontana and Douglas J. Besharov, *The Maltreated Child: The Maltreatment Syndrome in Children: A Medical, Legal and Social Guide*, 5th ed. (Springfield, IL: Charles C. Thomas, 1996), 3–4.

15. Vincent J. Fontana, *The Maltreated Child: The Maltreatment Syndrome in Children* (Springfield, IL: Charles C. Thomas, 1964), 8–9.

16. See: Allen and Morton, *This Is Your Child*, 16; Ebling, "Thoughts on Intervention," 7; David R. Walters, *Physical and Sexual Abuse of Children* (Bloomington: Indiana University Press, 1975), 18; Mary Hanemann Lystad, "Violence at Home: A Review of the Literature," in *Child Abuse and Violence*, ed. David G. Gil (New York: AMS Press Inc., 1979), 393–94; Samuel X. Radbill, "Children in a World of Violence: A History of Child Abuse," in *The Battered Child*, 3rd ed., ed. C. Henry Kempe and Ray E. Helfer (Chicago: University of Chicago Press, 1980), 11; Mulford, "Historical Perspective," 3; Kadushin and Martin, *Child Welfare Services*, 221–22. For an account of how these erroneous facts surrounding Mary Ellen's case have crept into the child welfare literature of the social work profession, see: Lela B. Costin, "Unraveling the Mary Ellen Legend: Origins of the 'Cruelty' Movement," *Social Service Review* 65 (June 1991): 203–23.

17. Walters, *Physical and Sexual Abuse*, 18.

18. Turner, *Reckoning with the Beast*; Kathleen Kete, *The Beast in the Boudoir: Petkeeping in Nineteenth-Century Paris* (Berkeley: University of California Press, 1995); Harriet Ritvo, *The Animal Estate: The English and Other Creatures in the Victorian Age* (Cambridge, MA: Harvard University Press, 1989).

19. Harold D. Guither, *Animal Rights: History and Scope of a Radical Social Movement* (Carbondale: Southern Illinois University Press, 1998), 1; Gary Francione, *Animals, Property, and the Law* (Philadelphia: Temple University Press, 1995), 123–24; Turner, *Reckoning with the Beast*, 54–59; Thomas G. Kelch, "Toward a Non-Property Status for Animals," *New York University School of Law Environmental Law Journal* 6 (1998): 540; Jordan Curnutt, *Animals and the Law: A Sourcebook* (Santa Barbara: ABC Clio, 2001), 28–30; Daniel S. Moretti, *Animal Rights and the Law* (London: Oceana Publications, 1984), 1. With respect to SPCCs, see: Lela B. Costin, Howard Jacob Karger, and David Stoesz, *The Politics of Child Abuse in America* (New York: Oxford University Press, 1996), 47, 67–75; Shauna Vey, "Good Intentions and Fearsome Prejudice," *Theatre Survey* 42 (May 2001): 53–66.

20. Linda Gordon, "Family Violence, Feminism, and Social Control," *Feminist Studies* 12 (Fall 1986): 453–78; Gordon, *Heroes of Their Own Lives*; Sherri Broder, "Informing the Cruelty: The Monitoring of Respectability in Philadelphia's Neighborhoods in the Late Nineteenth Century," *Radical America* 21 (1987): 34–47; Broder, *Tramps, Unfit Mothers and Neglected Children*; Robertson, *Crimes against Children*.

21. Gordon, "Family Violence, Feminism, and Social Control"; Unti, "Quality of Mercy," esp. 4–7; Beers, *For the Prevention of Cruelty*, esp. 19–38. A generally middle-of-the-road assessment is also given by Freitag, "The Peril and Promise of Nineteenth Century Child Protection." For Britain, see: Hilda Kean, *Animal Rights: Political and Social Change in Britain since 1800* (London: Reaktion Books, 1998).

22. The phrase "long Progressive Era" is Rebecca Edwards's. Edwards, *New Spirits: Americans in the Gilded Age* (New York: Oxford University Press, 2006), 7.

23. "Waifs and Strays," *New York Times*, 11 April 1874.

24. James Baldwin, "Everybody's Protest Novel," in *Notes of a Native Son* (1955; repr., Boston: Beacon Press, 1970), 14.

25. Dan McKanan, *Identifying the Image of God: Radical Christians and Nonviolent Power in the Antebellum United States* (New York: Oxford University Press, 2002), 5; Philip Fisher, *Hard Facts: Setting and Form in the American Novel* (New York: Oxford University Press, 1987), 100.

26. Gillian Silverman, "Sympathy and Its Vicissitudes," *American Studies* 43 (Fall 2002): 5; Ruth Bloch, "Utopianism, Sentimentalism, and Liberal Culture in America," *Intellectual History Newsletter* 24 (2002): 48–49; Glenn Hendler, *Public Sentiments: Structures of Feeling in Nineteenth-Century America* (Chapel Hill: University of North Carolina Press, 2001), 3.

27. "Terrible Cruelty to a Child," *New York Daily Tribune*, 10 April 1874; "Cruelty to a Child," *New York Daily Tribune*, 14 April 1874.

28. Quoted in Shelman and Lazoritz, *Out of the Darkness*, 328.

29. Untitled, *New York Times*, 10 April 1874.

30. "Terrible Cruelty to a Child."

31. "Cruelty to a Child."

32. "A Child's Suffering," *New York Daily Tribune*, 11 April 1874; "Cruelty to a Child."

33. NY-SPCC, *Twentieth Annual Report, December 31, 1894* (New York: s.n., 1895), 5.

34. For the transformation in reform attitudes and strategies, see: George M. Fredrickson, *The Inner Civil War: Northern Intellectuals and the Crisis of the Union* (New York, 1965); John L. Thomas, "Romantic Reform in America, 1815–1865," *American Quarterly* 17 (1965): 656–81; John Higham, *From Boundlessness to Consolidation: The Transformation of American Culture, 1848–1860* (Ann Arbor, 1969); Lori D. Ginzberg, *Women and the Work of Benevolence: Morality, Politics, and Class in the Nineteenth-Century United States* (New Haven, 1990); Gaines M. Foster, *Moral Reconstruction: Christian Lobbyists and the Federal Legislation of Morality, 1865–1920* (Chapel Hill, 2002). There is some dispute over the timing of these changes in attitude and method. Foster and Frederickson, for example, make the war itself a primary causative factor, while Higham and Ginzberg find changes afoot in the late 1840s and in the 1850s. Nevertheless, the changes detected in the 1850s are the result of a debate that is essentially extended and answered by the war experience: namely, the efficacy and desirability of political-legal versus individual-moral means for producing social change. Indeed, in the late 1840s this debate split the antislavery movement between the Garrisonian suasionists and the newly formed Liberty Party.

35. Donald Pizer, ed., *The Cambridge Companion to American Realism and Naturalism* (Cambridge: Cambridge University Press, 2002); Amy Kaplan, *The Social Construction of American Realism* (Chicago: University of Chicago Press, 1992); Michael Davitt Bell, *The Problem of American Realism: Studies in the Cultural History of a Literary Ideal* (Chicago: University of Chicago Press, 1996); Henry May, *The End of American Innocence: A Study of the First Years of Our Own Time, 1912–1917* (New York: Columbia University Press, 1959); Ann Douglas, *Terrible Honesty: Mongrel Manhattan in the 1920s* (New York: Farrar, Strauss & Giroux, 1996). On the transition from Victorianism to Modernism generally, see: John Kasson, *Amusing the Million: Coney Island at the Turn of the Century* (New York: Hill and Wang, 1978); Daniel Singal, *The War Within: From Victorian to Modernist Thought in the South, 1919–1945* (Chapel Hill: University of North Carolina Press, 1982); Singal, "Towards a Definition of American Modernism," *American Quarterly* 39 (1987): 7–26; Miles Orvell, *The Real Thing: Imitation and Authenticity in American Culture, 1880–1940* (Chapel Hill: University of North Carolina Press, 1989); Christine Stansell, *American Moderns: Bohemian New York and the Creation of a New Century* (New York: Metropolitan Books, 2000).

36. Louis Menand, *The Metaphysical Club: A Story of Ideas in America* (New York: Farrar, Straus & Giroux, 2002).

37. For one of the few scholarly treatments of sentimentalism after the Civil War, and for an argument about the "concrete social institutionalization" of sentimentalism through reform practices, see: Laura Wexler, *Tender Violence: Domestic Visions in an Age of U.S. Imperialism* (Chapel Hill: University of North Carolina Press, 2000), esp. chap. 3; Michele Landis Dauber, "The Sympathetic State," *Law and History Review* 23 (2005): http://www.historycooperative.org.turing.library.northwestern.edu/journals/lhr/23.2/dauber.html (12 March 2007). Dauber argues that the legal and political

justification for the federal welfare state was crafted in the nineteenth century through disaster relief administration, and that such practices were shaped by narratives of innocent suffering and by the ideal of what she calls the "sympathetic state." Congressmen advocating relief measures argued that it was the duty of the state to relieve suffering; some even developed "a theory of the state based upon compassion and charity" (paragraph 31).

38. This definition of liberalism relies on the following: Ruth Bloch, "Utopianism, Sentimentalism, and Liberal Culture in America," 47; Amy Dru Stanley, *From Bondage to Contract: Wage Labor, Marriage, and the Market in the Age of Slave Emancipation* (Cambridge: Cambridge University Press, 1998), 4–17; Joyce Appleby, *Liberalism and Republicanism in the Historical Imagination* (Cambridge, MA: Harvard University Press, 1992), 1–11. For the world-historical importance of American liberalism, see: Dorothy Ross, "Liberalism and American Exceptionalism," *Intellectual History Newsletter* 24 (2002): 72–83.

39. "Waifs and Strays."

40. "Prevention of Cruelty to Children."

41. "Prevention of Cruelty to Children."

42. "Terrible Cruelty to a Child."

43. Wheeler, *Story of Mary Ellen*, 1.

44. "Prevention of Cruelty to Children."

45. For a classic definition of this distinction, see: Sidney Fine, *Laissez Faire and the General-Welfare State: A Study of Conflict in American Thought, 1865–1901* (Ann Arbor: University of Michigan Press, 1956).

46. For general accounts that cover both the Gilded Age and the Progressive Era, see: Fine, *Laissez Faire and the General-Welfare State*; Samuel P. Hays, *The Response to Industrialism: 1885–1914* (Chicago: University of Chicago Press, 1957); Robert Wiebe, *The Search for Order, 1877–1920* (New York: Hill & Wang, 1967); Nell Irvin Painter, *Standing at Armageddon, The United States, 1877–1919* (New York: W. W. Norton & Company, 1987); Alan Dawley, *Struggles for Justice: Social Responsibility and the Liberal State* (Cambridge, MA: Belknap Press of Harvard University Press, 1991); Michael McGerr, *A Fierce Discontent: The Rise and All of the Progressive Movement in America* (New York: Oxford University Press, 2005); Eric Foner, *The Story of American Freedom* (New York: W. W. Norton & Company, 1998), chaps. 6 and 7; Sheldon Stromquist, *Reinventing "The People": The Progressive Movement, the Class Problem, and the Origins of Modern Liberalism* (Urbana: University of Illinois Press, 2006); T. J. Jackson Lears, *Rebirth of a Nation: The Making of Modern America, 1877–1920* (New York: Harper, 2009). On interdependence as a crucial concept in this period, see: Thomas Haskell, *The Emergence of Professional Social Science: The American Social Science Association and the Nineteenth Century Crisis of Authority* (Urbana: University of Illinois Press, 1977). Among these surveys there are, of course, a number of different interpretations of the Gilded Age and the Progressive Era. Most, however, represent the Progressive Era as a departure from the Gilded Age rather than as an extension of it. In Dawley's language, the Gilded Age is a period when industrialization creates problems that produce an imbalance between state and society that is corrected by the Progressive attempt to transform the state, to bring its powers into line with the

reality of the scale and depth of the post–Civil War transmogrification of the United States from agrarian to industrial economy. For the few historians who represent the Progressive Era as an extension of logics or activities set in motion in the Gilded Age, see: Nancy Cohen, *The Reconstruction of American Liberalism, 1865–1914* (Chapel Hill: University of North Carolina Press, 2001); Edwards, *New Spirits*.

47. William Novak, "The Myth of the 'Weak' American State," *American Historical Review* 113 (2008): 752–72. See also: Novak, "The Pluralist State: The Convergence of Public and Private Power in America," in *American Public Life and the Historical Imagination*, ed. Wendy Gamber et al. (Notre Dame: University of Notre Dame Press, 2003), 27–48; Novak, *The People's Welfare: Law and Regulation in Nineteenth-Century America* (Chapel Hill: University of North Carolina Press, 1996). For a suggestive account of the expansion of public authority through SPCCs, see: Michael Grossberg, "'A Protected Childhood': The Emergence of Child Protection in America," in *American Public Life and the Historical Imagination*, 213–39.

48. Stephen Skowronek, *Building a New American State: The Expansion of National Administrative Capacities, 1877–1920* (Cambridge: Cambridge University Press, 1982); Morton Keller, *Affairs of State: Public Life in Late Nineteenth Century America* (Cambridge, MA: Belknap Press of Harvard University Press, 1977); Drew Gilpin Faust, *This Republic of Suffering: Death and the American Civil War* (New York: Knopf, 2008).

49. James Bryce, *The American Commonwealth*, vol. 2 (London: MacMillan and Co., 1888), 407, 409.

50. Novak, *The People's Welfare*; Bryce, *American Commonwealth*; Fine, *Laissez Faire and the General Welfare State*, 353–62; quote is from James H. Eckels, "The Menace of Legislation," *North American Review* 165 (August 1897): 244.

51. Ernest Nusse, "The Protection of Children," *Bay State Monthly* 2 (November 1884): 89–96.

CHAPTER ONE

1. McCrea, *The Humane Movement*, 136.

2. Fisher, *Hard Facts*, 99–102.

3. "The Children," *Humane Journal* 5 (October 1877): 4; Illinois Humane Society, "A New Service in an Old Tradition" (Chicago: s.n., 1966), 3; *Doings of the First Annual Meeting of the International Humane Society* (Boston: A. J. Wright, 1877), 5.

4. *Doings of the Seventh Annual Meeting of the American Humane Association, Held at Washington, D.C., on Wednesday, Dec. 5, and Thursday, Dec. 6, 1883* (Boston: Wright & Potter, 1884), 58.

5. John G. Shortall, "Child-Saving Work of the Humane Societies," (unpublished speech, 1897), 3.

6. No official reasons for the decision to include both animals and children under the Mercy mantle were ever recorded. The original Department of Mercy reports refer only to promoting kindness to animals, but in 1902 the department begins to report remonstrances against cruelty to children as well as animals. WCTU, *Report of the*

*Twenty-Ninth Annual Convention, National Woman's Christian Temperance Union* (Chicago: Woman's Temperance Publishing Association, 1902), 315.

7. Floyd Morse Hubbard, *Prevention of Cruelty to Animals in the States of Illinois, Colorado and California*, Bulletin of Social Legislation on the Henry Bergh Foundation for the Promotion of Humane Education, no. 4, ed. Samuel McCune Lindsay (New York: Columbia University Press, 1916), 37, 59; WCTU, *Report of the Thirty-First Annual Convention, National Woman's Christian Temperance Union* (Chicago: Woman's Temperance Publishing Association, 1904), 78; WCTU, *Report of the Thirty-Second Annual Convention, National Woman's Christian Temperance Union* (Chicago: Woman's Temperance Publishing Association, 1905), 84.

8. Thomas Clarkson, "To His Excellency, William Pennington, Governor of New Jersey," *The Friend; a Religious and Literary Journal*, 19 December 1840, 96; A Subscriber, "Society of Friends—Slavery, and the Slave Trade," *The Friend; a Religious and Literary Journal*, 3 June 1837.

9. "Lynn Women's A. S. Society," *Liberator*, 11 August 1843; Thomas D. Morris, *Southern Slavery and the Law, 1619–1860* (Chapel Hill: University of North Carolina Press, 1996), 229.

10. Wisconsin Humane Society, *First Biennial Report for the Two Years Ending November 29, 1881* (Milwaukee, 1882), 1; Edward P. Buffett, *The Animals' Magna Charta: An Ethnic History and Ethical Truth* (Boston: American Humane Education Society, 1925), 7. NY-SPCC, *Twenty-Second Annual Report, December 31, 1896* (New York, 1897), 10; NY-SPCC, *Twenty-Seventh Annual Report, December 31, 1901* (New York, 1902), 9; "We Speak for Children," *Humane Journal* 16 (February 1888): 18; "Societies for the Prevention of Cruelty," *Humane Journal* 17 (January 1889): 10; *In Memoriam, Henry Bergh, Died March 12, 1888* (New York: G. P. Putnam's Sons, 1888), 9.

11. Samuel J. Levick, PSPCA secretary, to unknown, June 26, 1876, PSPCA Papers, Historical Society of Pennsylvania; PSPCA, *Fourth Annual Report of the Pennsylvania Society for the Prevention of Cruelty to Animals* (Philadelphia: s.n., 1872); "Animals Only," *Our Dumb Animals* 8 (August 1875): 20; "Cruelty to Children," *Our Dumb Animals* 6 (January 1874): 74; "Cruelty to Children," *Our Dumb Animals* 8 (January 1876): 60.

12. Mrs. C. M. Fairchild, *Pleadings of Mercy for the Animal World, and All Other Defenseless Creatures* (Chicago: A. W. Landon, 1883), 23.

13. NY-SPCC, *Second Annual Report* (New York: s.n., 1877), 5.

14. Wisconsin Humane Society, *Reports for the Years 1895, 1896, 1897, 1898, and 1899* (Milwaukee: s.n., 1899), 63.

15. "Work of the Illinois Humane Society," *Humane Journal* 8 (August 1880): 9.

16. Shortall, "Child-Saving Work," 2.

17. Illinois Humane Society, *Eighth Annual Report* (Chicago: s.n., 1879), 6. Other humane societies received similar complaints. See: Floyd Morse Hubbard, *Prevention of Cruelty to Animals in New York State*, Bulletin of Social Legislation on the Henry Bergh Foundation for the Promotion of Humane Education, no. 3, ed. Samuel McCune Lindsay (New York: Columbia University Press, 1915), 41–45.

18. Illinois Humane Society, *Ninth Annual Report* (Chicago: s.n., 1880), 5.

19. Illinois Humane Society, *Tenth Annual Report* (Chicago: s.n., 1881), 9.

20. Illinois Humane Society, *Fourteenth Annual Report* (Chicago: s.n., 1884), 17.

21. Shortall, "Child-Saving Work," 2.

22. Connecticut Humane Society, *Thirty-First Annual Report* (Hartford: Case, Lockwood & Brainard Company, [1912]), 9.

23. O. L. Dudley to John Shortall, 8 October 1884, Illinois Humane Society Records—supplement, box 2, folder 19, case records, Sept.–Nov 1884, University of Illinois at Chicago, Special Collections.

24. *Sixth Annual Report of the Fox River Valley District of the Wisconsin Humane Society . . . For the Year Ending October 1894* (Oshkosh, WI: s.n., 1895), 21–27; *Annual Report of the St. Paul Humane Society* (St. Paul: s.n., 1899), 7–8.

25. Broder, *Tramps, Unfit Mothers, and Neglected Children*, 38; Pleck, *Domestic Tryanny*, 83; Gordon, *Heroes of Their Own Lives*, 70–71.

26. Nancy Cott, *The Bonds of Womanhood: "Woman's Sphere" in New England, 1780–1835*, 2d. ed. (New Haven: Yale University Press, 1997); Mary Ryan, *Cradle of the Middle Class: The Family in Oneida County, New York, 1790–1865* (Cambridge: Cambridge University Press, 1981); Jeanne Boydston, *Home and Work: Housework, Wages, and the Ideology of Labor in the Early Republic* (New York: Oxford University Press, 1993); Carl Degler, *At Odds: Women and the Family in America from the Revolution to the Present* (New York: Oxford University Press, 1980): 8–9, 66–85; Barbara Welter, "The Cult of True Womanhood, 1820–1860," *American Quarterly* 18 (1966): 151–74; Amy Dru Stanley, "Home Life and Morality of the Market," in *The Market Revolution in America: Social, Political, and Religious Expressions, 1800–1880* (Charlottesville: University of Virginia Press, 1996), 74–96.

27. Quoted in *The Child and the State*, vol. 1, *Legal Status in the Family, Apprenticeship and Child Labor, Selected Documents*, ed. Grace Abbott (Chicago: University of Chicago Press, 1938), 51.

28. Mary Ann Mason, *From Father's Property to Children's Rights: The History of Child Custody in the United States* (New York: Columbia University Press, 1994), 2–13, 30–31, 46–47; Michael Grossberg, *Governing the Hearth: Law and Family in Nineteenth-Century America* (Chapel Hill: University of North Carolina Press, 1985), 4; Peter Bardaglio, *Reconstructing the Household: Families, Sex, and the Law in the Nineteenth-Century South* (Chapel Hill: University of North Carolina Press, 1995), 23–28; Grace Abbott, "Introduction" and "Early History of Child Labor in the United States," in *The Child and the State*, 3–8, 270–76; Thomas P. Mason, "Child Abuse and Neglect Part 1: Historical Overview, Legal Matrix, and Social Perspectives," *North Carolina Law Review* 50 (1972): 299–300.

29. Degler, *At Odds*, 66–75; Ryan, *Cradle of the Middle Class*, 157–73; Viviana A. Zelizer, *Pricing the Priceless Child: The Changing Social Value of Children* (New York: Basic Books, 1985); Steven Mintz, *Huck's Raft: A History of American Childhood* (Cambridge, MA: Belknap Press of Harvard University Press, 2004), 75–93; Peter N. Stearns, *Childhood in World History* (New York: Routledge, 2006), 54–63; Bernard Wishy, *The Child and the Republic: The Dawn of Modern American Child Nurture* (Philadelphia: University of Pennsylvania Press, 1968); Daniel Beekman, *The Mechanical Baby: A Popular History of the Theory and Practice of Child Raising* (Westport, CN: Lawrence

Hill & Company, 1977); Christina Hardyment, *Dream Babies: Three Centuries of Good Advice on Child Care* (New York: Harper & Row, 1983).

30. On colonial and early American childrearing ideas and practice, see: John Demos, *A Little Commonwealth: Family Life in Plymouth Colony* (Oxford: Oxford University Press, 1970), esp. 100–106, 134–36; Philip Greven, *The Protestant Temperament: Patterns of Child-Rearing, Religious Experience, and the Self in Early America* (New York: Alfred A Knopf, 1977), 28–43; On changes in theology, see: Ann Douglas, *The Feminization of American Culture* (New York: Knopf, 1977); Lydia Maria Child, *The Mother's Book*, 6th ed. (New York: C. S. Francis, 1844), 3; electronic reproduction made available by the Gerritsen Collection of Women's History online: http://nucat .library.northwestern.edu/cgi-bin/Pwebrecon.cgi?BBID=4749704; Jacqueline S. Reiner, *From Virtue to Character: American Childhood, 1775–1850* (New York: Twayne Publishers, 1996), 73, 90–91, 101.

31. On American romanticism, see: Philip F. Gura, *American Transcendentalism: A History* (New York: Hill & Wang, 2007). On romantic views of children, see: Jacqueline S. Reiner, *From Virtue to Character: American Childhood, 1775–1900* (New York: Twayne, 1996), 99–101; Peter Coveney, *Poor Monkey: The Child in Literature* (London: Rockliff, 1957), 1–14; M. H. Abrams, *Natural Supernaturalism: Tradition and Revolution in Romantic Literature* (New York: W. W. Norton & Company, 1971), 380–82, 411–15; Gura, *American Transcendentalism*, 84–90; Megan Marshall, *The Peabody Sisters: Three Women Who Ignited American Romanticism* (Boston: Houghton Mifflin, 2005), 315; Mintz, *Huck's Raft*, 76–81; Terry Ogel, "The Background of the Images of Childhood in American Literature," *Western Humanities Review* 33 (1979): 281–97; Emerson quoted in Abrams, *Natural Supernaturalism*, 412–13.

32. David Perkins, *Romanticism and Animal Rights* (Cambridge: Cambridge University Press, 2003); Christine Kenyon-Jones, *Kindred Brutes: Animals in Romantic-Period Writing* (Aldershot: Ashgate, 2001); Karin Calvert, *Children in the House: The Material Culture of Early Childhood, 1600–1900* (Boston: Northeastern University Press, 1992), 32–33, 125–27. See also: Greven, *Protestant Temperament*, 29.

33. "About Babies," *Putnam's Monthly Magazine of American Literature, Science, and Art* 6 (August 1855): 140; George Ackerley, *On the Management of Children* (New York: Bancroft and Holley, 1836), 61, quoted in Wishy, *The Child and the Republic*, 43; Caroline Winterer, "Avoiding a 'Hothouse System of Education': Nineteenth-Century Early Childhood Education from the Infant Schools to the Kindergartens," *History of Education Quarterly* 32 (1992): 289–314.

34. Katherine C. Grier, "Animal House: Pet Keeping in Urban and Suburban Households in the Northeast, 1850–1900," *Dublin Seminar for New England Folklife Annual Proceedings* 18 (1993): 109–29.

35. "Pet," in *Oxford English Dictionary Online* (Oxford University Press, 2003); Leo Spitzer, "On the Etymology of Pet," *Language* 26 (1950): 533–38.

36. Lori Merish, *Sentimental Materialism: Gender, Commodity Culture, and Nineteenth-Century American Literature* (Durham: Duke University Press, 2000), 5, 151–64.

37. Grier, "Animal House," 119–20; Unti, "The Quality of Mercy," 48–55; Grier, "Childhood Socialization and Companion Animals: United States, 1820–1870," *Society*

*and Animals* 7 (1999): 95–120; Grier, *Pets in America: A History*, 127–81. For the historic suspicion of petkeeping, see: James Serpell, *In the Company of Animals: A Study of Human-Animal Relationships* (New York: Basil Blackwell, 1986), 34–47; Louise E. Robbins, *Elephant Slaves and Pampered Parrots: Exotic Animals in Eighteenth-Century Paris* (Baltimore: Johns Hopkins University Press, 2002), 140–49, shows how a critique of the idleness of nobility and the vanity of women was expressed through criticism of their idle and indulged animals.

38. *Kindness to Animals, Illustrated by Stories and Anecdotes* (London: W. & R. Chambers, 1877), 182.

39. E. Oakes Smith, "Pets in Prison," *Our Dumb Animals* 8 (April 1876): 81.

40. Grier, "Animal House," 120; Grier, "Childhood Socialization," 109–13. Other historians have explored the symbolic use of animals to naturalize social relations in a British context. See: Moira Ferguson, *Animal Advocacy and Englishwomen, 1780–1900: Patriots, Nation, and Empire* (Ann Arbor: University of Michigan Press, 1998); Harriet Ritvo, *The Animal Estate: The English and Other Creatures in the Victorian Age* (Cambridge, MA: Harvard University Press, 1987). For Germany, see: Boria Sax, *Animals in the Third Reich: Pets, Scapegoats, and the Holocaust* (New York: Continuum, 2000).

41. Mrs. S. Colman, *The Little Keepsake for 1844* (Boston: T. H. Carter & Co., 1844), 29–33.

42. "In the Schoolroom and the Church," *Humane Journal* 10 (April 1882): 54.

43. "Animals for Children," *Humane Journal* 12 (January 1884): 5.

44. Anna Harris Smith, *Report of the Chairman of the Executive Committee for the Six Months Ending November 1, 1899* (Boston: Animal Rescue League, [1899]), 10, 14.

45. Emma Elizabeth Page, *Heart Culture: A Text Book for Teaching Kindness to Animals, Arranged for Use in Public and Private Schools* (San Francisco: Whitaker & Ray Co., 1897), i.

46. Page, *Heart Culture*, 96, 113, 253.

47. Page, *Heart Culture*, 96.

48. Grier, "Childhood Socialization," 99, 105–8.

49. "Kitten and Woodpecker," *Our Dumb Animals* 8 (March 1876): 79.

50. On thoughtlessness rather than innate evil as the source of boys' cruelty, see: Henry Bergh, "Dangerous Education," in *In Memoriam*, 16–17; "Early Influences," *Our Animal Friends* 19 (January 1892): 97. On boys' regular "play" as cruel, see: Wakefield, *Instinct Displayed, in a Collection of Well-Authenticated Facts, Exemplifying the Extraordinary Sagacity of Various Species of the Animal Creation* (Boston: Cummings and Hilliard, 1816), 297; J. Lamb, *The Dog* (Burlington: Chauncey Goodrich, 1830), 13–14; Jane Taylor, *Original Poems for Infant Minds* (Boston: Munroe and Francis, 1845), 115–18, 126; *The History of Beasts* (Portland: Bailey & Noyes, [187–?]), 2; "An Appeal on Behalf of the Illinois Humane Society" (Chicago: s.n., 1871), 4; "Cruelty to Animals Culminating in Murder," *Our Dumb Animals* 4 (August 1871): 126; "Dive, Boys, Dive," *Our Dumb Animals* 4 (September 1871): 134; *The Centennial Frog, and Other Stories* (Philadelphia: Claxton, Remsen & Haffelfinger, 1877), 27–34; Thomas Hill, *Ways of Cruelty*, 22, 26–27, 29; "Turn About Is Fair Play," *Humane Journal* 11 (April 1883): 53; F. W. Holbrook, "Only a Cat," *Humane Journal* 11 (June 1883): 89; Jessie Mae Watt,

"How Howard Reformed," *Humane Journal* 12 (June 1884): 90; Sarah J. Eddy, *Friends and Helpers*, (Boston: Ginn & Co., 1899), 84–85; Animal Rescue League, *Fourth Annual Report* (Boston: s.n., 1903), 4.

51. Grier, "Childhood Socialization," 105–6, 109–10.

52. *The Bird's Nest and Other Stories* (New York: Leavitt & Allen, n.d.), 2–3.

53. See: Taylor, *Original Poems*, 9; *Stories About Birds and Beasts* (New York: Clark, Austin & Co., 1851), 9–14; "Birds Robbing Child's Nests," *Our Dumb Animals* 4 (July 1871): 118; "Bird Love," *Our Dumb Animals* 7 (July 1874): 14; "The Bird's Petition," *Our Dumb Animals* 8 (July 1875): 14; "Frightened Birds," *Our Dumb Animals* 8 (October 1875): 38; "The Little Builders," *Our Dumb Animals* 8 (April 1876): 86; *Kindness to Animals*, 124; Aunt Clara, "Lost—Three Little Robins," in *Selections for School Exhibitions and Private Reading, Illustrating and Advocating Mercy to the Dumb Creation*, 2d. ed., compiled by the Massachusetts Society for the Prevention of Cruelty to Animals (Boston: s.n., 1878), n.p.[repr., *Humane Journal* 10 (March 1882): 42]; "Do They Not Love—and Suffer?" in *Pleadings of Mercy*, 68; "The Lost Nestlings," *Humane Journal* 24 (January 1896): 12; Mary A. Dana, "The Birds' Convention," *Humane Journal* 24 (August 1896): 121; Sarah Nelson Carter, *For Pity's Sake; a Story for the Times, Being Reminiscences of a Guest at a Country Inn, Dedicated to My Horse, My Dog, and My Cat* (Boston: American Humane Education Society, [1897]), 92; "A Great Summer Prize Competition" *Humane Journal* 25 (July 1897): 109; "Don't Rob the Birds Boys," in *Songs of Happy Life*, comp. Sarah J. Eddy (Providence: Art and Nature Study Publishing Company, 1897), 99; Eddy, *Friends and Helpers*, 173; Annie L. Hannah, "A Little Story," *Our Animal Friends* 26 (June 1899): 233–34; John T. Dale , "Senator George F. Hoar and the Birds," in *Heroes and Greathearts and their Animal Friends* (Chicago: Fairfax Publishing Company, 1908), 123–26.

54. "Stealing a Bird's Nest," *Humane Journal* 9 (August 1881): 2.

55. The story of Theodore Parker is as follows: he is walking in the woods one day and comes across a turtle sunning itself on a rock. He picks up a stick, thinking he will strike it, as he has seen other boys do on countless occasions. As he begins, however, he hears a voice inside his head telling him that it is wrong. He is scared by this voice, stops himself, and runs home to tell his mother the story. She responds that the voice young Theodore heard was God's. See: "The Inner Voice," *Our Dumb Animals* 1 (July 1868): 11; Frederic Rowland Marvin, *Christ among the Cattle: A Sermon Preached in the First Congregational Church, Portland, Oregon. A New and Revised Edition* (Portland: Oregon Humane Society, 1885), 9; Wisconsin Humane Society, *Fifth Annual Report of the Wisconsin Humane Society, 1883–1884* (Wisconsin: s.n., 1884), 60; George Angell, *Humane Leaflet, No. 1: 8 Leaflets, 100 Selections, for Schools, Sunday Schools, Bands of Mercy, and Homes* (Boston: MSPCA, n.d.), 4; Rev. D. Sutherland, "The Rights of Animals," *Union Signal* 22 (November 26, 1896), 3. Although subject to slight modifications in time and place, Abe Lincoln's story is as follows: while out riding his horse on his circuit as a country lawyer, he stopped and disappeared back into the woods for a while. His colleagues asked him where he had gone, and he replied that he'd seen a baby bird that had fallen out of its nest a ways back. He hadn't felt right leaving it there, and so he'd gone back to restore it to its nest, reuniting it with its squawking siblings. See: untitled, *Our Dumb Animals* 8 (June 1875): 6; Ralph Waldo Trine, *Every Living Crea-*

ture; or, Heart-Training through the Animal World (New York: TY Crowell & Company, 1899), 40; Eddy, Friends and Helpers, 210; Page, Heart Culture, 74–75; Dale, Heroes and Greathearts, 19–21; "Abraham Lincoln," Humane Journal 11 (February 1883): 25; "Lincoln's Tenderness," Humane Journal 13 (October 1885): 149; "Lincoln's Humanity," Humane Journal 15 (January 1887): 4; "Abraham Lincoln," Humane Journal 18 (July 1890): 105; "What Makes a Boy Popular," Humane Journal 19 (April 1891): 61.

56. Jacob Abbot, Bruno; or, Lessons of Fidelity, Patience, and Self-Denial Taught by a Dog (New York: Harper & Brothers, 1854), 159. For other historical homages to the loyal dog, see: Faithful Friends: Dogs in Life and Literature, ed. Frank Jackson (New York: Carroll & Graf Publishers, Inc., 1997).

57. George Angell, Humane Leaflet, No. 4: 8 Leaflets, 100 Selections, for Schools, Sunday Schools, Bands of Mercy, and Homes (Boston: MSPCA, n.d.), 3–4. See also: "Which Is the Better Soldier?" Our Dumb Animals 6 (January 1874): 68; "Editor's Easy Chair," Harper's New Monthly Magazine 84 (February 1892): 475; Jennifer A. Mason, "Civilized Creatures: Animality, Cultural Power, and American Literature, 1850–1901" (Ph.D. diss., University of Texas, 2000), 10.

58. Grier, "Animal House," 121; Grier, Pets in America, 167–72.

59. Kete, Beast in the Boudoir, 76–96.

60. "Marrying for the Sake of a Dog," Riverside Magazine (February 1867): 64–66.

61. JTF, "A Church-Going Dog," Ark 1 (February 25, 1875): 1.

62. Little Pet (Boston: Henry A. Young, 1872).

63. Grace Greenwood, History of My Pets (Boston: Ticknor, Reed, and Fields, 1851); Frank, Fourteen Pet Goslings, and Other Pretty Stories of My Childhood (Boston: J. E. Tilton & Co., 1858); Southey, "On the Death of a Favorite Spaniel," in Selections for School Exhibitions and Private Reading.

64. On child-pet portraiture, see: Grier, "Animal House," 121.

65. "Pet," in Oxford English Dictionary Online (Oxford University Press, 2003).

66. "Children and Young Animals," Humane Journal 8 (November 1880): 3.

67. The Pet Fawn, and Other Stories (New York: Leavitt & Allen, n.d.), 4.

68. "Miss Murphy," Our Animal Friends 24 (July1897): 250–53. See also: Jane Boudinot Keith, "The Two Little Cripples," Our Animal Friends 26 (March 1899): 159–60.

69. Florence V. Barry, A Century of Children's Books (New York: George H. Doran Company, 1923), 135–37.

70. The Council of Dogs (Philadelphia: Johnson & Warner, 1809); Taylor, Original Poems; The Life and Perambulations of a Mouse (Philadelphia: George S. Appleton; New York: D. Appleton & Co, 1846); "A Very Old Barn-Yard Hen," Ark 1 (February 26, 1875): 1; Bucephalus, "An Equine Epistle," Ark 1 (March 2, 1875): 1 Esther, "A Dog's Letter," Humane Journal 5 (May 1877): 3; The Centennial Frog; A. T. Shockly, "History of Dobbin Gray as Told by Himself," Humane Journal 10 (March 1882): 42; "A Little Conversation between Jack and Rover," Humane Journal 11 (January 1883): 10; "The Convention of Rats," Humane Journal 12 (June 1884): 85; "Adventures of Snobblegoster," Our Animal Friends 19 (January1892): 113–14; Teufel the Terrier; or, the Life and Adventures of an Artist's Dog (New York: G. P. Putnam's Sons, [1892]); Mary H. Krout, "Friends at Court," Humane Journal 22 (November 1894): 150–51; Annie

L. Hannah, "The Other Side Heard From," *Our Animal Friends* 26 (February 1899): 137–38; Annie L. Hannah, "A Little Story," *Our Animal Friends* 26 (June 1899): 233–34; Mrs. Neville Peel, *The Autobiography of a Bulldog* (London: National Societies Depository; New York: Thomas Whittaker, [1899]); Miranda Eliot Swan, *Daisy: The Autobiography of a Cat* (Boston: Noyes Brothers, [1900]); John S. Owen, M.D., *Gramma: The Autobiography of a Cat* (Detroit: American Publishing Company, [1900]); Richard Harding Davis, *The Bar Sinister* (New York: Scriber, 1903); "Prof. Bow Wow Gives a Lecture," *Humane Advocate* (November 1910): 27–28.

71. New York [City] Board of Education, *An Outline of Study Recommended for the Teaching of Humane Education* (New York: Board of Education, 1920).

72. Susan Chitty, *The Woman Who Wrote Black Beauty: A Life of Anna Sewell* (London: Hodder and Stoughton, 1971), 214–17.

73. "New Publications," *Humane Journal* 18 (April 1890): 52; "To Chicago Students," *Humane Journal* 19 (January 1891): 5; "'Black Beauty' in Kansas," *Humane Journal* 19 (January 1891): 5; "Black Beauty in Our Schools," *Humane Journal* 19 (March 1891): 36; Miss N. S. Dennis, "Blowing Rock, N.C.," *American Missionary* 45 (July 1891): 271; "Lessons from Black Beauty, No.1," *Humane Journal* 19 (December 1891): 18; "At Last They Speak," *Humane Journal* 20 (September 1892): 132; "Closing Exercises at Santee, Nebraska," *American Missionary* 48 (September 1894): 331; Alta, "Our Silent Servants" *Humane Journal* 24 (September 1896): 134; Eddy, *Songs of Happy Life*, 163, 165.

74. Jacob Abbott, *Gentle Measures in the Training and Management of the Young* (New York: Harper & Brothers, 1871), electronic reproduction, The Making of America, http://name.umdl.umich.edu/ABE5535.0001.001.

75. Myra C. Glenn, *Campaigns against Corporal Punishment: Prisoners, Sailors, Women, and Children in Antebellum America* (Albany: State University of New York Press, 1984), 29.

76. Glenn, *Campaigns against Corporal Punishment*, 28, 41–42, 121.

77. Richard Brodhead, *Cultures of Letters: Scenes of Reading and Writing in Nineteenth-Century America* (Chicago: University of Chicago Press, 1993), 17–18. See also: Pleck, *Domestic Tyranny*, 39–40.

78. Brodhead, *Cultures of Letters*, 18–21. Both Glenn and Brodhead connect these changes in disciplinary methods to the broad shift from premodern to modern technologies of power described by Michel Foucault. See: Michel Foucault, *Discipline and Punish: The Birth of the Prison* (New York: Vintage Books, 1979).

79. Wisconsin Humane Society, *Reports for the Years 1900, 1901, 1902, and 1903* (Milwaukee: s.n., 1903), 42.

80. For antebellum corporal punishment reform, see: Glenn, *Campaigns against Corporal Punishment*.

81. B. A. Ulrich, "The Family Circle," *Humane Journal* 10 (August 1882): 118.

82. Samuel Smiles, "The Effect of Parental Severity upon Children," in *Fifth Annual Report of the Wisconsin Humane Society, 1883–1884* (Milwaukee: s.n., 1884), 66–67.

83. Hill, *Ways of Cruelty*, 24.

84. Hill, *Ways of Cruelty*, 16.

85. ASPCA, *A Brief Account of Some of the So-Called Vices Practised by Horses; Such as Baulking, or Inability to Proceed; Cribbing, or Gnawing Mangers and Stalls; Tearing of their Blankets, etc., With Some Suggestions for their Corrections* (New York: s.n., 1866), 15.

86. Emma Rood Tuttle, *Angell Prize-Contest Recitations to Advance Humane Education in All its Phases. 'Nil desperandum.' Compiled to be Used in Entertainments Managed by Churches, Societies, Lyceum, Sunday Schools, Bands of Mercy, or Individuals Aiming to Establish Right over Wrong, Kindness over Cruelty, Knowledge over Ignorance, and Justice over All* (Chicago: J. R. Frances; Berlin Heights, OH: Hudson Tuttle, 1896), 75–78; "Kate Thorn's Defense of Cats," *Our Dumb Animals* 7 (September 1874): 27; T. T. Munger, *The Rights of Dumb Animals* (Hartford: Connecticut Humane Society, 1898), 18. For this sentiment about dogs, see also: Wesely Mills, *How to Keep a Dog in the City* (Toronto: Canadian Kennel Gazette Office, 1891), 11.

87. *Footsteps to the Natural History of Beasts* (Philadelphia: Jacob Johnson, 1804), 9–10; Samuel Osgood, *Gospel among the Animals; or, Christ with the Cattle* (New York: Samuel R. Wells, 1867), 12. For other examples extolling Arabs' humane horse training, see: *History of Domestic Animals* (New York: Kiggins & Kellog, n.d.), 4; *The Book of Beasts for Young Persons* (Banbury: J. G. Rush, Printer, 1840), 11; "Rarey, the American Horse-Tamer, in the Arabian Desert," *Living Age* 65 (June 23, 1860): 767; Abram Soles, *Original and Interesting Book on the Horse* (Schenectady: Young & Graham, 1860), 32; John G. Whittier, "Our Dumb Relations," *Ark* 1 (1875), 1; *Kindness to Animals*, 11–12; Marvin, *Christ among the Cattle*, 12; Colonel T. A. Dodge, "Some Oriental Riders," *Harper's New Monthly Magazine* 87 (October 1893): 772; Eddy, *Songs of Happy Life*, 52–61; Dale, *Heroes and Greathearts*.

88. "Arab Horse Maxims," *Humane Journal* 5 (July 1877): 4.

89. *The History of Beasts* (New York: S. Wood & Sons, 1816), 13. This story is also in *The Book of Beasts for Young Persons*, 11.

90. Soles, *Original and Interesting*, 32.

91. Frank C. Bostock, *The Training of Wild Animals* (New York: Century Company, 1903), xvi. For dogs, see: *The General Character of the Dog: Illustrated by a Variety of Original and Interesting Anecdotes of that Beautiful and Useful Animal, in Prose and Verse* (New York: George G. Sickels, 1829); Henry William Herbert, ed., *The Dog. By Dinks, Mayhew, and Hutchinson. Compiled, Abridged, Edited, and Illustrated by Frank Forester. Revised Edition* (New York: Stringer & Townsend, 1857).

92. For changes in horse training and the image of the horse, see: Jennifer A. Mason, "Animal Bodies: Corporeality, Class, and Subject Formation in The Wide, Wide World," *Nineteenth Century Literature* 54 (2000): 503–33. In addition to a new training regime, the horse itself comes to be seen as a more self-regulating being and less an unruly bundle of passions. Traveling animal trainers or tamers had been a source of entertainment since the eighteenth century, and they usually highlighted exotic, wild, or "learned" animals. I am suggesting that what is new with the horse tamers and whisperers of this sort is that display of mastery through kindness. For earlier animal entertainment, see: Peter Benes, "To the Curious: Bird and Animal Exhibitions in New England, 1716–1825," *Dublin Seminar for New England Folklife Annual Proceedings*

(1993): 147–63. For accounts of the popular mania for demonstrations of horse breaking, see: "Horse Taming," *Scientific American* 13 (May 1, 1854): 269.

93. Willis J. Powell, *Tachyhippodamia, or Art of Quieting Wild Horses in a Few Hours, As Discovered by the Author, in the Year 1814* (New Orleans: Observer Office, 1838), 4–5, 30. Sullivan is fairly legendary too in America. He is mentioned in: Wakefield, *Instinct Displayed*, 298; Thomas Craige, *A Conversation between a Lady and Her Horse* (Philadelphia: Thomas Craige, 1851), 63; "Animal Teaching," *Our Dumb Animals* 6 (1874): 71.

94. For contemporary coverage of Rarey's exploits, see: "American Horse-Tamer in London," *Scientific American* 13 (February 20, 1858): 189; "Rarey's Method of Subduing Vicious Horses," *Scientific American* 13 (April 17, 1858): 253; "The Horse-Taming Secret Again—Another Theory," *Scientific American* 13 (May 22, 1858): 293; "A Rarey Show," *Living Age* 57 (May 29, 1858): 694–97; "Mr. Rarey's Teaching," *Living Age* 58 (July 10, 1858): 120–21; "Horse-Taming," *Scientific American*, n.s. 1 (December 3, 1859): 365; "Rarey, the American Horse-Tamer, in the Arabian Desert,"; "The Horse and His Rider," *Living Age* 68 (January 26, 1861): 243–45; "Horses and Billiards—Rarey and Berger," *Scientific American*, n.s. 4 (January 26, 1861): 54; "How to Treat Horses," *Scientific American*, n.s. 4 (February 2, 1861): 74; "Rarey the Horse-Tamer—Exciting Exhibition," *Scientific American*, n.s. 4 (February 16, 1861): 106; T. B. Thorpe, "Rarey, the Horse-Tamer," *Harper's New Monthly Magazine* 22 (April 1861): 615–24; "Editor's Easy Chair," *Harper's New Monthly Magazine* 31 (November 1865): 808–9.

95. John Solomon Rarey, *Taming, or Breaking the Horse by a New and Improved Method, as Practiced with Great Success in the United States and in all the Countries of Europe* (New York: Brother Jonathan Office, 1861), 5, iii, 48.

96. Thorpe, "Rarey the Horse-Tamer," 624.

97. Rev. T. Jackson, "Cure for a Vicious Horse," *Our Dumb Animals* 1 (1868): 21.

98. For other positive invocations of Rarey in humane publications, see: R. Weaver, "Baulky Horses," *Our Dumb Animals* 1 (1868): 44–45; "Kindness for Its Own Sake and for Our Own Sake," *Our Dumb Animals* 3 (1871): 73; Paul Ketchum, "A Horse College," *Our Dumb Animals* 8 (1875): 24; "Kindness to Animals," *Humane Journal* 23 (1895): 188; Eddy, *Friends and Helpers*, 79–80. For more examples of general testimony of the power of kindness, or stories of animal redemption, see: "Landseer's Whip," *Our Dumb Animals* 7 (1874): 2; "Kindness Does It," *Our Dumb Animals* 6 (1874): 99; "What the Owner of a Trick Horse Says," *Our Dumb Animals* 8 (1876): 66; "Treatment of Dogs," *Our Dumb Animals* 8 (1876): 82; "A Word Not a Whip," *Humane Journal* 8 (February 1880): 6; "The Education of Horses," *Humane Journal* 9 (January 1881): 6; "Equine Paradox," *Humane Journal* [of the Saratoga Springs SPCA & C] 1 (1881): 22; Wisconsin Humane Society, *Fifth Annual Report*, 60; "Lessons in Politeness," *Our Animal Friends* 25 (1898): 134.

99. Thorpe, "Rarey the Horse-Tamer," 622; "A Rarey Show," 697; "Mr. Rarey's Teaching," 120.

100. Jesse Haney, *Haney's Art of Training Animals. A Practical Guide for Amateur or Professional Trainers. Giving Full Instructions for Breaking, Taming and Teaching All Kinds of Animals, Including an Improved Method of Horse Breaking, Management of Farm Animals, Training of Sporting Dogs; Serpent Charming, Care and Tuition of*

*Talking, Singing and Performing Birds; and Detailed Instructions for Teaching All Circus Tricks, and Many Other Wonderful Feats. Illustrated with over Sixty Engravings* (New York: Jesse Haney & Co. Publishers, 1869), 17, 15.

101. *Kindness to Animals*, 8. For an example of confrontation between man and beast that stresses their antagonism and the necessity of beastly fear of man, see: H. Frost, *A Brief Biographical Sketch of I. A. Van Amburgh, and an Illustrated and Descriptive History of the Animals Contained in This Mammoth Menagerie and Great Moral Exhibition, Comprising More in Number and a Greater Variety than All Other Shows in the United States Combined* (New York: Samuel Booth, [184–?]); James Capen Adams, *The Hair-Breadth Escapes and Adventures of "Grizzly Adams," in Catching and Conquering the Wild Animals Included in His California Menagerie* (n.p.: 1860). These accounts tended to stress man's physical prowess and his God-given superiority over animals, themselves figured as innately savage rather than innately good and willing. The tamer's prowess consisted of his ability to subdue animals, while the thrill of the show depended, paradoxically, on convincing audiences that wild animals could never really be tamed, hence the tamer's constant danger and the source of the show's dramatic tension.

102. "The Most Savage Animals May Be Ruled by Kindness," *Humane Journal* 14 (November 1886): 170. For another example, see: Mrs. Charles Bray, "Free Animals That Are Useful, Harmless, or Beautiful," *Our Dumb Animals* 4 (July 1871): 118.

103. "Bruin Controlled by Kindness," *Humane Journal* 15 (January 1887): cover page.

104. P. T Barnum and Hyatt Frost, *Illustrated and Descriptive History of the Animals Contained in Barnum & Van Amburgh's Museum and Menagerie Combination* (New York: Samuel Booth, 1866); Haney, *Haney's Art of Training*, 175.

105. *The Bird Cage* (Concord: Rufus Merrill, 1852), 24. See also: *Kindness to Animals*, 148; "Whisk and His Friends," *Our Dumb Animals* 8 (March 1876): 78; "Reason in Lower Animals," *Humane Alliance* 26 (April 1899): 52; Mrs. H. B. Paul, "Only a Cat; or, the Autobiography of Tom Blackman," *Our Animal Friends* 19 (March 1892): 162–63.

106. "Rarey the Horse-Tamer," 622.

107. John Hildrop, *Free Thoughts upon the Brute Creation; or, an Examination of Father Bougeant's Philosophical Amusement &c. In Two Letters to a Lady. Letter II* (London: R. Minors, Bookseller and Stationer, [1742]), 10–24; Humphrey Primatt, *A Dissertation on the Duty of Mercy and Sin of Cruelty to Brute Animals* (London: R. Hett, 1776), 295–303; Osgood, *Gospel among the Animals*, 5–6; Mary O. Ayers, "My Brother's Keeper," *Humane Journal* 12 (January 1884): 6; Marvin, *Christ among the Cattle*, 3–5; AHA, *Report of the Proceedings, Fourteenth Annual Meeting of the American Humane Association for the Prevention of Cruelty to Children and Animals* (Cincinnati: s.n., 1890), 7.

108. "Mr. Rarey's Teaching," 120.

109. "Rarey, the Horse-Tamer," 624.

110. Oliver Wendell Holmes, "Crime and Automatism," *Atlantic Monthly* 35 (April 1875): 476, 479–80.

111. "The Rarey Method," *Harper's New Monthly Magazine* 26 (February 1863): 377–84.

112. "Rarey, the Horse-Tamer," 617–18.

113. Craige, *A Conversation between a Lady and Her Horse*, 45; Ketchum, "A Horse College," 24. See also: Murray, *The Perfect Horse, How to Know Him, How to Train Him, How to Breed Him, How to Shoe Him, How to Drive Him* (Boston: James R. Osgood and Company, 1873), 154.

114. Hill, *Ways of Cruelty*, 37.

115. "Breaking the Child's Will," *Our Dumb Animals* 6 (1874): 64.

116. "Grace Webster Hinsdale," A Woman and a Balky Horse," *Our Dumb Animals* 8 (1875): 96.

117. "How to Bring Up Children," *Humane Journal* 10 (April 1882): 54.

118. "A Schoolboy's Troubles," *Humane Journal* 8 (January 1880): 4.


## CHAPTER TWO

1. Illinois Humane Society, *Fourteenth Annual Report*, 10.

2. Michel de Montaigne, *Essays*, trans. with an introduction by J. M. Cohen (1580; repr., London: Penguin Books, 1993), 187.

3. John Locke, quoted in *Political Theory and Animal Rights*, ed. Paul A. B. Clarke and Andrew Linzey (London: Pluto Press, 1990), 119. Orig. publ. "Some Thoughts Concerning Education" [1693], in *The Works of John Locke in Ten Volumes*, 10th. ed. (London: 1801), vol. 9. Locke's advice was reprinted on this side of the Atlantic in, among other places, *The Spirit of Humanity and Essence of Morality: Extracted from the Productions of the Enlightened and Benevolent of Various Ages and Climes. Illustrated with Engravings* (Albany: O. Steele and D. M'Kercher, 1835), 18–22.

4. William Hogarth, *Anecdotes of William Hogarth, Written by Himself* (1833; repr., London: Cornmarket Press Limited, 1970), 233–37. Nineteenth-century humane literature often referred to Hogarth and/or reprinted the *Stages*. See, for instance: Henry Crow, *Zoophilos; or, Considerations on the Moral Treatment of Inferior Animals* (London: J. Seeley, 1819), 82; *The Spirit of Humanity and Essence of Morality*, 155–69; Henry Bergh, *An Address by Henry Bergh, Esq., President of the American Society for the Prevention of Cruelty to Animals, Delivered in the Great Hall of the Putnam County Agricultural Society; On the Occasion of the Late Fair, Held at Carmel, on the 19th of September, 1867* (New York: ASPCA, 1868), 3–4; Marvin, *Christ among the Cattle*, 9.

5. Harriet Beecher Stowe, *Uncle Tom's Cabin; or, Life among the Lowly* (1852; repr., with an introduction by Ann Douglas, New York: Penguin Books, 1981), 488.

6. "Annual Meeting of the Illinois Humane Society," *Humane Journal* 8 (May 1880): 7.

7. "Cruelty to Horses, Inhuman Practices Which Can Not Be Condemned Too Strongly," *Humane Journal* 24 (November 1896): 165.

8. Untitled, *Our Dumb Animals* 1 (1869): 72.

9. Gordon, *Heroes of Their Own Lives*, 27. Gordon argues that SPCCs made child abuse into a "social problem" by linking it to social disorder.

10. Norman S. Fiering, "Irresistible Compassion: An Aspect of Eighteenth-Century Sympathy and Humanitarianism," *Journal of the History of Ideas* 37 (1976): 199–200. For the development of this sensibility, see also: Karen Halttunen, "Humanitarianism

and the Pornography of Pain in Anglo-American Culture," *American Historical Review* 100 (1995): 303–34; Keith Thomas, *Man and the Natural World: A History of the Modern Sensibility* (New York: Pantheon Books, 1983). Because the moral sense philosophers assumed that benevolence was natural and ahistorical, they felt no need to explain *why* the humanitarian sensibility, the urge to benevolence, might arise. This, however, has been the subject of some debate among historians. Keith Thomas views the rise of humanitarianism through the lens of how men and women have viewed their relationship to nature.

Other historians have also sought the origins of benevolence in economic changes. See, for instance, Thomas Haskell in "Capitalism and the Origins of the Humanitarian Sensibility, Part 1" and "Capitalism and the Origins of the Humanitarian Sensibility, Part 2," in *The Antislavery Debates: Capitalism and Abolitionism as a Problem in Historical Interpretation*, ed. Thomas Bender (Berkeley: University of California Press, 1992), 107–60. Haskell argues that capitalism gave rise to humanitarian sentiment, not through "the medium of class interest," but through "changes the market wrought in *perception* or *cognitive style*" (111).

Some, however, turn from economic to the realm of psychology and culture proper. Lynn Hunt, for instance, has recently noted that the idea of universal human rights has its origins in what she calls "new practices of selfhood." Specifically, from the eighteenth century on, the "increasing sense of separation of bodies from each other," combined with "an increasing sense of empathy between psyches across space," helped to create the idea that all humans are autonomous. Empathy provided evidence of that fundamental likeness and functioned as "the psychological foundation of democracy and human rights." Crucially, Hunt argues that novels served as an important means of cultivating these new practices of selfhood by providing a forum in which, through empathetic identification with its characters, men and women learned to imagine distant others as being essentially similar to themselves. See: Hunt, *Inventing Human Rights: A History* (New York: W. W. Norton, 2007).

11. Fiering, "Irresistible Compassion," 202.

12. Fiering, "Irresistible Compassion," 205–8.

13. Halttunen, "Humanitarianism and the Pornography of Pain," 306–7. For more on the Smithian spectator, see: Luc Boltanski, *Distant Suffering: Morality, Media and Politics*, trans. Graham Burchell (Cambridge: Cambridge University Press, 1999); Gillian Silverman, "Sympathy and Its Vicissitudes," *American Studies* 43 (Fall 2002): 5–28.

14. Ann Douglas, *The Feminization of American Culture* (New York: Alfred A. Knopf, 1977), 121–64; John L. Thomas, "Romantic Reform in America, 1815–1865," *American Quarterly* 17 (1965), 658–59.

15. Esther Cohen, "The Animated Pain of the Body," *American Historical Review* 105 (2000): 36–68; "Address of Rev. Phillips Brooks, at our Annual Meeting, March 29, 1870," *Our Dumb Animals* 3 (August 1870): 17–18.

16. Elizabeth Clark, "'The Sacred Rights of the Weak': Pain, Sympathy, and the Culture of Individual Rights in Antebellum America," *Journal of American History* 82 (1995): 476. David Reynolds discusses how the evangelical emphasis on spectatorship, on moral reform through exposure to immoral practices and their resultant evils, could easily lead into what he calls "immoral didacticism" or "subversive reform." The emo-

tionalism of evangelical reform literature meant that the line between the didactic and the sensational was easily blurred. See: David Reynolds, *Beneath the American Renaissance: The Subversive Imagination in the Age of Emerson and Melville* (Cambridge, MA: Harvard University Press, 1988), chap. 2. Karen Halttunen also describes how the humanitarian imperative to expose pain could shade into what she calls a "pornography of pain." "The eighteenth-century cult of sensibility had proclaimed pain unacceptable, but simultaneously discovered it to be alluring" (322).

17. The quotation is from Clark, "Sacred Rights of the Weak," 472–73. For a fuller treatment of changed medical attitudes toward pain, see: Martin Pernick, *A Calculus of Suffering: Pain, Professionalism, and Anesthesia in Nineteenth-Century America* (New York: Columbia University Press, 1985), 77–82. Of course, as Protestants remained split throughout the nineteenth century (and, indeed, remain so today) over questions like predestination and the nature of God, the value of pain and suffering remained a subject of debate. Some religious men and women, for instance, were opposed to the use of anesthesia in the nineteenth century on predestinarian grounds; if one got sick and suffered, it was a sign from God. To cover the pain was to deny His will and sovereignty. For this controversy, see: Pernick, *Calculus of Suffering*, 42–58.

18. Pernick, *Calculus of Suffering*, 149–57.

19. Charles Sellers, *The Market Revolution: Jacksonian America, 1814–1846* (New York: Oxford University Press, 1994); Paul Johnson, *A Shopkeeper's Millennium: Society and Revivals in Rochester, New York, 1815–1837* (New York: Hill & Wang, 1979); Herbert Gutman, *Work, Culture, and Society in Industrializing America* (New York: Vintage, 1977); Paul Boyer, *Urban Masses and Moral Order in America, 1820–1920* (Cambridge, MA: Harvard University Press, 1992); Michael O'Malley, *Keeping Watch: A History of American Time* (New York: Viking, 1990), chap. 1. Quotes are from John F. Kasson, *Rudeness & Civility: Manners in Nineteenth Century-Urban America* (New York: Hill & Wang, 1991), 112, 147.

20. Louis P. Masur, *Rites of Execution: Capital Punishment and the Transformation of American Culture, 1776–1865* (New York: Oxford University Press, 1989); Glenn, *Campaigns against Corporal Punishment*; Johnson, *Shopkeeper's Millennium*; Clark, "Sacred Rights of the Weak."

21. Quotes are from Masur, *Rites of Execution*, 55, 57.

22. Masur, *Rites of Execution*, 61. The Rush quote is on page 64.

23. Note, "The Cruel and Unusual Punishment Clause and the Substantive Criminal Law," *Harvard Law Review* 79 (1966): 636–38; Anthony F. Granucci, "'Nor Cruel and Unusual Punishments Inflicted': The Original Meaning," *California Law Review* 57 (1969): 839–65.

24. Clark, "'The Sacred Rights of the Weak'," 488–90.

25. Robert L. Griswold, "Law, Sex, Cruelty, and Divorce in Victorian America, 1840–1900," *American Quarterly* 38 (1986): 721–45; Griswold, "The Evolution of Mental Cruelty in Victorian American Divorce, 1790–1900," *Journal of Social History* 20 (1986): 127–48; Griswold, "Sexual Cruelty and the Case for Divorce in Victorian America," *Signs* 11 (1986): 529–41. See also: Lawrence M. Friedman, *A History of American Law* (New York: Simon & Schuster, 1973), 437–40. Some North American anticruelty societies also absorbed marital abuse under their rubric. See: Judith Fingard, "The Prevention

of Cruelty, Marriage Breakdown and the Rights of Wives in Nova Scotia, 1880–1900," *Acadiensis* 22 (1993): 84–101.

26. G. W. Peck, "On the Use of Chloroform in Hanging," *American Review* (September 1848): 297.

27. Karen Haltunnen, *Murder Most Foul: The Killer and the American Gothic Imagination* (Cambridge, MA: Harvard University Press, 2000).

28. Henry Bergh, "Prevention of Cruelty to Animals," *New York Times,* 24 February 1867.

29. Cynthia Eagle Russett, *Darwin in America: The Intellectual Response* (San Francisco: W. H. Freeman and Company, 1976), 28–43; Ward quoted in Edwards, *New Spirits,* 154.

30. Rev. James T. Bixby, quoted in Robert W. Rydell, *All the World's a Fair* (Chicago: University of Chicago Press, 1984), 68.

31. Gail Bederman, *Manliness and Civilization: A Cultural History of Gender and Race in the United States, 1880–1917* (Chicago: University of Chicago Press, 1995), 25–40; Rydell, *All the World's a Fair,* 50–68; Christopher A. Vaughn, "Ogling Igorots: The Politics and Commerce of Exhibiting Cultural Otherness, 1891–1913," in *Freakery: Cultural Spectacles of the Extraordinary Body,* ed. Rosemarie Garland Thomson (New York: New York University Press, 1996), 219–33.

32. Lester Frank Ward, "Mind as a Social Factor," *Mind* 9 (October 1884): 570; General Rush C. Hawkins, "Brutality and Avarice Triumphant," *North American Review* 152 (June 1891): 656–70.

33. Robert G. Ingersoll, "Is Avarice Triumphant," *North American Review* 152 (June 1891): 671–81.

34. Illinois Humane Society, *Eighteenth Annual Report* (Chicago: s.n., 1888), 6.

35. *Sixth Annual Report of the Fox River Valley District of the Wisconsin Humane Society, for the Year Ending October 1894* (Oshkosh, WI: s.n., 1895), 3.

36. "Humane Education," *Union Signal* 23 (1897): 8.

37. "Progress and Humanity," *Humane Journal* 16 (January 1888): 2.

38. G. L. C., "Mr. Chaney's Words on Cruelty," *Ark* 1 (1875): 1; Osgood, *Gospel among the Animals,* 9. For other references to the gladiatorial games, see: Lord Chief Justice Coleridge, *The Lord Chief Justice of England on Vivisection* (Philadelphia: American Anti-Vivisection Society, 1884), 10; "Pigeon Shooting with Women at the Gun," *Our Animal Friends* 26 (June 1899): 217; Henry S. Salt, "Humanitarianism," *Humanitarian and Nature Student and Our Animal Friends* 36 (February 1910): 132.

39. ASPCA, *Seventh Annual Report* (New York: s.n., 1873), 27.

40. Mary F. Lovell, "The Degradation of Spain," *Union Signal* 22 (1896): 3. For other of her rants against Spain, see: "Cruel Teneriffe," *Union Signal* 21 (1895): 4; "The Amusement of a Semi-Barbarous Nation," *Union Signal* 22 (1896): 4–5.

41. Lovell, "The Church's Responsibility," *Union Signal* 23 (1897): 3.

42. Lovell, "The World's Great Object Lesson," *Union Signal* 24 (1898): 4.

43. Margaret E. Garvey, "Humanity as Applied to Dumb Animals," *Humane Journal* 16 (June 1881): 86. Rev. S. F. Stratton, "Kindness to Animals," *Humane Journal* 9 (June 1881): 8.

44. On horse drivers, see: Clay McShane and Joel A. Tarr, *The Horse in the City:*

*Living Machines in the Nineteenth Century* (Baltimore: Johns Hopkins University Press, 2007), chap. 2; Mrs. George E. Hill, "Alabama: Notes from Marion," *American Missionary* 34 (April 1880): 113–14; Women's Branch of the PSPCA, *Ninth Annual Report* (Philadelphia: s.n., 1878), 5.

45. "Cruelty to Animals," reprinted in *Humane Journal* 13 (January 1885): 2. For a discussion of the Picayune's anticruelty stance, see: Lamar W. Bridges, "An Editor's Views on Anti-Cruelty: Eliza Jane Nicholson of the Picayune," *Journal of Mississippi History* 39 (1977): 303–16.

46. AHA, *Fourteenth Annual Meeting*, 31–32.

47. On lynching and stereotypes of black criminality in the late nineteenth century, see: Christopher Waldrep, *The Many Faces of Judge Lynch: Extralegal Violence and Punishment in America* (New York: Palgrave Macmillan, 2002), 116–22; Bederman, *Manliness and Civilization*.

48. St. Paul Society for the Prevention of Cruelty, *Ninth Annual Report* (St. Paul, s.n.: 1896), n.p.; NY-SPCC, *Tenth Annual Report* (New York: s.n., 1885), 39; NY-SPCC, *Sixteenth Annual Report* (New York: s.n., 1891), 5–6.

49. Friedman, *History of American Law*, 517. On the abolition of corporal punishment generally, see: Glenn, *Campaigns against Corporal Punishment*. On the campaign to revive the whipping post, see: Elizabeth Pleck, "The Whipping Post for Wife-Beaters, 1876–1906," in *Essays on the Family and Historical Change* (College Station: Texas A & M Press, 1983), 127–49, quote on 127.

50. "The Lash for Criminals," *New York Times*, 29 July 1877, 5. See also: "Mr. Bergh Defines His Position," *New York Times*, 16 December 1880, 5; "Treatment of Criminals," *New York Times*, 26 December 1880, 9.

51. "The Lash for Wife Beaters," *New York Times*, 19 January 1881, 2.

52. Gerry was chairman of the New York State Committee on Capital Punishment, which in 1886 recommended replacing hanging with electrocution. Sydney Coleman, *Humane Society Leaders in America* (Albany: American Humane Association, 1924), 67; Elbridge T. Gerry, "Capital Punishment by Electricity," *North American Review* 149 (September 1889): 321325; "Fit Punishment for Brutes," *New York Times*, 4 October 1894, 1. On wrangling over Gerry's bill in the New York state legislature, see: "The Whipping-Post Bill," *New York Times*, 21 February 1895, 13; "The Whipping Post Bill," *New York Times*, 7 March 1895, 9; "An Affront to Mr. Gerry," *New York Times*, 8 March 1895, 1; "The Legislative Wasp," *New York Times*, 14 March 1895, 14.

53. Ronald Lee Boostrom, "The Personalization of Evil: The Emergence of American Criminology, 1865–1910," (Ph.D. diss., University of California, Berkeley, 1974), 41–84.

54. Elbridge T. Gerry, "Must We Have the Cat-O'-Nine Tails?" *North American Review* 160 (March 1895): 318–24; See also: "Whipping Post Advocated," *Humane Journal* 23 (January 1895): 183; "Corporal Punishment," *Humane Journal* 23 (February 1895): 21; Rev. Henry G. Perry, "To Prevent and Punish for Human Torture," *Humane Journal* 23 (March 1895): 36.

55. Mary Lovell, Jane Addams, and WCTU president Lillian Stevens all decried Gerry and Shortall. See: untitled, *Union Signal* 24 (1898): 2; Mary F. Lovell, "The Whipping Post," *Union Signal* 31 (1905): 4. Support for, and opposition to, the whipping post

did not break down on neat gender lines. For female support, see: Harriet J. Roworth, "The Whipping Post," *Union Signal* 31 (1905): 4. Even some prominent suffragists, most notably Lucy Stone, supported the lash for wife-beaters. Pleck, "The Whipping Post," 132–33.

56. Bederman, *Manliness and Civilization*, 23.

57. Adelle Octavia Clouston, *Some of New York's 400* (Boston: American Humane Education Society, 1898), 55. The title refers to the elite four hundred men and women who were considered truly fashionable by New York society maven Mrs. William Astor.

58. Clouston, *Some of New York's 400*, 90, 91.

59. "Editor's Easy Chair," *Harper's New Monthly Magazine* 73 (June 1886): 152–53.

60. Sarah Carter Nelson, *For Pity's Sake; a Story for the Times, Being Reminiscenses of a Guest at a Country Inn, Dedicated to My Horse, My Dog, and My Cat* (Boston: American Humane Education Society, [1897]), 92–93.

61. "Pigeon Shooting with Women at the Gun," *Our Animal Friends* 26 (June 1899): 217. Antivivisectionists also argued that female vivisectors were unsexed by practicing cruelty. Ellen Snow, *"Scientized" Juveniles; Little Pitchers Have Long Ears. One Phase of Woman's Progress at [the] Close of the Century* (Chicago: Press of the International Kindness to Animals Society, [1898]).

62. Mrs. Velma V. Beebe, "Cruelty in its Relation to Dress and Food," *Union Signal* 22 (May 14, 1896): 6.

63. On the relationship between civilization and sexual differentiation, see: Bederman, *Manliness and Civilization*, 25.

64. For comprehensive accounts of early animal protection organizations and their activities, see: Bernard Oreste Unti, "The Quality of Mercy: Organized Animal Protection in the United States, 1866–1930" (Ph.D. diss., American University, 2002); Roswell C. McCrea, *The Humane Movement: A Descriptive Survey* (New York: Columbia University Press, 1910); Floyd Morse Hubbard, *Prevention of Cruelty to Animals in New York State*, Bulletin of Social Legislation on the Henry Bergh Foundation for the Promotion of Humane Education (New York: Columbia University Press, 1915); Hubbard, *Prevention of Cruelty to Animals in the States of Illinois, Colorado and California*, Bulletin of Social Legislation on the Henry Bergh Foundation for the Promotion of Humane Education (New York: Columbia University Press, 1916); William J. Schultz, *The Humane Movement in the United States, 1910–1922* (New York: Columbia University Press, 1924).

65. Joel Prentiss Bishop, *Commentaries on the Criminal Law*, 6th ed. (Boston: Little, Brown and Company, 1877), 1:335.

66. Ronald L. Meek, *Social Science and the Ignoble Savage* (Cambridge: Cambridge University Press, 1976), 74–75, 153, 178, 183, 195, 201. Meek incidentally mentions the subordination of animals in liberal theory, but makes no note of it—his concern is how the idea of the "savage" contributed to early social scientific theories about the development and progress of societies. In such theories, societies advance from hunting/gathering to pasturage through agriculture and, finally, commerce. Animals are not only the first glimmer man has of property—in the hunting stage—but also their domestication is what marks the transition from hunting to pasturage, and their successful domestication and propagation prompts the transition from pasturage to agriculture.

67. Jerald Tannenbaum makes the argument that animals' property status does not preclude their having rights since property has always been regulated and protected. Property has never, liberal myths notwithstanding, conferred absolute dominion— indeed, owning property often entails a number of duties, which are correlated with the rights of those toward whom duties are owed. "Animals and the Law: Property, Cruelty, Rights," *Social Research* 62 (1995): 539–607.

68. Joel Prentiss Bishop, *Bishop's New Criminal Law* (Chicago: T. H. Flood and Company, 1892), 366.

69. Jordon Curnutt, *Animals and the Law: A Sourcebook* (Santa Barbara: ABC-Clio, 2001), 72–73.

70. "Henry Bergh and His Work," *Scribner's Monthly* 17 (1879): 872.

71. "Negligent Keeping of Animals," *Central Law Journal* 17 (1883): 307–10; Thomas Beven, "The Responsibility at Common Law for the Keeping of Animals," *Harvard Law Review* 22 (1909): 465–91.

72. Oscar L. Quinlan, "Have Animals Rights?" *Central Law Journal* 38 (1894): 160–61. See also: J. H. L., "Cruelty to Animals," *Law Notes* 6 (1902): 139–42. See also: J. H. L., "Cruelty to Animals," *Law Notes* 6 (1902): 139–42.

73. Bishop, *Commentaries on the Criminal Law*, 334–35; Bishop, *Bishop's New Criminal Law*, 366–67; Bishop, *Commentaries on the Law of Statutory Crimes* (Boston: Little, Brown, and Company, 1873), 676–77; W. W. Thornton, "Cruelty to Animals," *Criminal Law Magazine and Reporter* 12 (1880): 378; *Grise v. State*, 37 Ark. 456. See also: W. W. Thornton, "Cruelty to Animals," *Criminal Law Magazine and Reporter* 12 (1880): 378.

74. Charles A. Barnard, *Forms for Complaints, under Chapter 207 of the Public Statutes of Massachusetts, Relating to the Prevention of Cruelty to Animals, with Sundry Directions for Pleading* (Boston: Massachusetts Society for the Prevention of Cruelty to Animals, 1888), 10.

75. Wisconsin Humane Society, *First Biennial Report for the Two Years Ending November 29, 1881* (Milwaukee: s.n., 1882), 81; Illinois Humane Society, *Twelfth Annual Report* (Chicago: s.n., 1882), 31; Elbridge T. Gerry, "Cruelty to Children," *North American Review* 137 (July 1883): 68–75; "Complaints," *Our Animal Friends* 19 (January 1892): 98; ASPCA, *Manual of the American Society for the Prevention of Cruelty to Animals* (New York: s.n., 1895), 10–13; Edith Carrington, *Man's Helpers* (London: G. Bell & Sons, 1897), 170–72.

76. Carrington, *Man's Helpers*, 170; ASPCA, *Manual*, 10; Barnard, *Forms for Complaints*, 11.

77. *Commonwealth v. Lewis*, 1891 Pa. LEXIS 839, 4.

78. Bishop, *Commentaries on the Criminal Law*, Sixth Edition, 1:161–66.

79. W. W. Thornton, "Cruelty to Animals," *Criminal Law Magazine and Reporter* 12 (May 1890): 396–97; Barnard, *Forms for Complaints*, 12–13.

80. Thornton, "Cruelty to Animals," 398.

81. *State v. Avery*, 44 N.H. 392, 396–97.

82. Barnard, *Forms for Complaints*, 11–12.

83. *State v. Bogardus*, 4 Mo. App. 215, holds that pigeon shooting contests do not inflict "unnecessary" suffering because they have a legitimate end—to improve marks-

manship, which may in turn increase the citizen's value to the state as a potential soldier. By contrast, *Commonwealth v. Lewis*, 7 Pa. C.C. R. 558, found the defendant guilty of cruelty for participating in a pigeon-shooting match, arguing that such sports had no legitimate purpose and tended to corrupt the public morals, which the anticruelty statutes were designed to protect. This was reversed by a higher court in *Commonwealth v. Lewis*, 1891 Pa. LEXIS 839, on the grounds that since the object of the match, to shoot pigeons and develop marksmanship, was legitimate, the practice of it was, in this instance, neither needless nor inclined to produce more pain than necessary to achieve the state end—shooting pigeons. Unlike the lower court, the higher court was unwilling to consider the "necessity" of the act in question.

84. MSPCA, *Ninth Annual Report* (Boston: s.n., 1877), 11.

85. *Grise v. State*, 1881 Ark. LEXIS 124, 6–7.

86. *Commonwealth v. Turner*, 1887 Mass. LEXIS 76, 8.

87. Jordan Curnutt, *Animals and the Law: A Sourcebook* (Santa Barbara: ABC Clio, 2001), 73.

88. Quinlan, "Have Animals Rights?" *Central Law Journal* 38 (1894): 161.

89. J. H. L., "Cruelty to Animals," *Law Notes* 6 (1902): 141.

90. Gaines M. Foster, *Moral Reconstruction: Christian Lobbyists and the Federal Legislation of Morality, 1865–1920* (Chapel Hill: University of North Carolina Press, 2002), 2, 4, 74–76.

91. This equation was made forcefully also by antivivisection activists who saw vivisection as cruelty par excellence. For more on vivisection and temperance, see: Craig Buettinger, "Women and Vivisection in Late Nineteenth-Century America," *Journal of Social History* 30 (1997): 857–72.

92. Women's Branch of the PSPCA, *Ninth Annual Report* (Philadelphia: s.n., 1878), 9. White also brought up the affinity between temperance and anticruelty reform at the annual meeting of the American Humane Association. See: AHA, *Doings of the Fourth Annual Meeting of the American Humane Association, Held at Philadelphia, Penn., On Wednesday, Nov. 17, and Thursday, Nov. 18, 1880* (Boston: Wright & Potter, 1880), 19.

93. "Mr. Bergh's Whipping Post," *New York Times*, 11 April 1881, 8.

94. Velma C. Melville, "Among Ourselves," *Wisconsin Humane Herald* 4 (October 1915); PSPCA, *Annual Report of the Pennsylvania Society for the Prevention of Cruelty to Animals* (Philadelphia: s.n., 1869), 4.

95. "Fourteenth Annual Convention," *Union Signal* 13 (December 1, 1887): 10.

96. "From the Watch-Tower," *Union Signal* 14 (October 18, 1888): 9; "Bands of Mercy," *Union Signal* 14 (December 6, 1888): 8; "New Superintendents," *Union Signal* 15 (November 28, 1889): 12; Mary F. Lovell, "The Department of Mercy, and a Word about Vivisection," *Union Signal* 15 (February 21, 1889): 4; "The First World's and Eighteenth National Convention," *Union Signal* 17 (1891): 11.

97. Illinois Humane Society, *Twenty-Sixth Annual Report* (Chicago: s.n., 1895), 12–13.

98. WCTU, *Report of the Thirty-Third Annual Convention, National Woman's Christian Temperance Union* (Chicago: Woman's Temperance Publishing Association, 1906), 122.

99. Untitled, *Humane Journal* 8 (October 1880): 4.

100. "Man's Brutality to Brutes," *New York Times*, 27 August 1870.

101. "Which Was the Brute?" *Humane Journal* 11 (November 1883): 167. For a similar story, see: Richard Harding Davis, *The Bar Sinister* (New York: Scribner, 1903).

102. Herman Daggett, *The Rights of Animals: An Oration Delivered at the Commencement of Providence-College, September 7, 1791* (1792; repr., ASPCA: New York, 1926), 1, 8.

103. "Rum Does Not Always Do It," *Our Dumb Animals* 7 (September 1874): 28.

104. "The Vacant Place," *Humane Journal* 8 (April 1880): 8.

105. "The Rights of Animals," *New York Times*, 11 March 1866.

106. "Mr. Bergh and His Work," *New York Times*, 8 August 1869; "Mr. Bergh's Work," *New York Times*, 19 February 1870; Unti, "The Quality of Mercy," 436–37.

107. ASPCA, *Charge of His Hon. Recorder Hackett, in the Case of the Driver and Conductor of one of the Cars of the Bleecker Street and Fulton Ferry R.R.* (New York: s.n., 1868), 3.

108. "Beating Not the Only Cruelty," *Our Dumb Animals* 8 (December 1875): 52; Angell, "What Is Overloading, and How Proved," *Our Dumb Animals* 1 (August 4, 1868): 17–18; Bishop, *Commentaries on the Law of Statutory Crimes*, 689.

109. Typical practices by horse dealers (or "knackers," as they were derogatively called) might include giving arsenic to a horse, making its coat look glossier. See: "At the Old Bull's Head," *Scribner's Monthly* 17 (January 1879): 421–32; Abraham Soles, *Original and Interesting Book on the Horse, Showing the Characteristics of this Noble Animal, Interspersed with Anecdotes, Etc., Together with a Large Number of Valuable and Original Recipies, Collected During a Career of Thirty Years, among the Indians, and from Practical Experience, and Now Offered to the Public for the First Time* (Schenectady: Young & Graham, 1860), 5–7.

110. "Common Trading Stock—a Disgrace to Our State," *Wisconsin Humane Herald* 5 (September 1916): n.p.

111. David Swing, "Love," *Humane Journal* 14 (June 1886): 84.

112. "Culture and Progress," *Scribner's Monthly* 13 (December 1876): 277–78. Angell repeated this claim elsewhere: George T. Angell, *Ten Lessons on Kindness to Animals* (Boston: MSPCA, 1883), 24.

113. AHA, *Fourteenth Annual Meeting*, 45–47.

114. WCTU, *Report of the Thirty-Eighth Annual Convention, National Woman's Christian Temperance Union* (Chicago: Women's Temperance Publishing Association, 1911), 332.

115. Mary F. Lovell, "Humane Education," *Union Signal* 25 (August 31, 1899): 5. She makes similar claims in "The Fundamental Need of Humane Education," *Union Signal* 29 (January 15, 1903): 4.

116. WCTU, *Report of the Twenty-Ninth Annual Convention, National Woman's Christian Temperance Union* (Chicago: Woman's Temperance Publishing Association, 1902), 315, 319; "Humane Education Necessary," *Union Signal* 22 (May 31, 1900). For other assertions of the link between cruelty and crime, see: Mrs. C. M. Fairchild, *Pleadings of Mercy for the Animal World, and All Other Defenseless Creatures* (Chicago: A. W. Landon, 1883), 95; Hill, *Ways of Cruelty*, 29; Sarah J. Eddy, *Songs of Happy Life*

(Providence: Art and Nature Study Publishing Company, 1897), 162; Ralph Waldo Trine, *Every Living Creature; or, Heart-Training through the Animal World* (New York: T. Y. Crowell & Company, 1899), 3–5.

117. Mary Ann Mason, *From Father's Property to Children's Rights: The History of Child Custody in the United States* (New York, 1994), 2–13, 30–31, 46–47; Michael Grossberg, *Governing the Hearth: Law and Family in Nineteenth-Century America* (Chapel Hill: University of North Carolina Press, 1985), 4; Grossberg, "'A Protected Childhood,'" 221; Peter Bardaglio, *Reconstructing the Household: Families, Sex, and the Law in the Nineteenth-Century South* (Chapel Hill: University of North Carolina Press, 1995), 23–28; Grace Abbott, "Introduction" and "Early History of Child Labor in the United States," in *The Child and the State*, 3–8, 270–76; Thomas P. Mason, "Child Abuse and Neglect Part 1: Historical Overview, Legal Matrix, and Social Perspectives," *North Carolina Law Review* 50 (1972): 299–300; Minnesota Society for the Prevention of Cruelty, *Annual Report for 1895*, 21;

118. NY-SPCC, *Thirteenth Annual Report* (New York, 1887), 8; Marilyn Irvin Holt, *The Orphan Trains: Placing Out in America* (Lincoln: University of Nebraska Press, 1992); Charles Loring Brace, "The Children's Aid Society of New York," in *History of Child Saving in the United States*, ed. C. D. Randall et al. (Boston, 1893), 1–36.

119. George A. H. Scott, "Anti-Cruelty Laws and Their Relation to Dependent, Neglected and Delinquent Children," *Humane Advocate* 8 (January 1913): 53; Illinois Humane Society supplement 1, Special Collections Library, University of Illinois at Chicago (hereafter IHS Supp I); Wisconsin Humane Society, *First Biennial Report for the Two Years Ending November 29, 1881* (Milwaukee, 1882), 9.

120. AHA, *Fourteenth Annual Report*, 16.

121. On SPCCs' commitment to a middle-class domestic ideal, see: Robertson, *Crimes against Children*, 23; on expanding definitions of cruelty, see: Grossberg, "'A Protected Childhood,'" 222.

122. O. C. Gibbs, "Neglected Childhood," *Humane Journal* 9 (August 1881): 7.

123. Case 466, Illinois Humane Society Records—supplement, box 4, folder 44, case records, May 1895–September 1902, University of Illinois at Chicago, Special Collections. In this and all IHS case records names have been changed. For another argument about how the poor's violation of domestic ideas became a social problem, see: Christine Stansell, "Women, Children and the Uses of the Street: Class and Gender Conflict in New York City, 1850–1860," *Feminist Studies* 8 (Summer 1982): 309–35.

124. Dr. W. A. Robertson, "The Vital Importance of Child Rescue and Conservation," *National Humane Review* 2 (February 1914): 32–33, 46; "No Peace for Shiftless Fathers in Tennessee," *National Humane Review* 4 (January 1916): 15; Walter Trattner, *From Poor Law to Welfare State: A History of Social Welfare in America*, 6th ed. (New York: Free Press, 1999), chap. 5; Stanley, *From Bondage to Contract*, chap. 3.

125. Robertson, *Crimes against Children*, 25–26; case 7958, Minneapolis Humane Society, Minnesota Historical Society, box 17, 144.H.17.3(F).

126. Nicola Beisel, *Imperiled Innocents: Anthony Comstock and Family Reproduction in Victorian America* (Princeton: Princeton University Press, 1997); Alison M. Parker, *Purifying America: Women, Cultural Reform, and Pro-Censorship Activism, 1873–1933* (Urbana: University of Illinois Press, 1997), 36–37.

127. Riis, *Children of the City*, 5–6, 132–33, 138–40.

128. For the Massachusetts cases, see: "Cruelty to Children," *Our Dumb Animals* 6 (1874): 75; Cruelty to Children," *Our Dumb Animals* 8 (1876): 60. For details of the New York law and its enforcement, see: Shauna Vey, "Good Intentions and Fearsome Prejudice: New York's 1876 Act to Prevent and Punish Wrongs to Children," *Theatre Survey* 42 (2001): 53–68. Elbridge Gerry, "Children of the Stage," *North American Review* 151 (1890): 15–19.

129. "Prevention of Cruelty to Children," *Humane Journal* 8 (April 1880): 2; Wisconsin Humane Society, *First Biennial Report for the Two Years Ending November 29, 1881* (Milwaukee: s.n., 1881), 16. For the efforts of other SPCCs and humane societies to regulate or prohibit children's performances, see: "Work of Kindred Societies," *Humane Journal* 8 (1880): 5–6; Wisconsin Humane Society, *Fifth Annual Report of the Wisconsin Humane Society, 1883–1884* (Milwaukee, s.n., 1884), 36; Wisconsin Humane Society, *Eleventh Annual Report of the Wisconsin Humane Society for the Prevention of Cruelty, 1889–1890* (Milwaukee, s.n., 1890), 22; "Position of the Humane Society," *Humane Journal* 19 (1891): 90; Illinois Humane Society, *Twenty-Third Annual Report* (Chicago: s.n., 1892), 10; Illinois Humane Society, *Twenty-Fourth Annual Report* (Chicago: s.n., 1893), 8; "Humane Society Notes," *Humane Journal* 22 (1894): 82; "Recent Legislation on Child Abuse," *Humane Journal* 23 (1895): 117; Illinois Humane Society, *Twenty-Eighth Annual Report* (Chicago: s.n., 1897), 10–11; Illinois Humane Society, *Twenty-Ninth Annual Report* (Chicago: s.n., 1898), 17.

130. A. J. McKelway, "Child Labor and Democracy," *Child Labor Bulletin* 1 (1912): 127; Owen Lovejoy, "Employment of Children on the Stage," *Child Labor Bulletin* 1 (1912): 72–82; "An Unattained Ideal of Juvenile Protection," unpublished manuscript, n.d., Juvenile Protective Association Papers, folder 77, University of Illinois at Chicago, Special Collections. On the JPA objection to child actors, see also: "Where the Appeal of Childhood Has a Commercial Value," unpublished manuscript, [c. 1924], JPA papers, folder 27; F. Zeta Youmans, "Childhood, Inc.," reprinted from *The Survey*, July 15, 1924, JPA papers, folder 27; Youmans, "The Significance of Jackie Coogan," unpublished manuscript, JPA papers, folder 78; "Stage Children and the Law," unpublished manuscript, n.d., JPA papers, folder 77. On the JPA, see: Elizabeth J. Clapp, *Mothers of All Children: Women Reformers and the Rise of Juvenile Courts in Progressive Era America* (University Park: Pennsylvania State University Press, 1998), 185–90.

131. ASPCA, *Nineteenth Annual Report for 1884* (New York: s.n., 1885), 6–7.

CHAPTER THREE

1. "Prevention of Cruelty to Children."

2. Michael Grossberg, "Children's Legal Rights? A Historical Look at a Legal Paradox," in *Children at Risk in America: History, Concepts, and Public Policy*, ed. Roberta Wollons (Albany: SUNY Press, 1993), 111–40, quote on 119. See also: David S. Tanenhaus, "Between Dependency and Liberty: The Conundrum of Children's Rights in the Gilded Age," *Law and History Review* (Summer 2005), http://www.historycooperative.org/ journals/lhr/23.2/tanenhaus.html (4 September 2009); Joseph M. Hawes, *The Children's Rights Movement* (Boston: Twayne Publishers, 1991), esp. chap. 2; Martha

Minow, "Rights for the Next Generation: A Feminist Approach to Children's Rights," *Harvard Women's Law Journal* 9 (1986): 1–24. Linda Gordon describes how SPCCs challenged patriarchy without advocating the destruction of the family or the liberation of children. *Heroes of Their Own Lives*, 55–57.

3. Harriet Beecher Stowe, "Rights of Dumb Animals," *Our Dumb Animals* 1 (February 1869): 69. Stowe's article was originally published in *Hearth & Home*.

4. "Extract from a Letter Received," *Our Dumb Animals* 1 (July 1868): 12.

5. Eric Foner, "Rights and the Constitution in Black Life during the Civil War and Reconstruction," *Journal of American History* 74 (1987): 863–83; Foner, *Reconstruction: America's Unfinished Revolution, 1863–1877* (New York: Harper & Row, 1988), esp. 77–123; Laura Edwards, *Gendered Strife and Confusion: The Political Culture of Reconstruction* (Urbana: University of Illinois Press, 1997); Bardaglio, *Reconstructing the Household*, esp. 116–34; Carole Shammas, *A History of Household Government in America* (Charlottesville: University of Virginia Press, 2002), esp. chap. 5; Amy Dru Stanley, *From Bondage to Contract: Wage Labor, Marriage, and the Market in the Age of Slave Emancipation* (Cambridge: Cambridge University Press, 1998).

6. "Prevention of Cruelty to Children"; Sydney Coleman, *Humane Society Leaders in America* (Albany: American Humane Association, 1924), 33. Modern animal rights activists often also make this comparison between the status of slaves and that of animals. See especially: Marjorie Spiegel, *The Dreaded Comparison: Human and Animal Slavery* (Philadelphia: New Society Publishers, 1988).

7. Leslie Butler, *Critical Americans: Victorian Intellectuals and Transatlantic Liberal Reform* (Chapel Hill: University of North Carolina Press, 2007), 89; *Mercury* quoted in Zulma Steele, *Angel in Top Hat* (New York: Harper and Brothers Publishing, 1942), 45.

8. Nancy Fraser and Linda Gordon, "A Genealogy of Dependency: Tracing a Keyword of the U.S. Welfare State," *Signs* 19 (1994): 309–36; Grossberg, *Governing the Hearth*, 5–9; Linda K. Kerber, *Women of the Republic: Intellect and Ideology in Revolutionary America* (Chapel Hill: University of North Carolina Press, 1980), 139–55; Linda K. Kerber, *No Constitutional Right to Be Ladies* (New York: Hill and Wang, 1998), 11–15; Mary Beth Norton, *Founding Mothers and Fathers: Gendered Power and the Forming of American Society* (New York: Knopf, 1996); Kathleen M. Brown, *Good Wives, Nasty Wenches and Anxious Patriarchs: Gender, Race, and Power in Colonial Virginia* (Chapel Hill: University of Chapel Hill Press, 1996), 13–41; Holly Brewer, *By Birth or Consent: Children, Law, and the Anglo-American Revolution in Authority* (Chapel Hill: University of Chapel Hill Press, 2005), 17–29; John Fabian Witt, "From Loss of Services to Loss of Support: The Wrongful Death Statutes, the Origins of Modern Tort Law, and the Making of the Nineteenth-Century Family," *Law & Social Inquiry* 25 (2000): 722–26; Laura F. Edwards, "Status without Rights: African Americans and the Tangled History of Law and Governance in the Nineteenth-Century U.S. South," *American Historical Review* (April 2007), http://www.historycooperative.org/journals/ahr/112.2/edwards.html (24 July 2007). Edwards is challenging the notion that dependents have no access to the law and no ability to make claims on the state, but she nonetheless shows how the claims of those with "status" but no "rights" must be framed as issues of public order or peace.

9. Joan Gunderson, "Independence, Citizenship, and the American Revolution," *Signs* 13 (1987): 59–77; Nancy Isenberg, *Sex and Citizenship in Antebellum America* (Chapel Hill: University of North Carolina Press, 1998), 7–8, 22–24, 26–27; Fraser and Gordon, "A Genealogy of Dependence," 312–13; John Adams, "On the Importance of Property for the Suffrage," *Annals of America* (Chicago: Encyclopedia Britannica), 2:422–23.

10. Sean Wilentz, *Chants Democratic: New York City and the Rise of the American Working Class, 1788–1850*, 20th anniversary ed. (New York: Oxford University Press, 2004); Sellers, *Market Revolution*; Foner, *Free Soil, Free Labor, Free Men*; David Roediger, *Wages of Whiteness: Race and the Making of the American Working Class* (New York: Verso, 1999); Elizabeth Clark, "Matrimonial Bonds: Slavery and Divorce in Nineteenth-Century America," *Law and History Review* 8 (1990): 25–54; Amy Dru Stanley, "Conjugal Bonds and Wage Labor: Rights of Contract in the Age of Emancipation," *Journal of American History* 75 (1988): 471–500; Henry Clay, quoted in Lydia Maria Child, *An Appeal in Favor of that Class of Americans Called Africans* (1836; reprint, New York: Arno Press, 1968), 77–78.

11. Fraser and Gordon, "A Genealogy of Dependency"; Rowland Berthoff, "Conventional Mentality: Free Blacks, Women, and Business Corporations as Unequal Persons, 1820–1870," *Journal of American History* 76 (1989): 753–84; *Journal of the Convention to Form a Constitution for the State of Wisconsin, with a Sketch of the Debates, Begun and Held at Madison, on the Fifteenth Day of December, Eighteen Hundred and Forty-seven* (Madison: W. T. Tenney, Holt, & Smith, 1848), 130, quoted in Berthoff, "Conventional Mentality," 761; Ellen Carol Dubois, "Outgrowing the Compact of the Fathers: Equal Rights, Woman Suffrage, and the United States Constitution, 1820–1878," *Journal of American History* 74 (1987): 836–62.

12. Tennessee Freedman's Bureau official quoted in Eric Foner, *Reconstruction: America's Unfinished Revolution, 1863–1877* (New York: Harper & Row, 1988), 152; Foner, *Reconstruction*, 77–123, 164–68; Foner, *The Story of American Freedom* (New York: Norton, 1998), 100–105; Heather Cox Richardson, *The Death of Reconstruction: Race, Labor, and Politics in the Post-Civil War North, 1865–1901* (Cambridge, MA: Harvard University Press, 2001); Stanley, *From Bondage to Contract*, 98–137, quote on 105.

13. Clark, "Matrimonial Bonds"; Stanley, "Conjugal Bonds and Wage Labor."

14. Quoted in Stanley, *From Bondage to Contract*, 84.

15. Stanley, *From Bondage to Contract*; Fraser and Gordon, "A Genealogy of Dependency"; Leon Fink, *Workingmen's Democracy: The Knights of Labor and American Politics* (Urbana: University of Illinois Press, 1983), 3–15; Linda K. Kerber, *A Woman's Wage: Historical Meanings and Social Consequences* (Lexington: University Press of Kentucky, 1990), 8–12.

16. Shammas, *History of Household Government*; Sir Henry Maine, *Ancient Law* (1861; reprint, Tucson: University of Arizona Press, 1986), 116, 162, 165.

17. William Graham Sumner, *What Social Classes Owe to Each Other* (1883; reprint, New York: Harper & Brothers, 1920), 25–27.

18. Grossberg, *Governing the Hearth*; Bardaglio, *Reconstructing the Family*; Shammas, *History of Household Government*. For exceptions, see: Witt, "From Loss of Ser-

vices to Loss of Support"; Karen Orren, *Belated Feudalism*: Labor, the Law, and Liberal Development in the United States (Cambridge: Cambridge University Press, 1991).

19. "Remarks of William L. Bowditch," *Liberator*, 18 September 1848, 1; "Who Is Responsible for the Existence of Slavery in America?" *Liberator*, 29 October 1855, 1; Garrison quoted in Amy Dru Stanley, "Home Life and the Morality of the Market," in *The Market Revolution in America: Social, Political, and Religious Expression*, ed. Melvyn Stokes and Stephen Conway (Charlottesville: University of Virginia Press, 1996), 86. See also: "Slavery in America," *Liberator*, 29 June 1849, 1; "Cruelty to Animals," *Liberator*, 27 June 1835, 103; "Anti-Slavery Meeting," *Liberator*, 4 October 1834, 159. Some discussion of cruelty to animals appears in the pages of the *Liberator*. See: "Unmerciful Beating of Animals," *Liberator*, 1 August 1856, 124; "A Few Random Thoughts on Cruelty to Animals," *Liberator*, 27 August 1847, 140; "Cruelty to Animals," *Liberator*, 7 April 1837, 60; "Cruelty to Animals," *Liberator*, 22 November 1834, 188.

20. René Descartes, *Discourse on Method and Meditations on First Philosophy*, 3d ed., trans. Donald A. Cress (Indianapolis: Hackett Publishing Company 1993). Descartes argues that animals have no reason, no language, and thus no soul; they are fundamentally different from man. Whatever animals are able to accomplish should be understood as the product of nature, or body, rather than mind. For an explanation of Descartes' innovative approach to separating humans and animals, see: Erica Fudge, *Brutal Reasoning: Animals, Rationality, and Humanity in Early Modern England* (Ithaca: Cornell University Press, 2006). For the influence of Cartesian dualism on the question of animal rights, see: Gary L. Francione, *Animals, Property, and the Law* (Philadelphia: Temple University Press, 1995), 8–10. Nineteenth-century animal protectionists were certainly aware that they were combating the legacy of Descartes. See: "What Epes Sargent Says," *Our Dumb Animals* 1 (July 1868): 14; "Are Animals Machines?" *Our Dumb Animals* 6 (January 1874): 64.

Reason, in turn, is the foundation of human equality and liberty in John Locke's classic account of the formation of the liberal state. John Locke, *Two Treatises of Government*, ed. with an introduction and notes by Peter Laslett (Cambridge: Cambridge University Press, 1988), sections 4–15. Though he explicitly excludes animals from the social contract, Locke does not speak to the question of animal intelligence in direct terms in the *Second Treatise*. His thoughts on the differences between humans and animals are developed in his *Essay Concerning Human Understanding*. See especially his discussion of human language, book 3, chap. 1. John Locke, *Essay Concerning Human Understanding* (Chicago: Henry Regenery Company, 1956). For the importance of reason to Locke's political theory of the liberal individual and the liberal state, see: Holly Brewer, *By Birth or Consent*; Uday Singh Mehta, *Liberalism and Empire* (Chicago: University of Chicago Press, 1999).

Although I am not concentrating on it here, animal protectionists did explicitly and vigorously argue that animals were rational (though there was not unanimity on this point). See: Susan Pearson, "The Rights of the Defenseless: Animals, Children, and Sentimental Liberalism in Nineteenth-Century America," (Ph.D. diss., University of North Carolina, Chapel Hill, 2004), 98–108.

21. Clark, "Sacred Rights of the Weak," 463–70.

22. Stowe, *Uncle Tom's Cabin*; "Men, Women and Babes Sold!," *Liberator*, 7 July 1832, 106; Lydia Maria Child, *An Appeal in Favor of Americans Called Africans* (1833; repr. New York: Arno Press, 1969), 10, 12, 188.

23. Clark, "Sacred Rights of the Weak," 471, 476.

24. Clark, "Sacred Rights of the Weak," 487–92. For the classic distinction between negative and positive liberties, see: Isiah Berlin, "Two Concepts of Liberty," in *Four Essays on Liberty* (Oxford: Oxford University Press, 1969), 118–72.

25. For the notion that rights are normally conceived in negative rather than positive terms, see: Jeremy Waldron, "Rights and Needs: The Myth of Disjunction," in *Legal Rights: Historical and Philosophical Perspectives*, ed. Austin Sarat and Thomas R. Kearns (Ann Arbor: University of Michigan Press, 1996), 97–98.

26. Witt, "From Loss of Services to Loss of Support," 722–26; Reeve quoted in Witt, *The Accidental Republic: Crippled Workingmen, Destitute Widows, and the Remaking of American Law* (Cambridge, MA: Harvard University Press, 2004), 52. With respect to harm to animals, see: Susan J. Pearson, "The Cow and the Plow: Animal Suffering, Human Guilt, and the Crime of Cruelty," in *Toward a Critique of Guilt: Perspectives from Law and the Humanities*, special volume of *Studies in Law, Politics and Society* 36 (2005): 77–101.

27. Untitled, *Our Dumb Animals* 8 (June 1875): 6; G. L. C., "Mr. Chaney's Words on Cruelty," *Ark* (March 2, 1875): 1.

28. "Cruelty to Animals in Their Lives and at Their Deaths," *Our Dumb Animals* I (July 1868): 10; American Humane Association, *Doings of the Third Annual Meeting of the American Humane Association* (Boston: Wright & Potter Printing, 1879), 7.

29. Animal Rescue League, *First Annual Report* (Boston: Animal Rescue League, 1900), 13, 6.

30. Henry Bergh, "Extracts from Address of President Bergh, of New York," *Our Dumb Animals* I (June 1868): 6. Bergh is here actually plagiarizing from another pamphlet at the time. For excerpts from the original text, see: Reverend Dr. Chalmers in *Kindness to Animals, Illustrated by Stories and Anecdotes* (London: W & R Chambers, 1877), 180–81.

31. "The Check Rein," *Our Dumb Animals* I (November 1868): 44.

32. "Thoughts for Drivers," *Our Dumb Animals* I (July 1868): 10.

33. "The Check Rein," *Our Dumb Animals* I (July 1868): 10.

34. "Is Turn About Fair Play?" *Our Dumb Animals* 4 (June 1871): 110; "How Do You Like This?" *Our Dumb Animals* 4 (June 1871): 110. Leslie Butler notes that the phrase "fair play" was popular among postbellum liberals who used it to articulate their conception of a just society. Butler, *Critical Americans*, 102–3.

35. "Birds Robbing Child's Nest," *Our Dumb Animals* 4 (July 1871): 118; "Dive, Boys, Dive," *Our Dumb Animals* 4 (September 1871): 134; "Geese Plucking!" *Our Dumb Animals* 4 (November 1871): 150.

36. Emma Elizabeth Page, *Heart Culture: A Text Book for Teaching Kindness to Animals, Arranged for Use in Public and Private School*s (San Francisco: Whitaker & Ray Co., 1897), 37–39; Mrs. C. M. Fairchild, *Pleadings of Mercy for the Animal World*,

and *All Other Defenseless Creatures* (Chicago: A. W. Landon , 1883), 56–58; Sarah J. Eddy, *Friends and Helpers* (Boston: Ginn and Company, 1899), 135–37; "An Eider-Down Dream," *Our Dumb Animals* 9 (June 1876): 1.

37. "Address of Rev. William R. Alger at the Annual Meeting of This Society, March 29, 1870," *Our Dumb Animals* 2 (1870): 113.

38. A. de Beaupre, "Animals Love Man," *Our Dumb Animals* 3 (October 1870): 34.

39. "Animal Affection," *Our Dumb Animals* 7 (September 1874): 35.

40. Lydia Maria Child, "Pussy Malta and Grizzly Tom," *Our Dumb Animals* 2 (April 1870): 105.

41. PSPCA, *Strange Story of a Dog* (Philadelphia: Brady, [1867]), 1.

42. Reverend Thomas Timmins, *The History and the Founding, Aims, and Growth of the American Bands of Mercy* (Boston: P. H. Foster & Co. Printers, 1883), 76.

43. "Golden Words from Rev. Dr. Putnam," *Ark* 1 (1875): 1. For other versions of this story, see: "Anecdote of a Dog," *Our Dumb Animals* 1 (1868): 29; George T. Angell, *Ten Lessons on Kindness to Animals* (Boston: MSPCA, 1883), 13; Timmins, *History and the Founding*, 35, 76; George T. Angell, *Humane Leaflet, No. 4: 8 Leaflets, 100 Selections, for Schools, Sunday Schools, Bands of Mercy, and Homes* (Boston: MSPCA, n.d.), 3; *Kindness to Animals: Illustrated by Stories and Anecdotes* (London: W & R Chambers, 1877), 54–56. The dedication of the dog to his dead master was a trope not confined to Bobby's story alone. See: Elizabeth Somerville, *Preludes to Knowledge; or, Amusing and Instructive Conversations on History, Astronomy, Geography, Optics, and the Division of Time in Different Countries. Interspersed with Stories, Moral and Entertaining* (London: W. Flint, 1803), 182; *The General Character of the Dog: Illustrated by a Variety of Original and Interesting Anecdotes of That Beautiful and Useful Animal, in Prose and Verse* (New York: George G. Sickels, 1829), 90; Samuel Griswold Goodrich, *Illustrative Anecdotes of the Animal Kingdom* (Boston: Bradbury, Soden & Co., 1845), 97; *Stories about Birds and Beasts* (New York: Clark, Austin & Co., 1851), 45–48; Grace Greenwood, *History of My Pets* (Boston: Ticknor, Reed, & Fields, 1851), 53–57; ASPCA, *Seventh Annual Report* (New York: Cushing, Bardua & Co. Printers, 1877), 42–44 [Elbridge T. Gerry, the ASPCA's chief counsel, is given a silver vase in appreciation of his work. It is engraved with, among other things, a picture of a dog lying on top of a freshly dug grave]; *Selections for School Exhibitions and Private Reading, Illustrating and Advocating Mercy to the Dumb Creation* (Boston: MSPCA, 1878), 34–36; "Affection of Animals," *Humane Journal* 6 (July 1878): 7; G. R. F., "Greyfriar's Bobby," *Our Animal Friends* 28 (February 1900): 127–29.

44. Dora Darmoore, "Animals Immortal," *Our Dumb Animals* 7 (December 1874): 50.

45. "Mother and Child," *Our Dumb Animals* 7 (October 1874): 38.

46. H. J. P., "A Plea for Animal Mothers," *Our Dumb Animals* 7 (May 1875): 91.

47. Lynn Hunt, *Inventing Human Rights*. Hunt suggests that the eighteenth-century novel's production of empathy was critical to the spread of the concept of human rights.

48. Angell, *Autobiographical Sketches and Personal Recollections* (Boston: American Humane Education Society, 1892), 94.

49. For some examples of the commercial use of this subtitle, see the following edi-

tions of *Black Beauty*: Lothrop, Lee & Shepherd (Boston: 1890); Rand, McNally & Co. (Chicago: 1892 and 1900); Frank Miller Company (New York: 1892, four editions); J. Howendon & Company (New York: 1894); H. M. Caldwell (New York: 1894); Charles E. Brown & Company (Boston: 1895); E. A. Weeks and Company (Chicago: 1895).

50. Angell, *Autobiographical Sketches*, 99.

51. Reverend J. B. Gross, *A Plea in Behalf of Our Domestic Animals against the Cruelties of Man* (Philadelphia: J. B. Lippincott & Co., 1869), 3.

52. The most extensive research on this point is that of Coleman O. Parsons, "The Progenitors of Black Beauty in Humanitarian Literature," parts 1–4, *Notes and Queries* 192 (1947): 156–58, 190–93, 210–12, 230–32. Parson's research largely explores the British context for Sewell's story, while my own research indicates not only that the same British humanitarian literature was widely circulated in the United States, but also that before Sewell's horse addressed readers directly, American writers experimented with this form quite explicitly. Parsons also fails to mention that the plot structure of Sewell's novel is borrowed most directly from a nonanimal, and American, source: *Uncle Tom's Cabin*. For more on this point, see: Robert Dingley, "A Horse of a Different Color: Black Beauty and the Pressures of Indebtedness," *Victorian Literature and Culture* 25 (1997): 241–51.

53. Other examples of direct appeal from horses include: *The Life of a Horse, Supposed to Be Written by Himself; Benevolence Rewarded; The Bird; Ingratitude Punished; The Accident; and, the Faithful Dog* (Boston: Munroe & Francis, [1824]), 1–10; Thomas Craige, *A Conversation between a Lady and Her Horse* (Philadelphia: Thomas Craige, 1851); American Humane Association, *How to Treat Horses* (Albany: American Humane Association, n.d.); untitled, *Our Dumb Animals* 8 (April 1876): 88; "Letter from 'Nellie,' a Family Horse," *Our Dumb Animals* 6 (September 1873): 38; Lucy Larcom, "The Car-Horse," *Ark* 1 (February 23, 1875): 1; Bucephalus, "An Equine Epistle," *Ark* 1 (March 2, 1875): 1; "The Horses' Prayer," in *The Horse Aid Society of New York, First Report, from March, 1910 to December, 1912* (New York: n.p., 1912), 12.

54. For the concept of "naïve reason," I am indebted to Peter Hollindale, "Plain Speaking: Black Beauty as a Quaker Text," *Annual of the Modern Language Association Division on Children's Literature and the Children's Literature Association* 28 (2000): 95–111.

55. Rob, "The Old Horse's Story," *Our Dumb Animals* 4 (November 1871): 151.

56. Eliza S. Turner, "Equine Correspondence, *Our Dumb Animals* 4 (July 1871): 119.

57. "An Excellent Example," *Our Dumb Animals* 8 (1875): 36.

58. James Macaulay, *Vivisection: Is It Scientifically Useful or Morally Justified? A Prize Essay by James Macaulay, A.M., M.D., Fellow of the Royal College of Surgeons, of Edinburgh. Reprinted from the English Edition* (Philadelphia: American Anti-Vivisection Society, 1884), 60–61.

59. Macaulay, *Vivisection*, 61.

60. T. T. Munger, *The Rights of Dumb Animals* (Hartford: Connecticut Humane Society, 1898), 12. On Munger as a Social Gospel advocate, see: Fine, *Laissez Faire and the General Welfare State*, 170; Hays, *The Response to Industrialism*, 77.

61. Munger, *Rights of Dumb Animals*, 4–6. This line of reasoning is also echoed in Gross, *Plea in Behalf of Our Domestic Animals*, 5–15. Animal welfare publications

constantly stressed the labor of horses, oxen, cows, and even dogs—portraying them as "servants," "slaves," and patient toilers. Further, in the early twentieth century, many large cities began "Work-Horse Parades," and during World War I, special committees for the care and relief of horse and dog "soldiers" were formed. All assumed that animals' service created a claim on humans.

62. Munger, *Rights of Dumb Animals*, 8–11.

63. Legal scholar Jeremy Waldron makes the point that contract is almost uniquely a domain of law where rights are strongly connected to duties—to obligations and responsibilities on the part of others. Waldron, "Rights and Needs," 100. Thus, while contract language has been identified by many historians as the chief scourge of laissez-faire liberalism and the cruel lynchpin of capitalism, Munger's use of a contract metaphor shows that the relational and reciprocal nature of contracts makes them an effective means of claiming rights, claiming what is owed to oneself.

64. Munger, *Rights of Dumb Animals*, 12–21. See also: Gross, *Plea in Behalf of Our Domestic Animals*, 4, 10–21.

65. Marcus Wood, *Blind Memory: Visual Representations of Slavery in England and America, 1780–1865* (Manchester: Manchester University Press), 260. There is an extensive literature on the question of whether the presentation of pain inspires sympathy, justice, and reform, or whether it inspires either compassion fatigue, narcissistic exploration of one's own suffering, or, worse, titillation. Much of this debate forms a part of the more general debate over the politics of sentimentalism, and much of it centers on the politics of white abolitionists' presentation of slave suffering in antebellum America. For some representative works addressing these questions, see: Clark, "Sacred Rights of the Weak"; Susan Sontag, *Regarding the Pain of Others* (New York: Farrar, Strauss & Giroux, 2003); Lacquer, "Bodies, Details, and the Humanitarian Narrative," 176–204; Boltanski, *Distant Suffering*; Haltunnen, "Humanitarianism and the Pornography of Pain in Anglo-American Culture," 303–34; Hinton, *The Perverse Gaze of Sympathy*; McKanan, *Identifying the Image of God*; Eppler, *Touching Liberty*.

66. For such critiques, see: Gillian Silverman, "Sympathy and Its Viccissitudes"; Gillian Brown, *Domestic Individualism: Imagining Self in Nineteenth-Century America* (Berkeley: University of California Press, 1990); Merish, *Sentimental Materialism*.

67. "Our Fair," *Our Dumb Animals* 3 (February 1871): 68.

68. Clark, "The Sacred Rights of the Weak," 465–70. Confinement is also central to Elaine Scarry's analysis of how torture replaces language and an embodied world with the reductionist experience of bodily pain. Scarry, *The Body in Pain: The Making and Unmaking of the World* (New York: Oxford University Press, 1985), 39–40.

69. Thomas Hill, *Ways of Cruelty* (Chicago: Albert W. Landon, 1883), 9.

70. Illinois Humane Society, *An Appeal in Behalf of the Illinois Humane Society* (Chicago: s.n., 1871), 4. For other complaints against leg tying in transport to market, see: "The Cattle," *Humane Journal* 10 (March 1882): 38; "Cruelty to Animals in Their Lives and at Their Deaths," *Our Dumb Animals* 2 July 7, 1868): 9; "Bleeding of Calves," *Our Dumb Animals* 1 (September 4, 1868): 26; "Tying Calves," *Our Dumb Animals* 2 (January 4, 1870): 80.

71. AHA, *Report of the Proceedings, Fourteenth Annual Meeting of the American Humane Association for the Prevention of Cruelty to Children and Animals* (Cincin-

nati: s.n., 1890). Also featured in: Wisconsin Humane Society, *Eleventh Annual Report of the Wisconsin Humane Society for the Prevention of Cruelty, 1889–1890* (Milwaukee: s.n., 1890); Wisconsin Humane Society, *Reports for the Years 1900, 1901, 1902 and 1903* (Milwaukee: s.n., 1903): 73.

72. "Editor's Easy Chair," *Harper's New Monthly Magazine* 84 (February 1892): 475.

73. "Bring the Dark Deeds to Light," *Humane Journal* 9 (October 1881): 7.

74. Emma Tuttle, *Angell Prize-Contest Recitations to Advance Humane Education in All Its Phases. 'Nil desperandum.' Compiled to Be Used in Entertainments Managed by Churches, Societies, Lyceum, Sunday Schools, Bands of Mercy, or Individuals Aiming to Establish Right over Wrong, Kindness over Cruelty, Knowledge over Ignorance, and Justice over All* (Chicago; J. R. Francis: 1896), 6.

75. On postbellum structural changes and the emergent sense of interdependence, see: Wiebe, *The Search for Order*; Louis Galambos, "The Emerging Organizational Synthesis in Modern American History," *Business History Review* 44 (1970): 279–90; Haskell, *The Emergence of Professional Social Science*, 27–43; Alfred Chandler, *The Visible Hand: The Managerial Revolution in American Business* (Cambridge, MA: Belknap Press, 1977); Alan Trachtenberg, *The Incorporation of America: Culture and Society in the Gilded Age* (New York: Hill & Wang, 1982); Galambos, "Technology, Political Economy, and Professionalization: Central Themes of the Organizational Synthesis," *Business History Review* 57 (1983): 471–93; Edwards, *New Spirits*.

76. George E. McNeill, "The Problem of Today," in *The Labor Movement: The Problem of Today*, ed. George E. McNeill (Boston: A. M. Bridgman & Company, 1887), 455; Haskell, *Emergence of Professional Social Science*, 39–43.

77. Barbara Young Welke, *Recasting American Liberty: Gender, Race, Law and the Railroad Revolution* (Cambridge: Cambridge University Press, 2001), xi, 43–57, 70, 83–101, 126–36; "Brief of Appellant," quoted in Welke, *Recasting American Liberty*, 121. See also: James Schmidt, "'How I Suffered': Industrial Violence and the Remaking of Working-Class Childhood, 1880–1930," paper presented at the Newberry Labor History Seminar, November 11, 2005; Witt, *Accidental Republic*; Dauber, "The Sympathetic State." Some political theorists have argued that a hallmark of modern citizenship is the mobilization of suffering and woundedness as grounds for the attention of the state and the recognition of rights. See: Wendy Brown, *States of Injury: Power and Freedom in Late Modernity* (Princeton: Princeton University Press, 1995), 52–76; Lauren Berlant, *The Queen of America Goes to Washington City: Essays on Sex and Citizenship* (Durham: Duke University Press, 1997), 25–54.

CHAPTER FOUR

1. John D. Wright, the first president of the New York Society for the Prevention of Cruelty to Children, made clear that, in their own view, what distinguished the SPCC from the city's other charities was that only the SPCC had been chartered to enforce laws against abuse, intervening in homes and removing children from them. NY-SPCC, *First Annual Report* (New York: s.n., 1876), 5.

2. Jacob Riis, *The Children of the Poor* (New York: Scribner and Sons, 1892), 142.

3. Untitled, *New York Times*, 10 April 1874.

4. Mark Warren Bailey, *Guardians of the Moral Order: The Legal Philosophy of the Supreme Court, 1860–1910* (Dekalb: Northern Illinois University Press, 2004), 24–84; Terence Martin, *The Instructed Vision: Scottish Common Sense Philosophy and the Origins of American Fiction* (Bloomington: Indiana University Press, 1961), 4–53; Perry Miller, *American Thought: Civil War to World War I* (New York: Holt, Rinehart and Winston, Inc., 1954), ix–xi; Sydney H. Alstrom, "The Scottish Philosophy and American Theology," *Church History* 24 (1955): 257–72; Henry F. May, *The Enlightenment in America* (New York: Oxford University Press, 1976), 308–58;

5. *A Catalogue of the Officers and Students of Dartmouth College, for the Academical Year, 1843–4* (Hanover: Dartmouth Press, 1843), 23; Francis Wayland, *Elements of Moral Science* (Boston: Gould and Lincoln, 1835), 50, 395–96.

6. Gregg Camfield, "The Moral Aesthetics of Sentimentality: A Missing Key to Uncle Tom's Cabin," *Nineteenth-Century Literature* 43 (1988): 328–29; G. Stanley Hall, "American College Textbooks," *Proceedings of the American Antiquarian Society* 9 (1894): 153.

7. W. A. Jones, "Children's Books," *United States Democratic Review* 15 (1844): 542.

8. American Sunday School Union, *Stories for Little Children in the Holiday Season* (Philadelphia: s.n., 1846). For the flowering of didactic literature for children in antebellum America, see: John C. Crandall, "Patriotism and Humanitarianism in Children's Literature, 1825–1860," *American Quarterly* 21 (1969): 3–22. For kindness to animals in this literature, see: Katherine C. Grier, "Childhood Socialization and Companion Animals: United States, 1820–1870," *Society and Animals* 7 (1999): 95–120.

9. Lydia Maria Child, *Isaac T. Hopper: A True Life* (1835; repr., New York: Negro University Press, 1969), 8–9, 16–23, vi.

10. Reverend David Swing, *Sermon Preached before the Central Church, Chicago, IL., October 12, 1879, Being the Sunday after the Third Annual Meeting of the American Humane Association, Held in That City* (Boston: Wright and Potter Printing Company, 1879), 4, 6, 16–17, 18.

11. Robert B. Carter, *A Brief Sketch of the Society for the Prevention of Cruelty to Animals* (Burlington, NJ: Burlington Co. District S.P.C.A., 1884), 7.

12. Zulma Steele, *Angel in Top Hat* (New York: Harper and Brothers Publishing, 1942), 2. Other biographical sources include: "Henry Bergh and His Work," *Scribner's Monthly* 17 (April 1879): 872–84; George Bungay, *Traits of Representative Men* (New York: Fowler & Wells, 1882), 186–94; Clara Morris, "Riddle of the Nineteenth Century: Mr. Henry Bergh," *McClure's Magazine* 18 (March 1902): 414–22; Gerald Carson, "The Great Meddler," *American Heritage* 19 (December 1967): 28–33, 94–97.

13. *In Memoriam, Henry Bergh, Died March 12, 1888* (New York: G. P. Putnam's Sons, 1888), 9.

14. "Editor's Easy Chair," *Harper's New Monthly Magazine* 83 (1891): 311–12; "Henry Bergh and His Work," 872.

15. Bungay, *Traits of Representative Men*, 192.

16. "Inherited Wealth," *Galaxy* 6 (August 1868): 276–77; "Work for the Idle," *New York Times*, 10 January 1868; "Grown Weary in Well-Doing," *New York Times*, 18 March 1868.

17. References to Bergh's sense of justice include: *In Memoriam*, 5–7; Robert G.

Ingersoll, "Thomas Paine," *North American Review* 155 (August 1892): 183; "Henry Bergh and His Work," 878; Morris, "Riddle of the Nineteenth Century: Mr. Henry Bergh," 422.

18. Steele, *Angel in Top Hat*, 35.

19. A. J. A., "Mr. Bergh. From a Lady Correspondent," *New York Times*, 19 February 1872.

20. "The American Society for the Prevention of Cruelty to Animals," *New York Times*, 3 May 1867. This is also emphasized in: "Bergh and His Work," 875; Bungay, *Traits of Representative Men*, 193. In emphasizing his dedication to selfless and principled service, Bergh was implicitly defending the idea of the moral sense (and intuitive moral philosophy) against the contemporary, countervailing current of utilitarianism. For a discussion of this battle in the nineteenth century, see: W. E. H. Lecky, *History of European Morals* (1869; repr., New York: George Braziller, 1955). Lecky makes a point of saying that though utilitarians, especially Bentham and Mill, had made an admirable effort to extend their theories to animals, a moral philosophy "which recognized no other end in virtue than the promotion of human happiness" could find little solid grounding for a concern with animal pleasure and pain (47–48).

21. Bungay, *Traits of Representative Men*, 193.

22. Wood, *Radicalism of the American Revolution*, 213–25.

23. Andrew Burstein, *Sentimental Democracy: The Evolution of America's Romantic Self-Image* (New York: Hill and Wang, 1999), xvii, 21, 290–92; Sarah Knott, "Sensibility and the American War for Independence," *American Historical Review* 109 (2003): 19–40.

24. Quoted in Steele, *Angel in Top Hat*, 35.

25. McCrea, *The Humane Movement*, 148.

26. "Henry Bergh and His Work," 875. Reportedly, these are the words of a citizen helping Bergh to reprimand "the ignorant foreman of a gang of gas-pipe layers" who has created a dangerous obstacle for the city's horse-drawn railroads.

27. "The Bergh Fountain Unveiled," *Humane Journal* 19 (May 1891): 75.

28. *Appeal in Behalf of the Illinois Humane Society*, 5.

29. Bungay, *Traits of Representative Men*, 193; "A Noble Life Ended," *Humane Journal* 16 (March 1888): 37; "Annual Meeting of the American Society for the Prevention of Cruelty to Animals, Address of President Haines," *Our Animal Friends* 25 (February 1898): 121; "Henry Bergh and His Work," 872. For other invocations of hostility to Bergh, see: "Henry Bergh," *Humane Journal* 11 (January 1883): 9; Carter, *A Brief Sketch of the Society for the Prevention of Cruelty to Animals*, 8; "Address of Daniel R. Noyes at Minneapolis Meeting of the A.H.A.," *Humane Journal* 23 (October 1895): 137; Morris, "Riddle of the Nineteenth Century," 414; George M. McCarthy, *The Evolution of a Sentiment* (Jersey City: Press of John L. Compton, 1905), 9; ASPCA, *Three Generations of Animal Protection in New York* (NY: s.n., 1941), 3.

30. Bruce Dorsey, *Reforming Men and Women: Gender in the Antebellum City* (Ithaca: Cornell University Press, 2002), 20–21, 74–75, 190–91; Illinois Humane Society, *Sixteenth Annual Report* (Chicago: s.n., 1886), 21. For the fear that womanly feeling might become hysteria, see: Carroll Smith Rosenberg, "The Hysterical Woman: Sex Roles and Role Conflict in Nineteenth-Century America," in *Disorderly Conduct:*

*Visions of Gender in Victorian America* (New York: Oxford University Press, 1985), 197–216. For an example of this concern about female hysteria within the animal protection movement, see: "Annual Meeting of the American Society for the Prevention of Cruelty to Animals, Address of President Haines," *Our Animal Friends* 28 (February 1900): 123.

31. Hoganson, *Fighting for American Manhood*, 20.

32. See note 8, above.

33. Ruth Bloch, "The Gendered Meanings of Virtue in Revolutionary America," *Signs* 13 (1987): 37–58; Barbara Welter, "The Cult of True Womanhood: 1820–1860," *American Quarterly* 18 (1966): 151–74; Nancy Cott, *The Bonds of Womanhood: "Woman's Sphere" in New England, 1780–1835*, 2d ed. (New Haven: Yale University Press, 1997); Mary Ryan, *Cradle of the Middle Class: The Family in Oneida County, New York, 1790–1865* (Cambridge: Cambridge University Press, 1981); Charles Sellers, *The Market Revolution: Jacksonian America, 1815–1846* (Oxford: Oxford University Press, 1991); Lori Ginzberg, *Women and the Work of Benevolence: Morality, Politics, and Class in the Nineteenth-Century United States* (New Haven: Yale University Press, 1990), 1–33; Paula Baker, "The Domestication of Politics: Women and American Political Society, 1780–1920," in *Unequal Sisters: A Multicultural Reader in U.S. Women's History*, ed. Ellen Carol DuBois and Vicki L. Ruiz (New York: Routledge, 1990), 66–91; Gail Bederman, *Manliness and Civilization* (Chicago: University of Chicago Press, 1995), 10–12; Susan Curtis, "The Son of Man and God the Father: The Social Gospel and Victorian Masculinity," in *Meanings for Manhood: Constructions of Masculinity in Victorian America*, ed. Mark C. Carnes and Clyde Griffen (Chicago: University of Chicago Press, 1990), 67–78; Adam Rome, "'Political Hermaphrodites': Gender and Environmental Reform in Progressive America," *Environmental History* 11 (2006): 440–63.

34. Illinois Humane Society, *Fourteenth Annual Report* (Chicago: s.n., 1884), 12.

35. NY-SPCC, *Fourteenth Annual Report, December 31, 1888* (New York: s.n., 1889), 10.

36. NY-SPCC, *Forty-Third Annual Report, December 31, 1917* (New York: s.n., 1918), 11.

37. Thomas Timmins, *The History of the Founding, Aims, and Growth of the American Bands of Mercy* (Boston: P. H. Foster & Co., Printers, 1883), 8.

38. MSPCA, *Tenth Annual Report* (Boston: s.n., 1878), 5–7; Mary F. Lovell, *An Interesting Re-Organization* (Philadelphia: n.p., [1923]).

39. Sarah J. Eddy, *Songs of Happy Life* (Providence: Art and Nature Study Publishing Company, 1897), 161.

40. "Bands of Mercy," *Humane Journal* 10 (November 1882): 163; AHA, *Doings of the Eighth Annual Meeting of the American Humane Association, Held at Pittsburgh, PA., on Wednesday, Nov. 19th, and Thursday, Nov. 20th, 1884* (Chicago: Office of the Humane Journal, 1885), 28–45; untitled, *Union Signal* 13 (June 30, 1887): 1; Young American Humane Union, *Report of the Young American Humane Union* (Philadelphia: s.n., 1905), 3.

41. Young American Humane Union, *Report of the Young American Humane Union* (Philadelphia: s.n., 1897), 14–15. Published Band of Mercy materials include: Eddy, *Songs of Happy Life*; Angell, *Ten Lessons in Kindness to Animals*; Angell,

*Humane Leaflet, No. 1.* Humane periodicals like *Our Dumb Animals*, the *Humane Journal*, and *Our Animal Friends* all printed Band of Mercy material.

42. Eddy, *Songs of Happy Life*, 5; Timmins, *History of the Founding*, 8, 43. For another reference to chivalry, see: American Anti-Vivisection Society, *Sixteenth Annual Report . . . for the Year 1898* (Philadelphia: s.n., 1899), 22.

43. "The Young Defenders' League," *Our Animal Friends* 28 (March 1900): 145; "Objects of the League," *Our Animal Friends* 27 (May 1900): 207.

44. *Report of the Proceedings of the Twenty-First Annual Convention of the American Humane Association* (Fall River, MA: s.n., 1897), 10.

45. "Humane Society Shield," *Humane Journal* 8 (August 1881): 2.

46. I am grateful to Caroline Winterer for identifying this figure as Minerva.

47. E. Johnson, "The Judge's Pets," *Riverside Magazine* (February 1869): 69–71.

48. Johnson, "The Judge's Pets," *Riverside Magazine* (March 1869): 109–10.

49. Johnson, "The Judge's Pets," *Riverside Magazine* (November 1869): 495–96.

50. John Day Smith, *What War Meant to a Maine Soldier, 1861–1865* (n.p., n.d.), Minneapolis Historical Society.

51. NY-SPCC, *Fifteenth Annual Report, December 31, 1889* (New York: s.n., 1890), 7; NY-SPCC, *Twenty-Fourth Annual Report, December 31, 1898* (New York: s.n., 1899), 7.

52. ASPCA, *Fifty-Fifth Annual Report* (New York, 1920), 61; ASPCA, *Thirty-Eighth Annual Report* (New York, 1904), 158–59.

53. "The Illinois Humane Society," *Humane Journal* 13 (August 1885): 118.

54. ASPCA, *Thirtieth Annual Report* (New York: s.n., 1896), 117; "A Word to Special Agents," *Humane Advocate* 6 (March 1911), 120–21; *Davis v. ASPCA*, 1878 N.Y. Lexis 872; "The Humane Agent," *Boulder News and Courier*, 27 April 1883, 2; *State v. Ashman*, 1914 Ohio Lexis 209.

55. Minnesota Society for the Prevention of Cruelty, *Annual Report for 1895* (St. Paul, 1895), 26; Elbridge T. Gerry, "The Law of Cruelty to Animals. A Lecture by Elbridge T. Gerry. Delivered before the Bar of Delaware County, New York, August 16, 1875 and Repeated before the Law School of Columbia College Feb. 16, 1876," unpublished manuscript, New-York Historical Society Library; Mrs. Edna Baker Oyler to John G. Shortall, July 17, 1901, box 541, folder 87, Illinois Humane Society Papers, University of Illinois at Chicago Special Collections (hereafter IHS Papers); William G. Kent to Illinois Humane Society, March 3, 1909, box 540, folder 78, IHS Papers; C. S. Tisdale to George Scott, May 10, 1911, box 538, folder 35, IHS Papers; "Policeman Died as He Had Wished—On Duty," *Humane Advocate* 11 (July 1916): 191; "Executive Secretary Marks 40 Years with Humane Society," *Chicago Daily News*, 30 April 1940, box 5, folder 55, IHS Papers, supplement 1 (hereafter IHS Supp.); report of Sergeant Bean, 1911, box 35, volume 3, Minneapolis Humane Society Records, Minnesota Historical Society Library (hereafter Mpls HS Papers). On the close identification—and relationship—of anticruelty organizations with the local police and judiciary, see: Robertson, *Crimes against Children*, 28–31; Gordon, *Heroes of Their Own Lives*, 52–55. On the fusion of public and private authority in SPCCs, see: Grossberg, "'A Protected Childhood'," 221–22.

56. *In re Goodell*, 39 Wisconsin 245, 242 (1875), quoted in Michael Grossberg, "Institutionalizing Masculinity: The Law as a Masculine Profession," in *Meanings for*

*Masculinity*, 146; Jannis Appier, *Policing Women: The Sexual Politics of Law Enforce-ment and the LAPD* (Philadelphia: Temple University Press, 1998), 9, 61–63 (even when women did win appointment to police forces in the early twentieth century, they were given specific tasks related to women and children rather than the general enforce-ment powers and duties of their male colleagues); "Here and There with Policewomen," *International Association of Policewomen* 3 (November–December 1927): 10–11, quoted in Appier, *Policing Women*, 63; Katz, *In the Shadow of the Poorhouse*, 60, 67–68, 81–82. There are, of course, exceptions to this generalization, particularly among women who had participated in the sort of organized wartime relief that presaged the more bureau-cratic, efficiency-oriented style of the postbellum scientific charity movement. Louisa Lee Schuyler, founder of the New York State Charities Aid Association in 1872, and Josephine Shaw Lowell, a founder of the Charity Organization Society of New York in 1882, are notable examples. George Fredrickson, *The Inner Civil War: Northern Intel-lectuals and the Crisis of the Union* (New York: Harper & Row, 1965), 211–13.

57. Unti, "Quality of Mercy," 153–55, 179–80; Women's Branch of the PSPCA, *Sixth Annual Report* (Philadelphia: s.n., 1875), 10; Mrs. E. F. Brady to IHS, [c. March 1899], box 535, folder 1, IHS Papers.

58. "Anti-Cruelty Society Meets," *Chicago Democrat & Dispatch*, 14 December 1899, box 544, scrapbook 1899–1900, IHS Papers; "Women Wear Police Badges," *Chicago Tribune*, 15 December 1899, box 544, scrapbook 1899–1900, IHS Papers; "Menace Brutal Teamsters," *Chicago Inter-Ocean*, 15 December 1899, box 544, scrapbook 1899–1900, IHS Papers; "Women Act as Police," *Chicago Democrat & Dispatch*, 15 December, 1899, box 544, scrapbook 1899–1900, IHS Papers; Angie Schweppe to John G. Shortall, [c. 1900], box 535, folder 2, IHS Papers; Emma Hamlin to IHS, July 9, 1912, box 544, folder 154, IHS Papers.

59. "Says Woman Can't Tell Horse from Cow," 27 February 1913, *Chicago Exam-iner*, box 538, folder 40, IHS Papers; *A Brief History of the Society of Humane Friends* (Chicago, s.n., 1911), box 543, folder 119, IHS Papers.

60. "1911 Report of Mrs. E. C. Bascomb," volume 3, Mpls HS Papers; 1911 Report of Miss Emilie L. Glorieux," volume 3, Mpls HS Papers; Appier, *Policing Women*, 46–49.

61. NY-SPCC, *Thirty-Ninth Annual Report, December 31, 1913* (New York: s.n., 1914), 14. Membership statistics based on count of lifetime and annual members in the NY-SPCC's *Thirteenth Annual Report* for 1887.

62. ASPCA, *Forty-Fifth Annual Report* (New York: s.n., 1911), 7.

63. WCTU, *Minutes of the National WCTU, 1888* (Chicago: Women's Temper-ance Publishing Association, 1888), 44; Mary F. Lovell, "Department of Mercy," *Union Signal* 19 (June 1, 1893): 13; "Twenty-Fifth Annual Convention of the National Woman's Christian Temperance Union, St. Paul, Minnesota," *Union Signal* 24 (December 8, 1898): 3; "Experience Corner," *Union Signal* 28 (June 12, 1902): 9; WCTU, *Report of the Thirty-Eighth Annual Convention, National Woman's Christian Temperance Union* (Chicago: Women's Temperance Publishing Association, 1911), 332–36; WCTU, *Report of the Forty-First Annual Convention, National Woman's Christian Temperance Union* (Chicago: Women's Temperance Publishing Association, 1914), 63, 78.

64. Ernst Fruend, *The Police Power: Public Policy and Constitutional Rights* (Chi-cago, 1904), 235.

65. Eric H. Monkkonen, *Police in Urban America, 1860–1920* (Cambridge: Cambridge University Press, 1981), 31, 35, 55, 62, 105–7, 127; James F. Richardson, *The New York Police: Colonial Times to 1901* (New York: Oxford University Press, 1970), 61–63; Roger Lane, *Policing the City: Boston, 1822–1885* (Cambridge, MA: Harvard University Press, 1967), 17, 83–84, 109, 114, 171–72, 191–93, 221; Robert M. Fogelson, *Big-City Police* (Cambridge, MA: Harvard University Press, 1977), 16–17. While all historians agree that the "modern" police force originated in 1820s London, there is a substantial debate about what prompted the formation of police both there and, later, in the United States. Some historians see it as a natural response to increasing crime, others as a mechanism of class control for a new industrial order, and others as part of the growth in the powers and function of municipal governments. For a synopsis of such debates, see: Monkkonen, *Police in Urban America*; Daniel Ernst, "Beyond Police History: A Systemic Perspective," *Maryland Historian* 16 (1985): 27–42.

66. Fogelson, *Big-City Police*, 2–6, 14–35; Timothy Gilfoyle, *City of Eros: New York City, Prostitution, and the Commercialization of Sex, 1790–1920* (New York: W. W. Norton & Company, 1992), 185–96.

67. Timothy J. Gilfoyle, "The Moral Origins of Political Surveillance: The Preventative Society in New York City, 1867–1918," *American Quarterly* 38 (1986): 637–52; Gilfoyle, *City of Eros*, 185–96; Lane, *Policing the City*, 214–15; Richardson, *New York Police*, 234. Pacific Society for the Suppression of Vice, Prevention of Cruelty to Children and Animals, *Annual Report and Supplement of the Pacific Society for the Suppression of Vice, Prevention of Cruelty to Children and Animals, for 1898 and 1899* (San Francisco: s.n., 1900), 8, Bancroft Library, University of California at Berkeley.

68. "The Employment of Pinkerton Detectives," House Report no. 2447, 52nd Congress, 2nd Session (Washington, D.C.: GPO, 1893), quoted in Robert P. Weiss, "Private Detectives and Labour Discipline in the United States, 1855–1946," in *Social History of Crime, Policing and Punishment*, ed. Robert P. Weiss (Ashgate: Dartmouth, 1999), 364; Frank Morn, *"The Eye That Never Sleeps": A History of the Pinkerton National Detective Agency* (Bloomington: Indiana University Press, 1982), vii–xi, 17–52; Lane, *Policing the City*, 101, 147; J. P. Shalloo, *Private Police, with Special Reference to Pennsylvania* (Philadelphia: American Academy of Political and Social Science, 1933), 35.

69. Floyd Morse Hubbard, *Prevention of Cruelty to Animals in the States of Illinois, Colorado and California* (New York, 1916), 83–87; William O. Stillman to George Scott, December 23, 1918, George Scott to R. T. Sundelius, June 12, 1925, box 545, folder 158, IHS Papers.

70. Coleman, *Humane Society Leaders*, 35.

71. Tisdale to Scott, August 8, 1911, box 538, folder 35, IHS Papers. See also: Henry Raab to Henry W. Clarke, October 21, 1889, box 536, folder 15, IHS Papers; AHA, *Report of the Proceedings of the Twenty-Third Annual Convention of the American Humane Association* (Fall River, 1899), 24; Mrs. Theodore Thomas, "Stars Prevent Cruelty," 28 January 1900, *Chicago Tribune*, clipping in box 544, scrapbook 1899–1900, IHS Papers; M. Easterday to IHS, December 3, 1909, box 536, folder 23, IHS Papers; minutes for June 25, 1891, box 35, volume 1, Mpls HS Papers.

72. "Stuart N. Dean," *Humane Advocate* 11 (July 1916): 191; Mrs. Edna Baker Oyler to IHS, July 17, 1901, box 541, folder 87, IHS Papers; John Keefe to IHS, May 3, 1899, box

541, folder 84, IHS Papers; "Report of Sargeant Bean" and "Report of Miss Emilie L. Glorieux," 1911, volume 3, Mpls HS Papers.

73. Wyoming State Board of Animal and Child Protection, *Fourth and Fifth Annual Report* (Cheyenne: s.n., 1912), 26; George T. Angell, *Five Questions Answered* (Boston: MSPCA, 1873), 4; June 25, 1891, volume 1, minutes, Mpls HS Papers; St. Paul Society for the Prevention of Cruelty, *Ninth Annual Report* (St. Paul, Minn.: s.n., 1896), 7; "Our Work," *Our Dumb Animals* 1 (July 1868): 1.

74. Pacific Society for the Suppression of Vice, Prevention of Cruelty to Children and Animals, *Annual Report . . . for 1898 and 1899*, supplement, 1–23; "Annual Meeting," *Humane Journal* 5 (1877): 5; Mrs. Jennie McOwin to John G. Shortall, July 25, 1901, box 536, folder 13, IHS Papers.

75. "Does This Jar You?" *Durango (CO) Democrat*, 11 January 1902, 1.

76. William Blackstone, *Commentaries on the Law of England*, vol. 4 (1769), 162, quoted in Markus Dirk Dubber, *The Police Power: Patriarchy and the Foundations of American Government* (New York, 2005), xii; Christopher Tomlins, *Law, Labor and Ideology in the Early American Republic* (Cambridge: Cambridge University Press, 1993), 35–59.

77. Novak, *The People's Welfare*; Freund, *The Police Power*, 3; Christopher G. Tiedeman, *A Treatise on State and Federal Control of Persons and Property in the United States, Considered from Both a Civil and Criminal Standpoint*, 2d ed. (St. Louis, 1900), 2:912.

78. "Lectures to Police," *Humane Advocate* 6 (November 1911), 26.

79. Tomlins, *Law, Labor, and Ideology*, 45–46; Morton J. Horowitz, *The Transformation of American Law, 1870–1960: The Crisis of Legal Orthodoxy* (New York, 1992), 27–29; Mark Warren Bailey, *Guardians of the Moral Order: The Legal Philosophy of the Supreme Court, 1860–1910* (Dekalb: Northern Illinois University Press, 2005), 128–40.

80. *Fagin v. Ohio Humane Society*, 1898 Ohio Misc. Lexis 186; *Fox v. Mohawk & Hudson River Humane Society*, 1897 N.Y. Misc. Lexis 358; *Polar Wave Ice and Fuel Company v. Alton Branch of the Illinois Humane Society*, 1910 Ill. App. Lexis 537; "Decision Interesting to Owners of Dogs," *Humane Journal* 25 (1897): 140–41. See also: "Decision of Supreme Court," *Creedle (CO) Candle*, 9 November 1907, 5.

81. *People v. Ewer*, 1894 N.Y. Lexis 1107, 5; NY-SPCC, *Twentieth Annual Report* (New York, 1895), 16. On how the Ewer case fits into the jurisprudence of the New York court of appeals, see: Felice Batalan, "A Reevaluation of the New York Court of Appeals: The Home, The Market, and Labor, 1885–1905," *Law and Social Inquiry* 27 (2002): 489–528. Batalan argues that the case is but one example of the courts' tendency to uphold and expand state regulation under the "police power."

82. I'm not so sure about how important the distinction between "rights" and "public welfare" justifications really is, but I've been trained to think it is important by reading the work of modern scholars of animal law, many of whom claim that the animal protection statutes I am discussing did not establish rights for animals. Among the reasons given is the fact that such statutes are housed under the "public morals" section of state legal codes; they thus appear to be about regulating human behavior for the sake of other human beings and not for the sake of animals. For this argument, see: Gary Francione, *Animals, Property, and the Law* (Philadelphia: Temple University

Press, 1995), 123–24; Thomas G. Kelch, "Toward a Non-Property Status for Animals," *New York University School of Law Environmental Law Journal* 6 (1998): 540; Jordan Curnutt, *Animals and the Law: A Sourcebook* (Santa Barbara: ABC-CLIO, 2001), 28–30; Daniel S. Moretti, *Animal Rights and the Law* (London: Oceana Publications, 1984), 1.

83. Novak, *The People's Welfare*, 240–45.

84. Dorsey, *Reforming Men and Women*; Steven Mintz, *Moralists and Modernizers: America's Pre–Civil War Reformers* (Baltimore: Johns Hopkins University Press, 1995); "Immediate, not Gradual," *Genius of Universal Emancipation* 3 (1832): 26–27.

85. For the transformation in reform attitudes and strategies, see: George M. Fredrickson, *The Inner Civil War: Northern Intellectuals and the Crisis of the Union* (New York: Harper & Row, 1965); John L. Thomas, "Romantic Reform in America, 1815–1865," *American Quarterly* 17 (1965): 656–81; John Higham, *From Boundlessness to Consolidation: The Transformation of American Culture, 1848–1860* (Ann Arbor: University of Michigan Press, 1969); Lori D. Ginzberg, *Women and the Work of Benevolence: Morality, Politics, and Class in the Nineteenth-Century United States* (New Haven: Yale University Press, 1990); Gaines M. Foster, *Moral Reconstruction: Christian Lobbyists and the Federal Legislation of Morality, 1865–1920* (Chapel Hill: University of North Carolina Press, 2002).

86. Fredrickson, *Inner Civil War*, 90, 183–97; McKanan, *Identifying the Image of God*, 174; John Thomas, "Romantic Reform in America, 1815–1865," 679–80.

87. William O. Stillman to [unknown], undated [c. 1905], box 35, folder 1, Mpls HS Papers; AHA, *Report of the Proceedings of the Twenty-First Annual Convention of the American Humane Association* (Fall River, 1897), 31; "The Illinois Humane Society," *Humane Journal* 13 (1885): 118.

88. See, for example: W. Perkins, "The Law of Kindness," *Our Dumb Animals* 8 (December 1875): 51.

89. W. P. Noble to IHS, May 1, 1890, box 536, folder 1, IHS Papers; PSPCA, *Second Annual Report of the Pennsylvania Society for the Prevention of Cruelty to Animals* (Philadelphia, 1870), 7.

90. Ferd W. Peck, "Prosecution of Offenders," *Humane Journal* 13 (1885): 166; Goldberg to Chase, MHS subject files; MN-SPCA, *Minnesota Society for the Prevention of Cruelty to Animals* (St. Paul, [c. 1875]), 10, MHS subject files. For other examples, see: Pliny Chase, "Second Report of the President and Secretary of the Proceedings during the Autumn of 1867, Read to the Executive Committee at Its Meeting on December 30, 1867," manuscript report, box 5, records of the Pennsylvania Society for the Prevention of Cruelty to Animals (hereafter, PSPCA papers), Historical Society of Pennsylvania.

91. Monkkonen, *Police in Urban America*, 40–42; Richardson, *New York Police*, 58; Lane, *Policing the City*, 34–35.

92. Case records are not uniformly available. Although I have done research in the records and publication of the NY-SPCC and SPCA, the Wisconsin, Illinois, Wyoming, Minnesota, and Minneapolis Humane Societies, and the Massachusetts and Pennsylvania SPCA, case files are available only for limited dates in records from Illinois, Minneapolis, and Pennsylvania. In Minneapolis, only children's case files are available.

93. Chase to Eskinrod, April 10, 1872, box 1, letterbook, PSPCA Records; Chase to Elijah Pennington, May 5, 1872, box 1, letterbook, PSPCA Records.

94. Case 198, box 2, folder 19, IHS Supp. In this and all other cases from the files of the Illinois Humane Society, respondents' names have been omitted or changed to protect their identity.

95. Case 460, Minneapolis Humane Society Papers, case files (hereafter, MHS-CF), Minnesota Historical Society. In this and all other cases from the files of the Minneapolis Humane Society, respondents' names have been omitted or changed to protect their identity.

96. MHS-CF, case 2449.

97. MHS-CF, case 2296.

98. Case 827, box 2, folder 25, IHS Supp; case 374, box 3, folder 29, IHS Supp.; case 206, box 2, folder 19, IHS Supp.

99. MHS-CF, case 4285.

100. MHS-CF, case 5815.

101. For a description of the old constable and magistrate system, see: Michael Willrich, *City of Courts: Socializing Justice in Progressive Era Chicago* (Cambridge: Cambridge University Press, 2003).

102. Gordon, *Heroes of Their Own Lives*; Broder, *Tramps, Unfit Mothers, and Neglected Children*; case 22, box 2, folder 25, IHS Supp.; MHS-CF, case 4591.

103. Case 466, box 4, folder 44, IHS Supp. See also: case 702–60, box 537, folder 28, IHS Papers; case 1–59, box 537, folder 27; case 120, box 2, folder 19, IHS Supp.; case 148, box 2, folder 19, IHS Supp.; case 500–559, box 537, folder 27, IHS Papers; MHS-CF, case 3361; MHS-CF, case 6889; MHS-CF, case 1; MHS-CF, case 613; MHS-CF, case 919; case 95, box 2, folder 19, IHS Supp.; case 138, box 2, folder 19, IHS Supp.

104. MHS-CF, case 1837.

105. Charles A. Williams to John G. Shortall, September 16, 1884, box 2, folder 19, IHS Supp.; MHS-CF, case 8547.

106. The New York SPCC fought a long battle with the State Board of Charities about whether it was a "charity," and thus subject to the board's inspection. Eventually, the SPCC won. The presiding judge declared that far from being a relief agency, the SPCC was "created for the purpose of enforcing laws . . . and that is the only object or purpose of its existence." *State Board of Charities v. The New York Society for the Prevention of Cruelty to Children*, 1900 Lexis, 1437.

107. "George Ellman Resigns," 7 August 1911, *Moline Mail*, box 538, folder 39, IHS Papers; MHS-CF, case 9487; "History of the Minneapolis Humane Society," undated manuscript, box 35, Mpls HS Papers. On criminalization of nonsupport as part of the progressive, and yet coercive, "socialization of the law," see: Willrich, *City of Courts*, 148–50.

108. Skowronek, *Building a New American State*, 5, 19–29; David S. Tanenhaus, *Juvenile Justice in the Making* (New York: Oxford University Press, 2004), 59; Grossberg, *Governing the Hearth*; Bardaglio, *Reconstructing the Household*, 137–213.

109. Monkkonen, *Police in Urban America*, 31, 150–52; Tomlins, *Law, Labor, and Ideology*, 19–34.

110. Gilfoyle, *City of Eros*, 187, 380–81, note 17. Gilfoyle categorizes SPCAs and SPCCs as, like vice societies, happy with existing laws and interested only in seeing that they be enforced. He contrasts them in this respect with other postbellum reform-

ers such as the WCTU, the Anti-Saloon league, the American Purity Alliance, and the YMCA. I disagree with this assessment; many anticruelty organizations in all sections of the country actively pursued, and often won, new legislation. In part, this is why the law enforcement activities of anticruelty organiztions cannot, as Gilfoyle argues, be understood simply and solely in terms of the *privatization* of state responsibility. Angell, *Five Questions Answered*, 4; "Growing in Summit," *Breckenridge (CO) Bulletin*, 28 April 1900, 2. See also: "Colorado Notes," *Summit County (CO) Journal*, 1 September 1900, 7.

111. Trattner, *From Poor Law to Welfare State*, 81–82.

112. NY-SPCC, *Twenty-First Annual Report, December 31, 1895* (New York: s.n., 1896), 5; NY-SPCC, *Twenty-Third Annual Report, December 31, 1897* (New York: s.n., 1898), 6–8.

113. NY-SPCC, *Twenty-Fourth Annual Report*, 6–7.

114. NY-SPCC, *Twenty-Fifth Annual Report, December 31, 1899* (New York: s.n., 1900), 122–31.

115. ASPCA, *Thirty-Eighth Annual Report* (New York: s.n., 1904), 157–61.

116. Floyd Morse Hubbard, *Prevention of Cruelty to Animals in the States of Illinois, Colorado and California* (New York: Columbia University Press, 1916), 36–38; "Summary of the Work of the Colorado Legislature," *Summit County (CO) Journal*, 2; "Colorado's Capital," *Summit County (CO) Journal*, 16 August 1902, 7; *General Laws of the State of Minnesota Passed during the Twenty-Sixth Session of the State Legislature* (Minneapolis: Harrison & Smith, 1905), 409–11; Wyoming Humane Society and State Board of Child and Animal Protection, *Biennial Report* (Cheyenne: s.n., 1914), 20–21; "State Humane Society in Annual Session," *Dallas News*, 23 May 1913, box 538, folder 40, IHS Papers; Texas Bureau of Child and Animal Protection, *First Biennial Report* (Austin: s.n., 1915), 5–6.

117. Colorado Humane Society, *Handbook of the Colorado Humane Society* (Denver: s.n., 1900), 3–4.

118. Michel Foucault, *Discipline and Punish: The Birth of the Prison* (New York: Vintage Books, 1977); Cynthia Halpern, *Suffering, Politics, Power: A Genealogy in Modern Political Theory* (Albany: SUNY Press, 2002); Karl Shoemaker, "The Problem of Pain in Punishment: Historical Perspectives," in *Pain, Death, and the Law*, ed. Austin Sarat (Ann Arbor: University of Michigan Press, 2001), 15–41; Austin Sarat, "Killing Me Softly: Capital Punishment and Technologies for Taking Life," in *Pain, Death, and the Law*, 43–70.

119. AHA, *Report of the Proceedings, Fourteenth Annual Meeting*, 40–44.

## CONCLUSION

1. The Horse Aid Society of New York, *First Report, from March, 1910 to December, 1912* (New York: s.n., 1912), 1–5.

2. Floyd Morse Hubbard, *Prevention of Cruelty to Animals in New York State*, bulletin of Social Legislation of the Henry Bergh Foundation for the Promotion of Humane Education, no. 3, ed. Samuel McCune Lindsay (New York: Columbia University Press, 1915), 15–16.

3. "International Humane Conference, Conducted under the Auspices of the American Humane Association," *Humane Advocate* 6 (November 1910): 11.

4. Wisconsin Humane Society, *First Biennial Report*, 11.

5. See chapter 1, note 46.

6. George Benjamin Mangold, *Problems of Child Welfare* (New York: MacMillan, 1916): 1. For progressive child welfare campaigns, see: Susan Tiffin, *In Whose Best Interest: Child Welfare Reform in the Progressive Era* (Westport, CT: Greenwood Press, 1982); Mintz, *Huck's Raft*, chap. 8; Hawes, *The Children's Rights Movement*, chap. 3.

7. Costin, Karger, and Stoesz, *The Politics of Child Abuse in America*, 47–48; 85–86; Gordon, *Heroes of Their Own Lives.*

8. Tiffin, *In Whose Best Interest*, chap. 6; Gordon, *Heroes of Their Own Lives.*

9. William O. Stillman, "An S.P.C.C. Criticized," *National Humane Review* 3 (August 1915): 186; Eugene Morgan, "Some Humane Legislative Problems," *National Humane Review* 2 (October 1914): 230; William O. Stillman, "Hostile Social Agencies," *National Humane Review* 2 (February 1914): 36–37.

10. William O. Stillman, "Duplicate Philanthropy," *National Humane Review* 1 (January 1913): 13; William O. Stillman, "Imitation S.P.C.C.s," *National Humane Review* 2 (April 1914): 84.

11. Robert J. Wilkin, "The True Mission of the S.P.C.C," *National Humane Review* 1 (February 1913): 27–28, 35. For similar arguments, see: Peter G. Gerry, "Problems in Child Rescue," *NHR* 1 (January 1913): 5; Thomas B. Maymon, "Practical Methods in Child Protection," *NHR* 2 (January 1914): 5; Ernest K. Coulter, "The Prevention of Cruelty to Children," *NHR* 3 (December 1915): 269, 287; Stillman, "What an S.P.C.C. May Do," *NHR* 3 (November 1915): 243–44, 263; Stillman, "The S.P.C.C. and Charity Work," *NHR* 3 (September 1915): 195–96, 215; Stillman, "Annual Address of William O. Stillman," *NHR* 3 (December 1915): 267–68; Nathaniel J. Walker, "Have S.P.C.C.s Outlived Their Usefulness," *NHR* 3 (February 1915): 27–28, 41; Wilkin, "The Birth of the Child Protection Movement," *NHR* 3 (October 1915): 223; Stillman, "Future of Child Protection," *NHR* 5 (August 1917): 150; John D. Lindsay, "More Than Legal Protection," *NHR* 8 (June 1920): 106–7.

12. William J. Schultz, *The Humane Movement in the United States, 1910–1922*, bulletin of Social Legislation of the Henry Bergh Foundation for the Promotion of Humane Education, no. 6, ed. Samuel McCune Lindsay (1924; repr., New York: AMS Press, 1968), 14–16, 204, 209.

13. Edwin F. Brown, "The Neglected Human Resources of the Gulf Coast States," *Child Labor Bulletin* 2 (May 1913): 112–14.

14. John P. Frey, "Social Cost of Child Labor," *Child Labor Bulletin* 1 (June 1912): 120; W. H. Oates, "Child Labor and Health," *Child Labor Bulletin* 2 (May 1913): 117–20.

15. G. Stanley Hall, "Evolution and Psychology," in *Fifty Years of Darwinism: Modern Aspects of Evolution* (New York: Henry Holt and Company, 1909): 251–67; Ross, *G. Stanley Hall*, 299–307, 310–11, 333, 368–75, 413–14; Strickland, "The Child and the Race." For Hall's vitalism, see: T. J. Jackson Lears, *No Place of Grace: Antimodernism and the Transformation of American Culture, 1880–1920* (Chicago: University of Chicago Press, 1994),

16. Dominick Cavallo, *Muscles and Morals: Organized Playgrounds and Urban Reform, 1880–1920* (Philadelphia: University of Pennsylvannia Press, 1981), esp. 50–55.

17. Daniel J. Kevles, *In the Name of Eugenics: Genetics and the Uses of Human Heredity* (Cambridge, MA: Harvard University Press, 1998); Barbara A. Kimmelman, "The American Breeders' Association: Genetics and Eugenics in an Agricultural Context, 1903–1913," *Social Studies of Science* 13 (1983): 163–204; W. E. D. Stokes, *The Right to Be Well Born; or, Horse Breeding in Its Relation to Eugenics* (New York: C. J. O'Brien, 1917), 10; Linda Gordon, "The Politics of Population: Birth Control and the Eugenics Movement," *Radical America* 8 (1974): 61–98; National Child Labor Committee, *The Child Workers of the Nation: Proceedings of the Fifth Annual Conference* (New York: American Academy of Political and Social Science, 1909), 37–38.

18. John J. Biddison, "'Better Babies,'" *Woman's Home Companion* (March 1913), 26. For more on the early-twentieth-century baby health contest, see: Susan J. Pearson, "Making Babies Better: Motherhood and Medicalization in the Progressive Era" (M.A. thesis, University of North Carolina, 1999); Alexandra Minna Stern, "Beauty Is Not Always Better: Perfect Babies and the Tyranny of Paediatric Norms," *Patterns of Prejudice* 36 (2002): 68–78; and "Making Better Babies: Public Health and Race Betterment in Indiana, 1920–1935," *American Journal of Public Health* (May 2002): 742–53.

19. AHA, *Report of the Proceedings of the Forty-First Annual Meeting of the American Humane Association* (Albany: s.n., 1917), 25.

20. T. Swann Harding, "The Rise of the United States Department of Agriculture," *Scientific Monthly* 53 (December 1941): 554–64; David E. Hamilton, "Building the Associative State: The Department of Agriculture and American State-Building," *Agricultural History* 64 (1990): 207–18.

21. Florence Kelley, *Some Ethical Gains through Legislation* (New York: MacMillan, 1905), 99–104; Lillian Wald, "Address to the House Committee Hearing on Establishing a Children's Bureau," in *Lillian D. Wald, Progressive Activist*, ed. Clare Coss (New York: Feminist Press at CUNY, 1993), 69; United States Senate, *Hearing before the Committee on Education and Labor on S. 8323, Establishment of Children's Bureau in the Interior Department, Sixtieth Congress, Second Session* (Washington, D.C.: Government Printing Office, 1909), 9.

22. 49 USC 80502; *United States v. Boston & A.R. Co., United States v. Fitchburg R. Co.*, 15 F. 209; 1883 U.S. Dist. Lexis 5; International Humane Society, *Doings of the First Annual Meeting of the International Humane Society* (Boston: A. J. Wright, 1877); American Humane Association, *Doings of the Third Annual Meeting of the American Humane Association, Held at Chicago, Ill., October 8, 9 and 10, 1879* (Boston: Wright & Potter Printing Company, 1879). On the interstate cattle trade, see: William Cronon, *Nature's Metropolis: Chicago and the Great West* (New York: W. W. Norton & Company, 1992), chap. 5.

23. Kelley, *Some Ethical Gains*, 91; "Opposed to Federal Children's Bureau," *New York Times*, 28 January 1912.

24. Stillman, "State Humane Bureaus," *National Humane Review* 1 (1913): 13; William R. Brock, *Investigation and Responsibility: Public Responsibility in the United. States, 1865–1900* (Cambridge: Cambridge University Press, 1984), 159–61.

25. Brock, *Investigation and Responsibility,* 222–26.

26. Illinois Humane Society, *Fourteenth Annual Report,* 10. For modern research on the link between animal and child abuse, see: Frank Ascione and P. Arkow, eds., *Child Abuse, Domestic Violence, and Animal Abuse: Linking the Circles of Compassion for Prevention and Intervention* (West Lafayette, IN: Purdue University Press).

27. Riis, *Children of the Poor,* 150.